India-Nepal Relations
Historical, Cultural and Political Perspective

India-Nepal Relations

India-Nepal Relations
Historical, Cultural and Political Perspective

Editor

Sanasam Sandhyarani Devi

VIJ BOOKS INDIA PVT LTD

NEW DELHI (INDIA)

Published by

Vij Books India Pvt Ltd
(Publishers, Distributors & Importers)
2/19, Ansari Road, Darya Ganj
New Delhi - 110002
Phones: 91-11-65449971, 91-11- 43596460
Fax: 91-11-47340674
web : www.vijbooks.com
e-mail : vijbooks@rediffmail.com

ISBN 13 : 978-93-80177-45-8

Price : ₹ 995.00

Printed in India
at Narula Printers, Delhi

Contents

Preface — *vii*

1. Indo-Nepalese Relations in Ancient and Medieval Times — 1
2. Emergence of Modern Nepal Relations with India — 27
3. India's Responsibility for the Defence and Foreign Policy of Nepal — 59
4. Modernization of Nepal — 71
5. Perspectives on Nepal-India Relations — 87
6. The Prospects for Democracy in Nepal — 127
7. Nepal China Relations and its Effects — 145
8. Maoist Problems and its Impact on India: Nepal Relations — 157
9. Nepali Citizens as Part of Indian Armed Forces: Impact on Relations — 175
10. Trafficking of Nepali Women in India — 183
11. Aspects of Cultural Policy in Nepal — 273
12. Problems and Prospects of India: Nepal Bilateral Trade Relations — 279

Bibliography — 295

Index — 301

Preface

India-Nepal relationship is wrought by the centuries old social-cultural, historical and geographic connections. India has over the years, consistently responded with a sense of urgency to the needs of the people and Government of Nepal in ensuring the success of the peace process and institutionalization of multi-party democracy through the framing of a new Constitution. It was India who first welcomes the restoration of democracy in Nepal.

Politically and culturally, the welfare of the people of the two countries is interlinked and developments in one country invariably have an impact on the other. Thus with Nepal, India needs to bring about a turnaround in the overall dysfunctional relationship and invest in long-term political linkages.

Identification and feasibility studies on small and medium projects were undertaken. The two Governments also decided to reinvigorate bilateral relations by ensuring effectiveness of all established institutional mechanisms. The two sides agreed to enhance bilateral trade on a sustainable basis.

India remains steadfast in its commitment to extend assistance for Nepal's economic development and political stabilization, with small run-of river projects starting to build in political confidence. India's support continues to be in accordance with the wishes and priorities of the people and Government of Nepal.

- Editor

1

Indo-Nepalese Relations in Ancient and Medieval Times

The Relationship between India and Nepal are very close, yet burdened with difficulties stemming from geography, economics, the problems inherent in big power-small power relations, and common ethnic, linguistic and cultural identities that overlap the two countries' borders. New Delhi and Kathmandu initiated their intertwined relationship with the 1950 Indo-Nepal Treaty of Peace and Friendshipý and accompanying letters that defined security relations between the two countries, and an agreement governing both bilateral trade and trade transiting Indian soil.

The 1950 treaty and letters stated that "neither government shall tolerate any threat to the security of the other by a foreign aggressor" and obligated both sides "to inform each other of any serious friction or misunderstanding with any neighboring state likely to cause any breach in the friendly relations subsisting between the two governments."

These accords cemented a "special relationship" between India and Nepal that granted Nepal preferential economic treatment and provided Nepalese in India the same economic and educational opportunities as Indian citizens. The history of Nepal is characterized by its isolated position in the Himalayas and its two dominant neighbors, India and China. Due to the arrival of disparate settler groups from outside through the ages, it is now a multi-ethnic, multi-cultural, multi-lingual country.

Its population is predominantly Hindu with significant presence of Buddhists, who were in majority at one time in the past. Nepal was split in three kingdoms from the 15th to 18th century, when it was unified under a monarchy. The national language of Nepal is called 'Nepali', a name given - long after unification of Nepal - to the language called Khas Kura. Nepal experienced a failed struggle for democracy in the 20th century. During the 1990s and until 2008, the country was in civil strife.

A peace treaty was signed in 2008 and elections were held in the same year. Many of the ills of Nepal have been blamed on the royal family of Nepal. In a historical vote for the election of the constituent assembly, Nepalis voted to oust the monarchy in Nepal.

In June 2008, Nepalis ousted the royal household. Nepal was formally renamed the Federal Democratic Republic of Nepal when it became a federal republic. The word Nepal is derived from Nepa; the old name of Kathmandu valley was Nepa in Nepal Bhasa, the language of Newars, who were the early inhabitants of the valley, long before the unification of Nepal.

The fact that Nepal Sambat, one of the three main calendars of Nepal, existed long before the unification of Nepal proves this historical fact.

Other toponym theories include:

- "Nepal" may be derived from the Sanskrit *nipalaya*, which means "at the foot of the mountains" or "abode at the foot", a reference to its location in relation to the Himalayas. Thus, it may be an Eastern equivalent of the European toponym "Piedmont."

- It has also been suggested that the name comes from the Tibetan *niyampal*, which means "holy land".
- A third theory suggests that Nepal came from compounding the words NE, which means wool, and PAL, which means a tented house; a long time ago, Nepal used to produce a lot of wool and the houses were used to store the wool - hence the word NE-PAL.
- The name Nepal is also supposed to be derived from the Sanskrit word "NEP", with the suffix "AL" added to it; though still under controversy, NEP were the people who use to be cow herders - the GOPALS - who came to the Nepal valley for the first time from the Ganges plain of India.
- According to Nepali scholar Rishikesh Shaha, the ancient chronicles report that a sage (*muni*) named Ne became the protector (*pâla*) of this land and the founder of its first ruling dynasty. The name of the country, Ne-pâla, therefore originally meant the land 'protected by Ne.'

EARLY AGES

PREHISTORY

Neolithic tools found in the Kathmandu Valley indicate that people have been living in the Himalayan region for at least 9,000 years. It appears that people who were probably of Kirant ethnicity lived in Nepal more than 2,500 years ago. The Kirant are a tribe of jungle and mountain people who migrated from various parts of India and the Himalayas.

LEGENDS AND ANCIENT TIMES

Though very little or sporadic things are known about the early history of Nepal, Asia, legends and documented references, like the following, reach back to the first millennium BCE:

- Also, the presence of historical sites, e.g., Valmiki ashram, indicates the presence of Sanatana (ancient) Hindu culture in Nepal at that period.

- The epic Mahabharata mentions the *Kiratas* among the inhabitants of Nepal. Kirati king Yalambar had the dubious honor of being slain in the battle of the Mahabharata, in which gods and mortals fought alongside each other. Legend credits him with meeting Indra, the lord of heaven, who ventured into the Valley in human guise. It is said that during the battle of Mahabharata, Yalamber went to witness the battle with a view to take the side of the losing party. Lord Krishna, knowing the intention of Yalamber and the strength and unity of the Kiratas, thought that the war would unnecessarily be prolonged if Yalamber sided with the Kauravas. So, by a clever stroke of diplomacy, Lord Krishna cut off Yalamber's head.
- According to some of the chronicles, the successors of Ne were the gopâlavaCœi or "Cowherd family", whose names often end in *-gupta* and are said to have ruled for some 491 years. They are said to have been followed by the mahaicapâlavaCœa or "Buffalo-herder Dynasty", established by an Indian Rajput named Bhul Singh.
- inscriptions found on archeological stoneworks, which list mostly the dates and commissioners of these constructions, also communicate royal edicts, religious mantras or historical notes sometimes and, through the corroboration of local myths with such evidence, a people prior to the Licchavi have been identified, known as the Kirata.

KIRAT PERIOD

Nepal's very first recorded or discovered history began with the Kiratis, who arrived in the 7th or 8th century BCE from the west to the Kathmandu valley (now the capital of Nepal). Little is known about them, other than their deftness as sheep farmers and great fondness for carrying long knives.

The Kirats ruled for about 1225 years (800 BCE-300 CE), their reign had a total of 29 kings during that time. Their first and best-remembered king was Yalambar, who is referenced in the epic Mahabharata. In the chronicle of Bansawali William Kirk Patrick mentions that the Kirat rule existed from about 900 BCE to 300 CE. During this long period altogether 29 Kirat Kings ruled over the country.

The 29 Kirat Kings were:

1. Yellung Hang or Yalambar
2. Pari Hang
3. Skandhar Hang
4. Balamba Hang
5. Hriti Hang
6. Humati Hang
7. Jitedasti Hang
8. Galinja Hang
9. Oysgja Hang
10. Suyarma Hang
11. Papa Hang
12. Bunka Hang
13. Swawnanda Hang
14. Sthunko Hang
15. Jinghri Hang
16. Nane Hang
17. Luka Hang
18. Thor Hang
19. Thoko Hang
20. Verma Hang
21. Guja Hang
22. Pushkar Hang
23. Keshu Hang
24. Suja Hang
25. Sansa Hang

26. Gunam Hang
27. Khimbu Hang
28. Paruka Hang
29. Gasti Hang

The 1st Kirat King Yalambar laid the foundation of the Kirat dynasty after defeating the last ruler of the Abhir dynasty. When Kirats occupied the valley, they made Matatirtha their capital. The Kirat kingdom during the rule of Yalambar had extended to Tista in the East and Trisidi in the West.

It is said Yalambar had gone to witness the battle of Mahabharata between the Pandavas and the Kauravas. He was so brave and powerful that Lord Krishna beheaded him prior to the battle suspecting he might fight for the Kauravas.

THE 7TH KIRAT KING 'JITEDASTI'

During the rule of the 7th Kirat King Jitedasti, Lord Gautam Buddha visited the valley with his several disciples. He visited holy places of Swayambhu, Guheswari, etc., and preached his religious teaching. The Kirats of the valley refused to follow his doctrine but welcomed Lord Buddha and his disciples.

THE 14TH KIIRAT KING 'STHUNKO'

During the rule of the 14th Kirat King Sthunko, the Indian Emperor Ashok came to the Kathmandu Valley with his daughter, princess Charumati.

During his stay in the valley, he had four stupas built in four directions and one in the centre of Patan. He arranged his daughter Charumati's marriage with a local young prince named Devpal.

Prince Devpal and his consort Charumati lived at Chabahil near Pashupati area. Later Charumati had the stupas of Devpatan built after the death of her husband in his memory. Charumati who had later on become a nun herself also got erected a convent where she resided and practiced Lord Buddha's doctrine.

THE 15TH KIRAT KING 'JINGHRI'

During the rule of the 15th Kirat King Jinghri, another religious doctrine, Jainism, was being preached by Mahavir Jain in India. In this regard, Bhadrabhau, a disciple of Mahavir Jain, came to Nepal. But Jainism did not gain as much popularity as Buddhism in Nepal.

THE 28TH KIRAT KING 'PARUKA'

During the rule of the 28th Kirat King Paruka, the Sombanshi ruler attacked his regime many times from the west. Although he successfully repelled their attacks, he was forced to move to Shankhamul from Gokarna. He had a royal palace called "Patuka" built there for him. The 'Patuka' palace can no longer be seen, except its ruins in the form of a mound. Patuka changed Shankhamul into a beautiful town.

THE 29TH KIRAT KING 'GASTI'

The last King of the Kirat dynasty was Gasti. He proved to be a dimpled or weak ruler and was overthrown by the Sombanshi ruler Nimisha. This ended the powerful Kirat dynasty that had lasted for about 1225 years. After their defeat, the Kirats moved to the Eastern hills of Nepal and settled down, divided into small principalities.

Their settlements were divided into three regions, i.e., 'Wallokirat' that lay to the East of the Kathmandu Valley (now the capital of Nepal), 'Majkirat' or Central Kirat region and 'Pallokirat' that lay to the far East of the Kathmandu valley (now the capital of Nepal). These regions are still heavily populated by Kirats.

BIRTH OF BUDDHA

One of the earliest confederations of South Asia was that of the Shakya clan, whose capital was Kapilvastu, Nepal. Siddhartha Gautama Buddha, Siddharta Gautama (563–483 BCE), who renounced his royalty to lead an ascetic life and came to be known as the *Buddha* ("the enlightened one") was born to the Shakya king Sudhodhan.

After finding enlightenment, Lord Gautam Buddha returned to his home place Kapilvastu Always a part of Nepal to teach his wife Yesodhara what he had learned. But by 260 BCE, most of North India and southern Nepal were ruled by the Maurya Empire. Buddha and his disciple Ananda visited the Kathmandu Valley and stayed for a time in Patan.

Although not all of Nepal was under Maurya occupation, there is evidence of at least the influence of Maurya Emperor Ashoka the Great, the legendary Buddhist proselytiser and ruler from 273 BCE to 232 BCE. Ashoka was a visitor to Kathmandu in this period and, as a follower of Buddhism, he visited Lumbini, the birthplace of Buddha, and erected 4 stupas in Kathmandu. His daughter married a local prince and further spread the religion. The remains of a Buddhist convent have been found in the Kathmandu Valley.

Before Nepal's emergence as a nation in the latter half of the 18th century, the designation 'Nepal' was largely applied only to the Kathmandu Valley. Thus up until the unification of the country, Nepal's history is largely the history of the Kathmandu Valley. References to Nepal in famous Hindu epics such as the Mahabharata, Puranas and also Buddhist and Jain scriptures, establish the country's antiquity as an independent political and territorial entity.

The Vamshavalis or chronicles, the oldest of which was written during the 14th century, are the only fairly reliable basis for Nepal's ancient history. The Vamshavalis mention the rule of several dynasties the Gopalas, the Abhiras and the Kiratas—over a stretch of centuries.

However, no extant historical evidence has yet authenticated the rule of these legendary dynasties. The documented history of Nepal begins with the Changu Narayan temple inscription of King Manadeva I (c. 464-505 A.D.) of the Lichavi dynasty.

LICHAVI DYNASTY

The Lichavis are said to have migrated into Nepal from north India in around 250 A.D. The first Lichavi king of historical importance was Manadeva 1. Another important Lichavi monarch was Anshuverma who opened trade routes to Tibet. One of his daughters, Bhrikuti, who was married to Tibetan ruler Tsrong-tsong Gompo, was instrumental in spreading the Gospel of the Buddha in Tibet and China.

Anshuverma has been referred to as a man of many talents in the accounts of the Chinese traveler Huen Tsang, who had visited India in the 7th century AD. Narendradeval another Lichavi king initiated friendly relations with China and his successors laid the foundations of friendship with India by entering into matrimonial alliances with the Indian royal families. The Lichchhavi rule spanned over a period of about 630 years, the last ruler being Jayakamadeva.

MALLA DYNASTY

After the fall of the Lichchhavis came the Malla period during which the foundation of the city of Kantipur (later Kathmandu) was laid. The early Malla rule started with Ari Malla in the 12th century and over the next two centuries grew into a large empire before disintegrating into small principalities which later became known as the Baise (i.e. the twenty-two principalities).

This was more or less coincidental with the emergence of the Chaubisi (i.e. twenty-four principalities). The history of these principalities remains shrouded up until the time when they joined other kingdoms, both large and small, to form the unified Kingdom of Nepal. Jayasthiti Malla, with whom commences the later Malla period in the Kathmandu Valley, reigned towards the end of the 14th century.

Though his rule was rather short, his place among the rulers in the Valley is eminent for the various social and economic reforms such as the 'Sanskritization' of the Valley people, new methods of land measurement and allocation etc. Yakshya Malla, the grandson of Jayasthiti Malla, ruled the Kathmandu Valley until almost the end of the 15th century.

After his demise, the Valley was divided into three independent Valley kingdoms—Kathmandu, Bhaktapur and

Patan—in about 1484 A.D. This division led the Malla rulers into internecine wars for territorial and commercial gains. Mutually debilitating wars gradually weakened them and by the time of King Prithvi Narayan ShahÕs invasion of the Valley, they had by themselves reached the brink of political extinction. The last rulers were Jaya Prakash Malla, Tej Narsingh Malla and Ranjit Malla of Kathmandu, Patan and Bhaktapur respectively.

SHAH DYNASTY, UNIFICATION OF NEPAL

Prithvi Narayan Shah (c 1769-1775), with whom we move into the modern period of Nepal's history, was the ninth generation descendant of Dravya Shah (1559–1570), the founder of the ruling house of Gorkha. Prithvi Narayan Shah succeeded his father King Nara Bhupal Shah to the throne of Gorkha in 1743 AD. King Prithvi Narayan Shah was quite aware of the political situation of the Valley kingdoms as well as of the Barsi and Chaubisi principalities.

He foresaw the need for unifying the small principalities as an urgent condition for survival in the future and set him self to the task accordingly. His assessment of the situation among the hill principalities was correct, and the principalities were subjugated fairly easily. King Prithvi Narayan Shah's victory march began with the conquest of Nuwakot, which lies between Kathmandu and Gorkha, in 1744.

After Nuwakot, he occupied strategic points in the hills surrounding the Kathmandu Valley. The ValleyÕs communications with the outside world were thus cut off. The occupation of the Kuti Pass in about 1756 stopped the ValleyÕs trade with Tibet. Finally, King Prithvi Narayan Shah entered the Valley. After the victory of Kirtipur, King Jaya Prakash Malla of Kathmandu sought help from the British and so the East India Company sent a contingent of soldiers under Captain Kinloch in 1767.

The British force was defeated at Sindhuli by King Prithvi Narayan Shahos army. This defeat of the British completely shattered the hopes of King Jaya Prakash Malla. The capture of Kathmandu (September 25. 1768) was dramatic. As the people of Kathmandu were celebrating the festival of Indrajatra, Prithvi Narayan Shah and his men marched into the city.

A throne was put on the palace courtyard for the king of Kathmandu. Prithvi Narayan Shah sat on the throne and was hailed by the people as the king of Kathmandu. Jaya Prakash Malla managed to escape with his life and took asylum in Patan.

When Patan was captured a few weeks later, both Jaya Prakash Malla and the king of Patan, Tej Narsingh Mallal took refuge in Bhaktapur, which was also captured after some time. Thus the Kathmandu Valley was conquered by King Prithvi Narayan Shah and Kathmandu became the capital of the modern Nepal by 1769.

King Prithvi Narayan Shah was successful in bringing together diverse religio-ethnic groups under one national. He was a true nationalist in his outlook and was in favor of adopting a closed-door policy with regard to the British. Not only his social and economic views guided the country's socio-economic course for a long time, his use of the imagery, 'a yam between two bouldersÕ in Nepal's geopolitical context, formed the principal guideline of the country`s foreign policy for future centuries.

The War with British - The Nepalese had differences of opinion with the East India Company regarding the ownership of the land strip of the western Terai, particularly Butwal and Seoraj. The outcome of the conflict was a war with the British. The British launched their attack on the Nepali forces at Nalapani, the western most point of Nepal's frontier at the close of 1814.

Though the Nepalese were able to inflict heavy losses to the British army on various fronts, the larger army and the superior weapons of the British proved too strong. The Nepali army evacuated the areas west of the Mahakali River and ultimately the treaty of Sugauli was signed with the British in 1816.

Among other things, this treaty took away a large chunk of the Terai from Nepal and the rivers Mahakali and Mechi were fixed as the country's western and eastern boundaries. At this time, King Girvana Yuddha Biktram Shah was on the throne of Nepal, and the power of state was in the hands of Prime Minister Bhimsen Thapa who wielded enormous power during the rule of King Girvana Yuddha Bikram Shah and his son King Rajendra Bikram Shah.

AGE OF PRINCIPALITIES

THREE CITY-STATES

After the 15th century, the Kathmandu Valley lost its central control and was ruled as three city-states: Kathmandu, Patan, and Bhadgaon. Many Nepalese architectural heritages, such as temples, palaces, including many UNESCO world heritage sites, were built during the rule of the Newar Kings. These include the Kathmandu Old Palace (Kathmandu Durbar Square), Patan Palace (Patan Durbar Square), Bhaktapur Palace (Bhaktapur Durbar Square) etc.

By this time, people living in and around Kathmandu Valley (irrespective of their ethnic origins) were called "Newars".

MAGAR PRINCIPALITIES

Magars are martial people that first established their kingdom in present day western Nepal. They were animistic and shamanic in their religious practices. The Kham Magar of the upper Karnali basin and their brethren of the mid-hills of Nepal had a flourishing and empirical kingdom. Much archaeological proof of their existence can be found in the western mid-hills of Nepal.

The Magar have a strong military and warrior tradition. However, their hospitality and concern for their fellow human beings is also legendary. Two waves of immigrants became the undoing of the Magar empire. Firstly, the Khasas were welcomed and assimilated within Magar empire. Secondly, due to the advance of Muslim forces into the Gangetic plains of India, the Brahmins entered the Magar empire as refugees.

These two groups were given sanctuary in the Magar empire. The latter group of refugees started to impose their view of Hinduism upon the Magars, while the former groups were given the status of Chettri by the latter group in accordance with their view of Hinduism.

This left the Magar people boxed into the third tier in their own kingdom (the first being the Brahmins, the second being the newly elevated Chettri, previously the Khasas). This meant that the one-time rulers of the Nepali mid-hills became the ruled upon. This was the start of the degradation of the Magar empire. The introduction of Hinduism in itself became the cataclysmic event in the undoing of the Magar empire.

HISTORY OF KIRAT

In the meantime, the History of Kirat covers much of the history and achievements of the Kirant people of Eastern Nepal/Kiratdesh from ancient period until the Gorkha conquest in the eastern Nepal.

HISTORY OF LIMBUWAN

History of Limbuwan shows the history and political development of the people of Limbuwan until their unification with the Kingdom of Gorkha in 1774 AD. During King Prithivi Narayan Shah's unification of Nepal, the present-day Nepal east of Arun and Koshi River was known as Pallo Kirant Limbuwan.

It was divided into ten Limbu Kingdoms of which the Morang Kingdom was the most powerful and had the central government. The capital of the Morang Kingdom of Limbuwan was Bijaypur, now Dharan.

After the Limbuwan-Gorkha War and seeing the threat of the rising power of the British East India Company, kings and ministers of all the ten Limbu Kingdoms of Limbuwan gathered in Bijaypur, present day Dharan, to agree upon the Limbuwan-Gorkha treaty. This Treaty formally united ten Limbu Kingdoms into the Gorkha Kingdom, but it also gave Limbuwan full autonomy under Limbuwan Kipat System.

KINGDOM OF NEPAL

GORKHA RULE

After decades of rivalry between the medieval kingdoms, modern Nepal was created in the latter half of the 18th century, when Prithvi Narayan Shah, the ruler of the small principality of Gorkha, formed a unified country from a number of independent hill states. Prithvi Narayan Shah dedicated himself at an early age to the conquest of the Kathmandu Valley and the creation of a single state, which he achieved in 1768.

The country was frequently called the Gorkha Kingdom. It is a misconception that the Gurkhas took their name from the Gorkha region of Nepal. The region was given its name after the Gurkhas had established their control of these areas. The Gurkha, also spelled Gorkha, are people from Nepal who take their name from the legendary eighth-century Hindu warrior-saint Guru Gorakhnath.

Gurkhas claim descent from the Hindu Rajputs and Brahmins of Northern India, who entered modern Nepal from the west. After Shah's death, the Shah dynasty began to expand their kingdom into what is present day North India. Between 1788 and 1791, Nepal invaded Tibet and robbed Tashilhunpo Monastery of Shigatse.

Alarmed, the Chinese emperor Qianlong appointed Fu Kangan commander-in-chief of the Tibetan campaign and Fu not only defeated the Gurkha army but also conquered Tibet. The Gurkhas were forced to accept surrender on China terms. After 1800, the heirs of Prithvi Narayan Shah proved unable to maintain firm political control over Nepal.

A period of internal turmoil followed. Rivalry between Nepal and the British East India Company - over the princely states bordering Nepal and India - eventually led to the Anglo-Nepalese War (1814–16), in which Nepal suffered a complete rout. The Treaty of Sugauli was signed in 1816, ceding large parts of the Nepali territories of Terrai and Sikkim, (nearly one third of the country), to the British, in exchange for Nepalese autonomy.

As the ceded territories were not restored to Nepal by the British when freedom was granted to the people of British India, these have become a part of the Republic of India even though it was mentioned that the treaties on behalf of the East India Company or British India would not be valid anymore. The Kingdom of Sikkim, which had already lost its Darjeeling region to British India in 1853, was annexed by the post-colonial Republic of India in April 1975 and, in the following month, Sikkim's people voted to join the Indian Union.

Royal coup by King Mahendra Declaring parliamentary democracy a failure, King Mahendra carried out a royal coup 18 months later, in 1960. He dismissed the elected Koirala government, declared that a "partyless" panchayat system would govern Nepal, and promulgated another new constitution on December 16, 1960. Subsequently, the elected Prime Minister, Members of Parliament and hundreds of democratic activists were arrested. (In fact, this trend of arrest of political activists and democratic supporters continued for the entire 30 year period of partyless Panchayati System under King Mahendra and then his son, King Birendra).

The new constitution established a "partyless" system of panchayats (councils) which King Mahendra considered to be a democratic form of government, closer to Nepalese traditions. As a pyramidal structure, progressing from village assemblies to a Rastriya Panchayat (National Parliament), the panchayat system constitutionalised the absolute power of the monarchy and kept the King as head of state with sole authority over all governmental institutions, including the Cabinet (Council of Ministers) and the Parliament.

One-state-one-language became the national policy in an effort to carry out state unification, uniting various ethnic and regional groups into a singular Nepali nationalist bond. King Mahendra was succeeded by his 27 year-old son, King Birendra, in 1972. Amid student demonstrations and anti-regime activities in 1979, King Birendra called for a national referendum to decide on the nature of Nepal's government: either the continuation of the panchayat system with democratic reforms or the establishment of a multiparty system.

The referendum was held in May 1980, and the panchayat system won a narrow victory. The king carried out the promised reforms, including selection of the prime minister by the Rastriya Panchayat. People in rural areas had expected that their interests would be better represented after the adoption of parliamentary democracy in 1990.

The Nepali Congress with support of "Alliance of leftist parties" decided to launch a decisive agitational movement, Jana Andolan, which forced the monarchy to accept constitutional reforms and to establish a multiparty parliament. In May 1991, Nepal held its first parliamentary elections in nearly 50 years. The Nepali Congress won 110 of the 205 seats and formed the first elected government in 32 years.

20TH CENTURY

In 1923 Britain and Nepal formally signed an agreement of friendship, in which Nepal and India (which was under British Rule at that time) negotiated and ended up exchanging some cities. Slavery was abolished in Nepal in 1924.

DEMOCRATIC REFORM

Popular dissatisfaction against the family rule of the Ranas had started emerging from among the few educated people, who had studied in various Indian schools and colleges, and also from within the Ranas, many of whom were marginalised within the ruling Rana hierarchy. Many of these Nepalese in exile had actively taken part in the Indian Independence struggle and wanted to liberate Nepal as well from the internal autocratic Rana occupation.

The political parties such as *The Prajaparishad* and *Nepali Congress* were already formed in exile by leaders such as B.

P. Koirala, Ganesh Man Singh, Subarna Sumsher Rana, Krishna Prasad Bhattarai, Girija Prasad Koirala, and many other patriotic-minded Nepalis who urged the military and popular political movement in Nepal to overthrow the autocratic Rana Regime. Among the prominent martyrs to die for the cause, executed at the hands of the Ranas, were Dharma Bhakta Mathema, Shukraraj Shastri, Gangalal Shrestha, and Dasharath Chand.

This turmoil culminated in King Tribhuvan, a direct descendant of Prithvi Narayan Shah, fleeing from his "palace prison" in 1950, to newly independent India, touching off an armed revolt against the Rana administration. This eventually ended in the return of the Shah family to power and the appointment of a non-Rana as prime minister.

A period of quasi-constitutional rule followed, during which the monarch, assisted by the leaders of fledgling political parties, governed the country. During the 1950s, efforts were made to frame a constitution for Nepal that would establish a representative form of government, based on a British model.

In early 1959, Tribhuvan's son King Mahendra issued a new constitution, and the first democratic elections for a national assembly were held. The Nepali Congress Party, a moderate socialist group, gained a substantial victory in the election. Its leader, Bishweshwar Prasad Koirala, formed a government and served as prime minister. After years of power wrangling between the kings (Tribhuvan and Mahendra) and the government, Mahendra dissolved the democratic experiment in 1960.

ROYAL COUP BY KING MAHENDRA

Declaring parliamentary democracy a failure, King Mahendra carried out a royal coup 18 months later, in 1960. He dismissed the elected Koirala government, declared that a "partyless" panchayat system would govern Nepal, and promulgated another new constitution on December 16, 1960.

Subsequently, the elected Prime Minister, Members of Parliament and hundreds of democratic activists were arrested. (In fact, this trend of arrest of political activists and democratic supporters continued for the entire 30 year period of partyless Panchayati System under King Mahendra and then his son, King Birendra).

The new constitution established a "partyless" system of panchayats (councils) which King Mahendra considered to be a democratic form of government, closer to Nepalese traditions. As a pyramidal structure, progressing from village assemblies to a Rastriya Panchayat (National Parliament), the panchayat system constitutionalised the absolute power of the monarchy and kept the King as head of state with sole authority over all governmental institutions, including the Cabinet (Council of Ministers) and the Parliament.

One-state-one-language became the national policy in an effort to carry out state unification, uniting various ethnic and regional groups into a singular Nepali nationalist bond. King Mahendra was succeeded by his 27 year-old son, King Birendra, in 1972. Amid student demonstrations and anti-regime activities in 1979, King Birendra called for a national referendum to decide on the nature of Nepal's government: either the continuation of the panchayat system with democratic reforms or the establishment of a multiparty system.

The referendum was held in May 1980, and the panchayat system won a narrow victory. The king carried out the promised reforms, including selection of the prime minister by the Rastriya Panchayat. People in rural areas had expected that their interests would be better represented after the adoption of parliamentary democracy in 1990.

The Nepali Congress with support of "Alliance of leftist parties" decided to launch a decisive agitational movement, Jana Andolan, which forced the monarchy to accept constitutional reforms and to establish a multiparty parliament. In May 1991, Nepal held its first parliamentary elections in nearly 50 years. The Nepali Congress won 110 of the 205 seats and formed the first elected government in 32 years.

CIVIL STRIFE

In 1992, in a situation of economic crisis and chaos, with spiralling prices as a result of implementation of changes in policy of the new Congress government, the radical left stepped up their political agitation. A Joint People's Agitation Committee was set up by the various groups. A general strike was called for April 6. Violent incidents began to occur on the evening before of the strike.

The Joint People's Agitation Committee had called for a 30-minute 'lights out' in the capital, and violence erupted outside Bir Hospital when activists tried to enforce the 'lights out'. At dawn on April 6, clashes between strike activists and police, outside a police station in Pulchok (Patan), left two activists dead. Later in the day, a mass rally of the Agitation Committee at Tundikhel in the capital Kathmandu was attacked by police forces.

As a result, riots broke out and the Nepal Telecommunications building was set on fire; police opened fire at the crowd, killing several persons. The Human Rights Organisation of Nepal estimated that 14 persons, including several onlookers, had been killed in police firing. When promised land reforms failed to appear, people in some districts started to organize to enact their own land reform and to gain some power over their lives in the face of usurious landlords.

However, this movement was repressed by the Nepali government, in "Operation Romeo" and "Operation Kilo Sera II", which took the lives of many of the leading activists of the struggle. As a result, many witnesses to this repression became radicalized. Nepal has traditionally maintained a non-aligned policy and enjoys friendly relations with neighboring countries, especially India and China.

As a small, landlocked country wedged between two larger and far stronger powers, Nepal maintains good relations with both China (People's Republic of China) and India. Constitutionally, foreign policy is to be guided by "the principles of the United Nations Charter, nonalignment,

Panchsheel [five principles of peaceful coexistence], international law and the value of world peace."

In practice, foreign policy has not been directed toward projecting influence internationally but toward preserving autonomy and addressing domestic economic and security issues. Nepal's most substantive international relations are perhaps with international economic institutions, such as the Asian Development Bank, the International Monetary Fund, the World Bank, and the South Asian Association for Regional Cooperation, a multilateral economic development association.

Nepal also has strong bilateral relations with major providers of economic and military aid, such as France, Germany, Japan, Switzerland, the United States, and particularly the United Kingdom, with whom military ties date to the nineteenth century. The country also maintains strong political relations with India and China, usually attempting to balance one against the other.

However, relations with India are fraught with trade and border disputes and Indian suspicions that Nepalese and Pakistani rebels use Nepal as a haven to attack India. Relations with Bhutan have been strained since 1992 over the nationality and possible repatriation of refugees from Bhutan. The Indo-Nepal Treaty of Peace and Friendship of 1950 is a bilateral treaty between Nepal and India establishing a close strategic relationship between the two South Asian neighbors.

The treaty was signed on July 31, 1950 by the then-Prime Minister of Nepal Mohan Shamsher Jang Bahadur Rana and Indian ambassador to Nepal, Chadreshwar Narayan Singh. The treaty allows for the free movement of people and goods between the two nations and a close relationship and collaboration on matters of defence and foreign affairs.

While India values the treaty as deflecting the influence of its regional competitor, the People's Republic of China, the treaty has been unpopular in many segments of Nepal, which often regards it as a breach of its sovereignty. The Himalayan federal republic of Nepal borders northern India in the south and east. During British rule in India, Nepal's ties were governed by the 1825 Treaty of Sugauli.

After the independence of India in 1947, the two nations sought to forge close strategic, commercial and cultural relations. The rise of Communist China in 1949 and the subsequent invasion of Tibet heightened security concerns in both India and Nepal — while India had maintained good relations with Tibet and was faced with border issues with China, Nepal feared that China would support the Communist Party of Nepal and sponsor a communist revolution overthrowing the state.

With heightening concerns over the security threat to India presented by Communist China, which was seen as seeking to projecting power and influence over Nepal, Sikkim and Bhutan and border disputes with India, the latter sought to strengthen its "Himalayan frontier" by forging an alliance on defence and foreign affairs with Nepal.

PROVISIONS

The Indo-Nepal Treaty of Peace and Friendship provided for an open border between the two nations, permitting free and unrestricted travel of people and goods and allowing the immigration of Indians to Nepal and of Nepalese people to India, granting equal rights to them. Both nations agreed to respect each others territorial integrity and independence.

The treaty also facilitated extensive cooperation on strategic issues, with both nations required to consult each other on affairs of regional security; while India was obligated to actively assist Nepal in national defence and military preparedness, and both nations resolved not to tolerate threats to each others security.

DETERIORATION OF BILATERAL RELATIONS

Although initially support enthusiastically by both sides, the treaty became the subject of increased resentment in Nepal, which saw it as an encroachment of its sovereignty and an unwelcome extension of Indian influence. After an abortive attempt in 1952 of the Communist Party of Nepal to seize power with Chinese backing, India and Nepal stepped up military and intelligence cooperation under treaty provisions, and India sent a military mission to Nepal, which was however regarded as an undue extension of Indian influence in Nepal.

In the late 1950s and 1960s, Nepal and China forged better relations, while relations with India deteriorated as Nepal forced the Indian military mission to leave and both nations began ignoring the treaty provisions. While temporarily brought closer after the Sino-Indian War in 1962 and the occupation of Aksai Chin by Chinese forces, Nepal resented the growth of India's regional power in the 1970s.

It also protested when Sikkim joined the Indian Union in 1975. The extensive Indian trade and economic influence was also resented in Nepal. Nepal began openly lobbying for renegotiation of the treaty and proposed itself as a "zone of peace" between India and China, effectively distancing itself from India.

PROPOSED SCRAPPING

Upon forming a coalition government after the 2008 Nepalese Constituent Assembly election, the leader of the Communist Party of Nepal (Maoist) Prachanda said on April 24, 2008 that the 1950 treaty would be scrapped and a new pact would be negotiated with India, which also signalled its willingness to review the treaty.

MULTILATERAL RELATIONS OF NEPAL

Nepal has played an active role in the formation of the economic development-oriented South Asian Association for Regional Cooperation (SAARC) and is the site of its secretariat. On international issues, Nepal follows a nonaligned policy and often votes with the Non-Aligned Movement in the United Nations.

Nepal participates in a number of UN specialized agencies and is a member of the World Bank, International Monetary Fund, Colombo Plan, and the Asian Development Bank.

HUMAN RIGHTS ISSUES

Police forces sometimes use excessive force in quelling violent demonstrations, or demonstrations that may upset 'friendly countries'. In addition, there have been reports of torture under detention and widespread reports of custodial abuse. In 2000, the government established the Human Rights Commission, a government-appointed commission with a mandate to investigate human rights violations. To date, the Commission has investigated 51 complaints.

Some restrictions continue on freedom of expression. Trafficking in women and child labour remain serious problems. Discrimination against women and lower castes is prevalent.

1950-1970

In the 1950s, Nepal welcomed close relations with India, but as the number of Nepalese living and working in India increased and the involvement of India in Nepal's economy deepened in the 1960s and after, so too did Nepalese discomfort with the special relationship.

Tensions came to a head in the mid-1970s, when Nepal pressed for substantial amendments in its favor in the trade and transit treaty and openly criticized India's 1975 annexation of Sikkim which was considered as part of Greater Nepal.

In 1975 King Birendra Bir Bikram Shah Dev proposed that Nepal be recognized internationally as a zone of peace; he received support from China and Pakistan.

In New Delhi's view, if the king's proposal did not contradict the 1950 treaty an extension of nonalignment, it was unnecessary; if it was a repudiation of the special relationship, it represented a possible threat to India's security and could not be endorsed.

In 1984 Nepal repeated the proposal, but there was no reaction from India. Nepal continually promoted the proposal in international forums, with Chinese support; by 1990 it had won the support of 112 countries.

1970-1980

In 1978 India agreed to separate trade and transit treaties, satisfying a long-term Nepalese demand. In 1988, when the two treaties were up for renewal, Nepal's refusal to accommodate India's wishes on the transit treaty caused India to call for a single trade and transit treaty.

Thereafter, Nepal took a hard-line position that led to a serious crisis in India-Nepal relations. After two extensions, the two treaties expired on March 23, 1989, resulting in a virtual Indian economic blockade of Nepal that lasted until late April 1990. Although economic issues were a major factor in the two countries' confrontation, Indian dissatisfaction with Nepal's 1988 acquisition of Chinese weaponry played an important role.

Treaties and letters exchanged in 1959 and 1965, which included Nepal in India's security zone and precluded arms purchases without India's approval. India linked security with economic relations and insisted on reviewing India-Nepal relations as a whole. Nepal had to back down after worsening ecconomic conditions led to a change in Nepal's political system, in which the king was forced to institute a parliamentary democracy. The new government sought quick restoration of amicable relations with India.

1990S

The special security relationship between New Delhi and Kathmandu was reestablished during the June 1990 New Delhi meeting of Nepal's Prime Minister Krishna Prasad Bhattarai and Indian prime minister V.P. Singh. During the December 1991 visit to India by Nepalese prime minister Girija Prasad Koirala, the two countries signed new, separate trade and transit treaties and other economic agreements designed to accord Nepal additional economic benefits.

Indian-Nepali relations appeared to be undergoing still more reassessment when Nepal's prime minister Man Mohan Adhikary visited New Delhi in April 1995 and insisted on a major review of the 1950 peace and friendship treaty. In the face of benign statements by his Indian hosts relating to the treaty, Adhikary sought greater economic independence for his landlocked nation while simultaneously striving to improve ties with China.

21ST CENTURY

In 2005, after King Gyanendra took over, Nepalese relations with India soured. However, after the restoration of democracy, in 2008, Prachanda, the Prime Minister of Nepal, visited India, in September 2008. He spoke about a new dawn, in the bilateral relations, between the two countries. He said, "I am going back to Nepal as a satisfied person. I will tell Nepali citizens back home that a new era has dawned. Time has come to effect a revolutionary change in bilateral relations. On behalf of the new government, I assure you that we are committed to make a fresh start." He met Indian Prime minister, Manmohan Singh, and Foreign Minister, Pranab Mukherjee. He asked India to help Nepal frame a new constitution, and to invest in Nepal's infrastructure, and its tourism industry.

In 2008, Indo-Nepali ties got a further boost with an agreement to resume water talks after a 4 year hiatus. The Nepalese Water Resources Secretary Shanker Prasad Koirala said the Nepal-India Joint Committee on Water Resources meet decided to start the reconstruction of breached Kosi embankment after the water level goes down. During the Nepal PM's visit to New Delhi in September the two Prime Ministers expressed satisfaction at the age-old close, cordial and extensive relationships between their states and expressed their support and cooperation to further consolidate the relationship.

The two issued a 22-point statement highlighting the need to review, adjust and update the 1950 Treaty of Peace and Friendship, amongst other agreements. India would also provide a credit line of up to 150 crore rupees to Nepal to ensure uninterrupted supplies of petroleum products, as well as lift bans on the export of rice, wheat, maize, sugar and sucrose for quantities agreed to with Nepal. India would also provide 20 crore as immediate flood relief.

In return, Nepal will take measures for the "promotion of investor friendly, enabling business environment to encourage Indian...investments in Nepal." Furthermore, a three-tier mechanism at the level of ministerial, secretary and technical levels will be built to push forward discussions on the development of water resources between the two sides.

Politically, India acknowledged a willingness to promote efforts towards peace in Nepal. Indian External affairs minister Pranab Mukherjee promised the Nepali Prime Minister Prachanda that he would "extend all possible help for peace and development." In 2008, the Bollywood film *Chandni Chowk to China* was banned in Nepal, because of a scene suggesting the Gautama Buddha was born in India. Some protesters called for commercial boycott of all Indian films.

2

Emergence of Modern Nepal Relations with India

NEPALESE CIVIL WAR

In February 1996, the Communist Party of Nepal (Maoist) started a bid to replace the parliamentary monarchy with a people's new democratic republic, through a Maoist revolutionary strategy known as the people's war, which led to the Nepalese Civil War. Led by Dr. Baburam Bhattarai and Pushpa Kamal Dahal (also known as "Prachanda"), the insurgency began in five districts in Nepal: Rolpa, Rukum, Jajarkot, Gorkha, and Sindhuli.

The Communist Party of Nepal (Maoist) established a provisional "people's government" at the district level in several locations. On June 1, 2001, Crown Prince Dipendra went on a shooting-spree, assassinating 9 members of the royal family, including King Birendra and Queen Aishwarya, before shooting himself. Due to his survival he temporarily became king before dying of his wounds, after which Prince Gyanendra (Birendra's brother) inherited the throne, according to tradition.

Meanwhile, the rebellion escalated, and in October 2001 the king temporarily deposed the government and took complete control of it. A week later he reappointed another government, but the country was still very unstable. In the face of unstable governments and a siege on the Kathmandu Valley in August 2004, popular support for the monarchy began to wane.

On February 1, 2005, Gyanendra dismissed the entire government and assumed full executive powers, declaring a "state of emergency" to quash the revolution. Politicians were placed under house arrest, phone and internet lines were cut, and freedom of the press was severely curtailed. The king's new regime made little progress in his stated aim to suppress the insurgents.

Municipal elections in February 2006 were described by the European Union as "a backward step for democracy", as the major parties boycotted the election and some candidates were forced to run for office by the army. In April 2006 strikes and street protests in Kathmandu forced the king to reinstate the parliament. A seven-party coalition resumed control of the government and stripped the king of most of his powers.

As of 15 January 2007 Nepal was governed by an unicameral legislature under an interim constitution. On December 24, 2007, seven parties, including the former Maoist rebels and the ruling party, agreed to abolish monarchy and declare Nepal a Federal Republic.. In the elections held on April 10, 2008, the Maoists secured a simple majority, with the prospect of forming a government to rule the proposed 'Republic of Nepal'.

An incident in a Nepali village, late one August afternoon in 1987, illustrates how people there have come to connect ideas about national development to healing. A young woman, Jethi, was pregnant for the third time. When her first baby was ten months old, the child fell sick and died within a day. Her second was stillborn. In her area of eastern Nepal, one kind of ghost-spirit, saruwa, is known to prey on pregnant women and infants, and Jethi has come to fear that a saruwa is attracted to her.

Her worried in-laws have sent her to stay with her own mother and father for a time so that she can be present at an elaborate family ritual that will be undertaken because of the bad fortune that has plagued the family for several years. A Brahmin in their village just happens to know the spells to chase off these spirits. They have called him to the house to make an amulet for Jethi, one of many measures they will take to protect her.

The healer, a dignified old man clad in the traditional homespun tunic and pants worn by old-fashioned farmers, sat in a corner of the outer room of the house while Jethi sat quietly in front of him, staring distractedly over her shoulder at an empty corner of the room. He has arranged five small piles of rice on a banana leaf, each with a flower laid on it. For several minutes he muttered a rapid succession of syllables - his mantra - punctuated by sharp, sucking intakes of breath, then wrote a protective formula on a piece of paper. He folded this neatly in plastic to make an amulet for Jethi to wear for the duration of her pregnancy.

Meanwhile, a man in store-bought shirt and pants arrived. He works in the Public Health Statistics Office in the nearby bazaar, and came with a dose of penicillin for Jethi's younger sister. A few days earlier, a painful boil had developed on the young woman's thigh, so she arranged for this neighbor to give her penicillin each day, for five days, on his way home from work.

There was no question of trying other remedies: "Why should I suffer from the stupid thing when I know that penicillin will cure it in a flash?" She immediately set to boiling water to sterilize the needle. "I won't have an injection at the clinic," she later declared, in response to my question. "You never know whether they've boiled the needle."

As each sister sat with the healers helping them, their father, sweaty from a day's work in the fields, strode into the house, a sickle swinging by his side. The juxtaposition he saw made him laugh aloud. "What's going on here? In one room injections and this ritual mumbo-jumbo in the other!" Then, noticing me sitting next to Jethi with a notebook open on my lap, he declared, still laughing: "See! In our Nepal it's like this!"

This ordinary event, and the amusement seen in its incongruities, says much about contemporary Nepal. The father's offhand comment is particularly significant for the contrast between traditional and Western healing that struck him, and the aspect of Nepalese social life that he saw represented in that juxtaposition. This chapter examines how local people see the medical pluralism brought about, directly or indirectly, by health development initiatives.

The ways local people maneuver in this pluralistic medical field is determined only in part by their access to therapies and their judgements about which works best for what. In Nepal, medical pluralism has a profound social symbolism for villagers as well. Its meaning, itself the result of specific historical experiences, is an important dimension in people's interactions with the various kinds of therapy available to them. Healing is a dense signifier of the social rifts now emerging as a result of a national agenda intensely focused on development.

Development activities and explanations are themselves, therefore, part of the contemporary ethnographic picture in Nepal. At the local level, simultaneous recourse to Western medicines and ritual therapies encapsulates contradictions in the social world of contemporary Nepal. The father's half-joking exclamation, that "in our Nepal it's like this," alludes to a relation between local traditions and things Nepali villagers call "modern." This relation is a paradox that assimilates the new while juxtaposing it with the traditional.

The scene described makes evident that people intermingle different kinds of therapy while at the same time being self-conscious about the relation between injections and amulets. This self-consciousness is an important social effect of development. Development does more than make drugs like penicillin available, or even change people's concepts of illness.

Development also transforms people's vision of who they are. The social divisions fostered by an ideology of modernization are at issue in people's understandings of medical pluralism. That people in Nepal avail themselves of diverse therapies, ranging from pharmaceuticals to shamanic rites, is not particularly remarkable. A vast literature in anthropology demonstrates that medical pluralism is the rule, not the exception, around the world.

Researchers have asked how these systems perpetuate themselves, how they change, and how actors operate within them. Much of the ethnographic work tracks the actor's trajectory through a complex field of medical possibilities.

The aims have been to document patterns of resort, to explain how and why people in a given context make choices among therapeutic options, and to show how actors use movement among healers to create complexly meaningful responses toward suffering. These approaches provide important insights into forces shaping the individual's path from illness to therapy.

One difficulty, however, is that as analysis narrows its focus to medical ideas, medical behaviors, and medical consequences, it is easy to lose sight of the ways that people's actions with respect to health and illness contribute to and are shaped by much broader social processes.

Comaroff argues strongly against an analytical distinction between social context and medical issues, noting that because "the context of healing affords privileged insight into the relationship between individual experience and the socio-cultural order" therapy systems, the changes that occur in them, and the ways individuals make sense of them must be understood in relation to wider processes of social change.

Her observation cuts two ways. It is important not only to take into account the social factors implicated in medical interactions (as anthropologists certainly realize), but also to consider how attention to the realm of healing can shed light on social concerns that are not strictly medical. More than just a field of therapeutic possibilities, medical pluralism is also an arena for the negotiation of social difference.

Several case studies highlight the ways that illness and healing power come to be imbued with an imagery of differentiation - a symbolics of ethnicity, race, gender, and class. Importantly, these cases illustrate that social differences are not simply variables influencing medical outcomes. Rather, the definition of medical problems and the interactions in medical encounters themselves contribute to the social experiences of difference.

For instance, in Bolivia medicine mediates ethnically marked class differences. People embark on certain therapeutic paths "not for medical, but for social reasons". Accordingly, "Campesinos, Methodists, and mestizos distinguish themselves from each other not by expressing different medical beliefs, but by perceiving themselves as holding different positions within the same medical universe".

For Colombia, Taussig (1987:218) argues that the logic of shamanic power has to be understood through the history of colonial social relations. Colonial images of the "savage other" project magical power onto those colonialism has marginalized, creating a logic that "folds the underworld of the conquering society into the culture of the conquered, the peon, the slave."

In Kalimantan, Tsing (1988) reports, ethnic power relations are played out through interactions between the distinctive discourses on healing and the body put forth by Muslim Banjar and Meratus Dyaks. In contemporary Nepal, the social difference most at issue in medical realms arises from Nepali ideas about modernization which make salient a distinction between traditional villager and modern cosmopolitans.

Complementary, competing, and blended medical systems have all been characterized as pluralistic, even though the relations involved are quite different. Bhattacharya (1983) shows that pluralism is found at institutional, cognitive, and structural levels, and that these are not necessarily congruent. Similarly, Waxler (1984) argues that pluralism is in the eye of the beholder.

While ayurvedic and Western medical practitioners in Sri Lanka distinguish between the two systems, patients do not.

"A pluralistic structure exists only to the extent that actors behave in such a way as to . . . differentiate various subsystems as distinct entities," Bhattacharya points out. Outside observers, be they anthropologists or development planners, may distinguish subsystems that the actors in a given locale do not.

What, then, makes certain distinctions significant from a local point of view? This chapter describes in general terms how people in one area of Nepal envision the significance of difference in medical pluralism. Local visions of the relation between traditional and Western-style healing stand in sharp contrast to the way medical pluralism is framed in the influential policy and planning discourse of development institutions.

Despite the intentions of many development initiatives to foster what they term "community participation" and to make use of what they see as "indigenous knowledge," the institutional priorities of development programs nearly always supersede responsiveness to local conditions. The presence of other authoritative, nonbiomedical systems of healing is problematic for development's fundamentally biomedical reform agenda.

It is difficult for planners and officials to listen to and learn from local approaches to health and illness when so much of their energy is concentrated on changing those very approaches. As a result, in health development especially, institutional concern with local perceptions rests solely on identifying the potential compatibility or incompatibility between what they call "beliefs and practices" and health development objectives.

The difference between so-called traditional medicine and the system development offers is viewed as self-evident. The medical pluralism perceived from the development perspective poses only questions of competition or possible collaboration; e.g., Do traditional practices interfere with our objectives? Can we train traditional medical practitioners? Do their shamans have useful medicinal knowledge? As shown below, people in rural Nepal have a different understanding of this difference, as well as of why it matters.

To the extent that health development planners concern themselves with local people's perceptions, the focus is on what they term "knowledge" (by which they mean familiarity with Western-style medicine) and "beliefs" (by which they mean nonbiomedical ideas about illness). Planners look to the attitudes and ideas about illness held by individuals in order to explain people's responses to Western-style medical practices.

Health education efforts are seen as ways of persuading people to adopt new health beliefs, or at the very least, to take sick family members to the health post sooner. Evaluations of specific programs typically measure changes in what they call "attitudes" as well as changes in morbidity and mortality. Implicit in this framework is a notion that all medical help seeking is a direct expression of discrete beliefs in people's heads. (As one American health official asked me upon learning the topic of my research: "Can you explain what is it in their culture that keeps them from going to the hospital'?")

This framework is not so much wrong - for culturally specific ideas about etiology and cures do exist - as overly narrow. Changes in health-related concepts occur in a social context that gives certain attitudes and knowledge a social meaning. Specifically, the people whose perspectives are reduced to sets of "ideas" and "attitudes" to be scrutinized for measurable changes know that they are participating in a wider process of social transformation. Not only are they affected by development, they reflect on what it means to be differentially affected by development.

This gives rural people an alternative perspective on what development is in Nepal and what its relation to local life might be. Medicine is central in Nepali people's constructions of the meaning of bikas (development). Nepalis are increasingly seeing their society in terms of contrasts between progress and backwardness, rationality and superstition, modernity and tradition.

When applied by Nepalis to other Nepalis, these polarizing categories ideologicaily reinforce growing economic disparities. As terms for flaming identity, the very ordinary ways individuals represent their place in a developing Nepal are acts through which a new, dominant vision of Nepal could eventually become entrenched and increasingly difficult to call into question. The concepts of tradition and development are key points around which reformulated views of identity are being constructed.

When people use the Nepali word bikas to talk about what we refer to as development, the connotations are specific to Nepalese experiences of this form of social change. Struggles over meaning emerge because development activities do more than implement a set of policies and programs, they reinforce an ideology of modernization.

Hegemony takes form in common sense and taken-for-granted assumptions about the world and how it works. A hegemonic order solidifies power by naturalizing a particular way of understanding the social world. In other words, hegemony is not the ability of a dominant class to impose its interests on other members of society, but is rather a particular combination of ideological elements that successfully links diverse interests, such that the interests of one class come to seem to be also the interests of others.

As Willlares has stressed, however, the ascendancy of any ideology can never be fully achieved. Tensions, contradictions, and contestations are part of the process by which structures of meaning are ambivalently appropriated and reproduced. Development initiatives in Nepal appear to have done little to better the lot of the poor, while opening up new opportunities to an emerging middle class. Yet the paradigm of modernization, with its stress on progress and backwardness, is to a great extent assimilated into the common sense governing everyday life even among rural farmers.

The ideology of modernization pivots on a social distinction between what are referred to in Nepal as traditional "village" and "modern" outlooks. That state-sponsored projects of development in much of the Third World draw heavily on a narrative of modern progress is clear. How people in diverse locales actually take up these notions and rework them, how they respond to being categorized through them and use them to understand themselves and others, has so far received little sustained attention, however, in the emerging literature on the construction of development discourse.

One exception is Woost's (1993) discussion of how factions in a Sri Lankan village use specifically nationalist images of development to justify their claims to benefits from development projects. Even while these villagers are critical of the injustices development forces on them, they have come to depend on development "not just for the scarce resources it offers from time to time, but for the symbols with which to construct their own histories of community development".

A similar transformation in self-understanding occurs in Nepal as the social categories of national development rhetoric intersect with and work to reshape a local sense of identity. It is what makes rural people self-conscious about their relationship to Western-style medicine in the first place. Yet, as we will later see, the common sense categories of the ideology of modernization are still open to contestation and alternative constructions.

THE SOCIAL IDENTITY

What it means to be a villager is as much a function of how images of villages figure in a national story about social transformation as it is an expression of social experience in actual villages. In much of the anthropological, touristic, and development policy writing on Nepal, the word village conjures up images of poverty, isolation, and unchanging tradition. Foreign observers and Nepalese cosmopolitan elites alike fall into the habit of attributing to villages and villagers dimensions of Nepalese social life that appear farthest from or most resistant to development and the ideals of modernization.

These narratives suggest that a gulf separates village Nepal from the "developed" sectors of society. As representations, they obscure the differences among and within the thousands of villages in Nepal and mask the significant ways that rural life in Nepal has already been transformed.

The process of national unification begun in the late eighteenth century, the exploitation that accompanied the state expansion, the ensuing changes in patterns of trade and land tenure, and the vulnerability of a nominally independent Nepal on the margins of the colonized subcontinent all contributed to transformations in rural life.

And while the broad economic contours of the processes leading to rural impoverishment can be traced, little is known of how people in the hills experienced and understood their position within these shifting political and economic realities. An ethnographic analysis of rural people's understanding of their position in a changing society is limited to contemporary expressions of identity.

This self-characterization is often articulated in relation to powerful images of the ahistorical village put forth in developmentalist ideology. The transformations associated with bikas, introduced abruptly in the mid-1950s, increasingly affect everyday life and define social identity. To be a villager in Nepal, these days, is to be poised between what people call "our hill people's customs" (hamro pahadko chal chalan) and the new manners people associate with "developed countries" (bikasit des).

This is particularly true where I conducted research. Bhojpur Bazaar and its surrounding villages are two-days' walk from the nearest motorable road, yet an airport, generator-powered mills, a college campus, a clinic, and numerous other amenities people associate with bikas are present.

Bikas is very much a part of people's lives in Bhojpur. They hear about it daily on Radio Nepal; they learn about it in school; they see it in the government offices that have sprung up in the bazaar in the last twenty years; they participate in it when they are able to bring electricity to their house or choose to vaccinate their children.

Together, these signs of bikas constitute a local experience of newness. Moreover, while subsistence farming and the daily demands of labor bind people to the land, the immediacy of this way of life is countered in the powerful images of other, more "developed places" (bikasit thaun) like Kathmandu and Hong Kong. Though tied to land and locality, the farmer-villager participates socially and economically in the much wider linkages between rural areas, cosmopolitan centers, and international circulations.

Some farmers in the area have salaried jobs in the bazaar; many have been soldiers in the British, Indian, or Nepalese Armies or have worked as laborers in India; most have relatives who have migrated to the Terai, Kathmandu, or beyond. These experiences and ties outside the local community lead people increasingly to contrast their village life with town-focused images of development and modernity. In comparison with these other places, Bhojpur appears poor and backward.

People in the Bhojpur area see themselves as more modern than the people of more remote areas yet more traditional than the elite of towns. This position in between different social worlds in Nepal is reflected in all aspects of people's daily life, including the ways they deal with illness.

LOCAL HEALERS

When people in Bhojpur get sick they turn to those who have special knowledge and insight. There are people who know about herbal medicines, people who are skilled at dream interpretation, people who know a mantra to cure snake bite or to set a broken bone, people who know a few spells to chase harmful spirits away from livestock.

There are also religious specialists whose skills can be applied to healing. Brahmin priests, Buddhist lamas, and Hindu religious devotees can recite phrases to protect people against inauspicious planetary configurations, perform rituals to insure the well-being of a household, or make protective amulets. There are healers known as phukne manchhe who are said to blow, sweep (jhar-phuk garne), and shoo away the various ghosts, spirits, and shades that frequently cling to people and make them sick.

Observed from the outside, this hererogenous mosaic of therapies bespeaks a long, dynamic history of intermingled religions and cultures. In the 1980s, however, local people did not see the history that brought about ethnic commingling reflected in these modes of healing. From a local perspective, these many kinds of healing are not seen as different systems, nor are they understood to form a single, coherently organized traditional form of medicine.

They merely constitute what is understood to be an open set of locally available options. Most prominent among local people who can heal are the various ritual specialists we call shamans. In eastern Nepal the generic term dhami or dhami-jhankri is used to refer to specialists who become possessed by spirits or go into trance and give divinations (jokhana), though people distinguish among different kinds of shamanic practitioners (such as bijuwa and baidhang). Shamans have magical and religious power acquired through their relationship with spirits (deuta).

They learn their songs and techniques through dreams, after having been chosen by a spirit. Initial possession appears first as uncontrolled trembling, fainting spells, or wild behaviour. Later, with the help of another shaman, the new shaman learns to control and channel possession and eventually to cure. A person does not choose to become a shaman; in fact, it is an onerous fate, especially for women.

Once chosen by spirits, shamans must continue to call their familiars to alight on their bodies and to follow certain ritual prescriptions. Though they are reimbursed for some of their services, no shaman makes a living exclusively by healing. People call shamans for many minor afflictions. A shaman sitting on a veranda muttering mantra over a sick child is a common sight. In cases of especially serious or intractable ailments shamans are called for nightlong sessions (chinta basnu) during which they call their spirits and send them “looking, searching” for the hidden forces that cause a person’s illness.

Often these spirits see the "stain" of witchcraft, and the shaman then uses his power to suck from the afflicted person's belly the bits of cloth, hair, or meat the witch has lodged there. These nightlong healing performances are infrequent, but memorable. Shamans drum, dance, sing, and give enigmatic divinations in gasping, syncopated verses for the people who have crowded into the dark house; they expose witches, engage in invisible battle with rivals, and sometimes perform dramatic cures.

In Nepal, everyone who has grown up in a village has firsthand experience with shamanic rituals, though in Bhojpur it was widely felt that shamans were not as powerful as they used to be. Although it is not uncommon for someone to accuse a shaman indirectly of being all performance and no power, or to voice skepticism whether these "magic acts" (jadu, chhal) can "really work," the meaning and relevance of shamanic intervention in troubled human lives is appreciated by all.

Shamans know how to appease, cajole, persuade, flatter, threaten, or chase away the myriad of extrahuman beings that plague people and cause them to suffer. They have extraordinary insight into the invisible world of restless, wandering ghosts, capricious local divinities, and malevolent human witches with whom people coexist. Shamans are necessary because they have the heightened sensitivity to serve as mediators between the extrahuman and human worlds. Thus they are key figures in local social life.

Without the help of shamans, ordinary people would have little hope of coping with the witches and spirits in their midst. But everyone comments that times have changed in Bhojpur, and now when someone is sick they are likely to consult both a shaman and a health worker, in hopes of getting Western-style medicine. They live within easy reach of a government-run general clinic, a tuberculosis clinic, and the family planning service's well-child clinic; or they can simply buy medicines themselves from a shop in the bazaar.

The therapies associated with doctors are well established in Bhojpur, even though a physician is rarely resident at the clinic there. It is health assistants, nurses, midwives, vaccinators, village health workers, and even the people who fetch tea in health offices who administer Western medicines. Nonetheless, it is the figure of the foreign-trained doctor - "come from cutting up people's hearts in England," as one man expressed it to me - that stands as a powerful symbol of Western medicine and the society from which it comes.

DEVELOPMENT IN TRANSFORMATION

The lack of roads, schools, industry, and, significantly, lack of hospitals and Western-style health care have long been used as indices of Nepal's economic backwardness. In recent decades, development programs ranging from road construction to education have come to have increasing impact on local communities. As roads bring more and more commodities to mountain villages, commercial medicines from India become more available to rural residents.

As the government, in conjunction with international donor agencies, establishes new programs for health development, rural people find health posts being built in their community, teams arriving to vaccinate their children, and radio messages exhorting them to go to the health post or hospital instead of to the shaman when they are sick. These are new experiences, according to people in Bhojpur. Prior to the push for national development, there were neither missionary hospitals nor state-sponsored health services. Local people were on their own.

Only those villagers who left the hills to work as laborers in India or who served in the British Army had any chance of encountering the institutions of Western-style medicine, let alone its cures. Thus the relationship between local and imported modes of healing is situated quite concretely within larger national processes of development and the ways these transform localities.

Obviously, Western-style medicine exists as a therapeutic alternative in Bhojpur in large measure as a direct result of Nepal's efforts to raise its standard of living through development. It is not surprising, then, that people in villages link the therapeutic practices associated with the people they call doctors to their experience of wider socioeconomic transformations in Nepal. They interpret healing through the social experience of development.

Intense efforts to build the nation through development began in Nepal quite abruptly in the mid-1950s. A political upheaval in 1950-51 ousted the Rana oligarchy, leading to the restructuring of national politics. The new state legitimated itself through its declared mission to, as it saw it, modernize Nepal. This watershed in national politics coincided with the postwar emergence of international development institutions.

Never colonized, a state that had carefully guarded its borders against direct foreign involvement embraced the technological, financial, and planning assistance offered by other nations.

Accordingly, the internally focused project of bikas has doubled as a vehicle for engagement with the world at large, both at the level of the state and that of everyday experience. The idea of bikas figures prominently in popular consciousness. Bikas is a reality for people not simply when programs or projects happen to involve them, but more importantly, in the way that the idea of bikas enters into people's imagination of their social world.

It has come to stand for a different way of life, a shadowy and elusive image of modernity formed from impressions of other places. Bikas has been promoted ideologicaily as a national mission for decades. The symbolism of development reaches further and faster into Nepalese society than do actual development initiatives. The things people equate with development were always preceded by the idea of bikas, an idea formed under specific historical conditions.

Planners and rural people understand bikas differently. From a policy perspective the development process is a matter of supplying villages with things, from credit to birth control devices, that were lacking before. No account is taken of the way that the very pursuit of development goals on a national scale itself creates a social and ideological milieu for the implementation of specific programs.

From the perspective of local people, however, the changes brought by development involve both the local incorporation of what they identify as modern elements coming from somewhere else and the re-evaluation of local values and practices. It is from within this local perspective that shamans and doctors acquire a specifically social symbolism.

To villagers, Western-style medicine can never come as a surprise, for two reasons. By the time it becomes conveniently available to people in a given locale, they already know of it and associate it with certain "developed places" beyond their locality. As a therapeutic form, furthermore, it already makes sense to people because they can fit it into a pre-existing framework for understanding illness and cure. This framework places ideas about illness causation and bodily processes within largely implicit propositions about medical knowledge.

People already know, for instance, that some illnesses are "inside" the body (bhitrako betha) while others are manifestations of external disturbances. They know that many kinds of influences affect people's well-being: the pull of the planets; the balance of hot and cold in the individual body; the relationships with ghosts and spirits; the malevolence of witches.

These influences all work simultaneously on a person. For example, a person affected by an inauspicious astrological configuration may be more vulnerable to attacks from a ghost or spells from a witch. People know, as well, that the way different influences combine to cause a person's suffering can make it difficult to pinpoint the precise cause of an illness.

They know that symptoms can be ambiguous because the same influences can manifest themselves differently at different times, showing up, say, as rashes in one case and as vomiting in another. They know that to cure an illness you have to deduce what kind of influence is primarily at work on the sick person; usually the only way you can know for sure what caused an illness is by seeing what cures it.

It is obvious, from the local perspective, that Western-style medicine works on the kinds of illnesses they identify as "sicknesses of the body" (jiuko betha). In searching for the cause of an illness, doctors gather knowledge directly from the body by taking temperatures, listening to heartbeats, checking the pulse, asking questions about appetite, digestion, physical symptoms. People equate these "tests" (janch) with the diagnostic processes, such as divinations, local healers use when they suspect a bodily illness.

Both are a way of seeing past the confusing aspect of symptoms into the true processes behind suffering. The difference, people note, is that doctors have much more powerful medicines that cure bodily illnesses quickly. It is equally obvious to people that the efficacy of Western-style medicine is limited to these bodily illnesses. Many people fail to be cured by the doctor's medicines because their illness is of a different nature. Some even get worse.

No one is startled by the novelty of Western-style medicine, nor by the theories of illness its practitioners expound. People consider the universe of influences that affect them to be open-ended, and they assume from the beginning that their knowledge of illness is incomplete. New ghosts and spirits may wander into the local community and be discovered, and new diseases may also come to be recognized. There is always more to learn.

Thus, people who have traveled and people from other places (for example, visiting shamans from other districts who might be especially powerful, wandering Indian holy men who might teach mantra to a local person, foreigners who might hand out medicines) are looked to for a contribution to the well-being of the community. These people may have bits of knowledge or medicines that would expand the local repertoire. Western-style medicine seems reasonable to people, and it is unproblematically incorporated into an existing local repertoire of healing practices.

Clearly, people view new medical options and ideas through the lens of familiar meanings. This kind of incorporation, accommodation, and interpretation of new medical possibilities within existing frameworks has been documented extensively. Thus, though Western-style medicine clearly originates outside the local community, the ideas and practices that make it possible for people to make it their own are locally based. Western-style medical facilities, pharmaceuticals, and trained personnel, however, are not reliably nor easily available in rural areas. Government-run health services provide care unevenly in the countryside; it is remote and inconvenient for some people, nearby and active for others.

Maintaining a supply of drugs to health posts is a constant problem, as is keeping health posts and district hospitals staffed with trained, active practitioners. Nor do most people in rural Nepal apprehend elements of the conceptual system, such as the germ theory of disease, that motivates the therapeutic actions of Western-style medicine.

Recognizing these longstanding, intractable problems in health care delivery, many planners in Nepal commonly voice a conventional view that it is futile to inquire into the ways people incorporate Western-style medicine because most people in the country do not have access to it. As a result, the administrative focus on issues of service delivery overshadows the equally important issue of how such services are received. But even in places where access is most minimal and sporadic, Western-style medicine is assimilated into local ideas about healing long before it becomes a practical possibility for people.

In Bhojpur, the clinic is a little far away, a little bit more inconvenient than calling on a neighbor. Trips to hospitals in distant towns such as Dharan are difficult to arrange, expensive, and reserved for cases of desperation. People have seen lives saved at the clinic in cases where everyone was convinced that the sufferer would die. People look with hope to "doctor's medicine" (daktarko dabai) for cures (though such cures are only possible, people say, if one can get the very best doctors, "not the kind we have here in Nepal").

Yet such hopes do not blind people to the limits to the doctor's medicine. People posit a division of labor, saying "there are things that they can cure at the hospital and things that only a shaman can cure." Still, both local healing and "doctor's medicine," though, are inevitably limited in the face of fate because they are all too human endeavors. "If it is your time to die, it is your time to die," one woman reflected in a conversation we had about how people choose which of many therapeutic options to seek out.

"No one can save you, not a shaman, not a doctor. If that wasn't true, why would our King Mahendra have died? You don't think he had the best doctors in the world? Still he died." Issues of efficacy, cost, or convenience are clearly not the only considerations involved in how people regard the medicine brought to them through bikas.

Doctors figure prominently in discussions about sickness and healing, about village life, about status differences, and about social change even though actual doctors, and even Western-style medical care, remain peripheral (even when available) to local life.

Local people express a vision of an ideal world in which both shamans and doctors are at their disposal, each contributing special expertise. Indeed, shamans in Bhojpur tell people to go to the clinic for certain symptoms that medicines are widely known to relieve. They offer first to take care of the other influences that may also be troubling a person. In their divinations, they help people sort out different aspects of their afflictions. They help them know, for example, that it would be a mistake to receive an injection without first appeasing a certain spirit. A young high school educated man who sometimes helped me with my research told people that shamans had been installed in an office in Bir hospital, a major hospital in Kathmandu.

"The doctors there won't treat people," he often declared, "until the shaman has first taken care of the spirits that might also be affecting a person." The image of doctors deferring to shamans in the heart of the capital city is a powerful one for people in Bhojpur, and particularly meaningful for this man, who often recounted this "fact" (not true, to my knowledge) in discussions with me and others about the nature and relevance of shamanic healing. Why?

As an image of medical pluralism, it is a direct challenge to the notion that shamans and doctors compete as mutually exclusive forms of authoritative knowledge. It suggests that shamans will prove to be necessary to the success of Western-style cures, thus vindicating existing village practice. Behind such visions of a harmonious integration of diverse forms of therapy lie the inherently pluralistic presuppositions about the multiple influences that lead to illness and about the partial nature of medical knowledge described earlier.

This vision of harmonious pluralism meshes with one aspect of people's local experience of development. Quite tangibly, through dealing with clinics, medicines, and health campaigns, people enact and come to tacitly understand the relationship of their village to the bikas they hear so much about. Stressing the fit between shamans and doctors is one way of asserting that the village can itself be a "developed place."

Incorporating bikas - in the form of a health post, or cataract surgery, or penicillin - is one way to be a "modern" villager in Nepal, at a time when villagers are increasingly stereotyped as backward and undeveloped. Villagers' tacit claims that they, too, are developed come up against contradictory messages in which villagers, their ways and their thoughts, are depicted as a problem in Nepal and an obstacle to development.

In their own interactions with institutions of development, villagers frequently feel themselves to be marked as inferior by their style of speech and dress, and by the very places and ways in which they live. The social disparities between village farmers and a growing, upwardly mobile class of salaried professionals and businessmen are increasingly salient in Nepal.

In this context, the propensity to incorporate Western-style medicine into the local schema for healing is paradoxically counterbalanced by a strong emphasis on the ways it remains alien to local ways. Doctors and shamans are as apt symbols for social ruptures as they are for processes of change.

Thus, people are as likely to emphasize the distinctiveness of these practitioners as to merge them into an integrated system. People are acutely aware that in "developed places" like America "there are no shamans, only doctors."

It is difficult for people who have never left Nepal to fully imagine a world in which the most ordinary of therapies, the jhar-phuk that blows away spirits, never takes place, but everyone knows that this is true. Often I was asked whether it is true that in my country we have no shamans.

Usually before I could muster an answer someone else would teasingly interject: "You idiot! In America they have hospitals everywhere. Why would they have shamans?" Such comments put the relationship between shamans and doctors in a different light. Shamans are markers of what is specific to the village, while doctors represent a modern world beyond.

As people in Nepal experience social change, they certainly have reason to reflect more and more on the relationships between these disparate social worlds and their own place in them.

Why would Nepalis so frequently emphasize the contrast between these practitioners rather than the equally plausible model of integration? The answer lies in the social symbolism of healing, not in any a priori natural contrast between two forms of medical knowledge.

The apparent naturalhess of the contrast between shamans and doctors is an artifact of a Western social imagination that places shamans and doctors as corresponding opposites. Consider the number of television documentaries about tribal wisdom, New Age books, New Yorker cartoons, and travel stories that use the device of the witch doctor to construct a commentary on the relation of the Western self to the exotic Other. Shaman and doctor serve as contrasting terms that align with other oppositions, such as magic to science, tradition to modernity, belief to reason, past to future.

Within this densely overdetermined symbolism, shamans and doctors must stand in contrast. Recognizing the social symbolism of shamans and doctors in the Western imagination, we are forced to look freshly at what is going on in Nepal and to ask why a contrast between shamans and doctors should ever be compelling to local people. What is it that reinforces people's sense that one can never be fully assimilated into the other?

Although villagers end up expressing a symbolic contrast that corresponds with the one familiar to us, the meaningfulness of this contrast is very much grounded in local life and experience. Although they may treat people in the same place, even in the same room, shamans and doctors operate in different worlds. The doctor is known locally to treat "bodily illnesses" (jiuko betha).

These kinds of illnesses are distinctive, in local understanding, not merely by being inside the body (in contrast to the many illnesses brought on by external disturbances), but also by being common to all humankind. They alone are classed as diseases (rog), and are known to occur all over the world. Villagers see these diseases as something they have in common with people of "developed countries," and that is why the kind of healing that evolved on the other side of the world also works for villagers in Nepal. It will be effective wherever it is administered.

Shamans, on the other hand, are specially skilled in dealing with the extrahuman beings that cause people so much sorrow and suffering. Numerous varieties of extrahuman creatures are recognized by people in Nepal. Cohabiting with people on the same hillsides, they form an extrasocial universe, an invisible world intimately connected to the human one.

People encounter these beings and interact with them daily, and the suffering these beings bring on people is a direct result of these interactions. They attack people they know because they are angry, or cling to perfect strangers because they are lonely, or follow people around because they are hungry. They need and desire things that only humans can provide.

They communicate their wishes and displeasures to specific people. Some attach themselves to people in specific social categories. Lineage divinities, for example, attack a member of the patriline when angered. Other beings attack whomever they encounter. Anonymous ghosts lurk in particular places: shady groves, stream beds, cremation sites, graves, the places where their human bodies suffered accidents or were murdered. Should you unwittingly encounter one of these creatures on the trail, you may fall victim.

One of the consequences of living in a village, therefore, is having to contend with these creatures. They are in the grove where you cut bamboo, they are at the water tap, they dart out on the trail you must travel late at night to check on the irrigation water to your fields. Villagers, constantly bothered by these creatures, offer them food and other things that they desire to send them off, at least temporarily. The shaman chases the ghost from your body, it scurries down the trail, only to afflict someone else. Thus villagers see themselves caught in an endless cycle of affliction. One man explained the situation this way:

Here we honorjangali, deu-deuta, khyak, these things. They get their hopes up and cling to people, causing them to be sick. But in places where people don't give them anything they don't have expectations and they don't bother anyone.

And he added: No matter what comes, it is best not to go to the shaman, it is better to go to the doctor, then whatever has come clinging will give up and go away. The doctor will tell you that this-or-that has gone wrong in your body and that is all there is to it. The problem is we keep honoring these creatures and they all keep cringing to us because we've raised their hopes.

This man's assertion that doctors can help villagers free themselves from their bonds to these creatures by refusing to acknowledge their existence points to what people think sets the village off from "developed places." Where these creatures do not afflict people, shamans are irrelevant. A worldly ex-soldier, ticking off all the countries he had been to and which ones had shamans declared to me and the others listening: "Shamans will never emerge in America because it has become a big country (thulo des) with much development (dherai bikas)."

It makes sense to everyone for a British doctor to come to Bhojpur to treat people's tuberculosis, but they find it a bit absurd to imagine a shaman from Bhojpur going to England. Shamans specialize in the problems that afflict people by virtue of their position in a local community. Their association with locality stems not only from the fact that they are local people themselves, but because their special knowledge revolves around the contingencies of place. They cure illnesses that people suffer from because of who they are and where they live.

By the same token, doctors represent things from outside the locality. The doctor's skills come to him through books, in the institutions of schools, through state bureaucracy. This kind of knowledge is accessible to anyone who can gain access to the institutions that impart it, and as a voluntarily acquired skill it differs from shamanic knowledge.

But while in theory this access to knowledge is democratic, in practice it is filtered through the Nepalese educational system, and is restricted to an elite. Doctors are associated with the institutions of a national society, especially institutions such as schools and hospitals that are common to those places that are bikasi. As individuals, doctors are also members of the elite, the most bikasi of Nepalis. Whereas doctors' knowledge is printed in books and taught in schools, shamans are selected by spirits who teach them through dreams. Learning with a more experienced shaman almost always accompanies this supernatural call.

This learning is informal, and it establishes a lifelong ritual bond between guru and disciple. Whether between spirits and human or guru and disciple, shamanic knowledge is transmitted through relationships that are highly personal, not institutional. Shamanic skill is a local product, while medical skill is produced in institutions to which villagers have little access.

Moreover, the magical implements shamans need, such as bones, quartz crystals, porcupine quills, etc., are also either found by the shaman himself or obtained through informal exchanges: they are not commodities in a cash economy. All the items that are part of a doctor's practice, in contrast, come from elsewhere, as the formidable difficulties in keeping rural health posts supplied attest.

The shiny equipment - stethoscopes and thermometers and blood pressure sleeves - bear the unmistakable stamp of foreignness and bikas, of manufacturing processes not located anywhere in Nepal, let alone in hill villages.

The medicines are powders and pills and ointments with long nonsense-syllable names like streptomycin whose contents no one could even guess at. No one can handle a foil packet of aspirin bought at a tea shop without being conscious that such items have to be brought from somewhere else.

This is not simply an issue of the logistics of trade and travel over daunting terrain, but of the overall symbolism of the flow of bikasi items up into the hills. For what these very ordinary things say to people is that bikas is something that exists elsewhere and can only be carried to villages in pieces that fit into a porter's basket.

The knowledge and the drugs of doctors (and most often the doctors themselves) come from a world that is and always will be, it seems to them, separate from the village. The contrast between doctors and shamans dramatizes the peripheral position of villages in the world of bikas.

To be a villager in the modern world is to live in an impoverished and provincial backwater, to live in a place defined by its deficits in relation to other places: "In America they have hospitals everywhere. Why would they have shamans?"

This image of the village as a place defined by its distance and difference from a world of bikas is part and parcel of an ideology of modernization expounded in contemporary Nepalese national society. This ideology, with its emphasis on progress, enlightenment, and advancement reconfigures people's representations of social identity and social difference.

The rhetoric of modernization and development makes it possible to blur ethnically and regionally specific social worlds in the broader, reified category of traditional ways which are considered backward or superstitious by definition. Furthermore, the intense focus on the need to develop villages fosters a widespread sense that it is villages that are the main obstacles to Nepal's development. Throughout Nepal, images of the backward village are elaborated, in tones varying from derision to compassion or humor, in public cultural forms such as films, short stories, television, and jokes.

Within this discourse, the "ignorance" of people classed as villagers are routinely blamed for the disappointing results of development initiatives, reflecting a new elite's sense of their own distinctively cosmopolitan sensibility. Urban elites and rural villagers alike speak of who is "modern" and who is "backward," who is "civilized" and who is "superstitious." They constantly compare Nepal to the images they have of "developed countries."

Villagers express concern over how they appear to people they see as modern. They discuss how local customs, habits, and ideas fit or do not fit with the picture of the modern they have formed. They are explicitly and self-consciously concerned with their social position as villagers. When villages are placed in relation to the kinds of places they are not, the social meaning of the village is altered. Local people come to see their home as a locus of backwardness.

They also become acutely aware that not all Nepalis live as they do; that some already appear to have the "modern" life to which the state exhorts them to aspire. For local people, development is every bit as much this new way of understanding what it means to be a villager as it is roads, electricity, or health posts. For them, bikas is not about progress, or a grand world transition from tradition to modernity. Rather, the national project of development introduces new ways of defining here and there, us and them.

Local approaches to illness and healing, involving as they do conceptions of identity and locality, take on an additional, socially laden meaning amidst competing representations of Nepalese society. As people call on shamans and doctors to cure their illnesses, and as they reflect on the relation between various modes of healing, they also experience different aspects of what it means to be a villager in Nepal. For people in Bhojpur, the symbolism of injections and amulets, of doctors and shamans, is bound up with the increasingly problematic identity of the villager in a Nepal struggling to transform itself.

People in Bhojpur do not separate the therapeutic aspect of healing from the social dynamics that produce, sustain, or deliver those therapies. Vying for primacy within this framework are two conflicting models. One integrates Western-style medicine into a local scheme of knowledge in a way that posits the possibility of a bikasi village. The other places the doctor's medicines and the shaman's mantra in separate worlds, thus reinforcing a definition of the village as the place development can never reach.

These models share a foundation in the actual ways people know and experience different forms of healing, and that is why they are both compelling. Only one, however, also has a life outside local experience. The model that insists that bikas and the village are distinct and mutually exclusive finds echoes in the messages of schoolbooks, the rhetoric of development, stereotypes of ethnic sensibilities, and the conventions of everyday speech. That the people in village Bhojpur currently find plausibility in both models indicates a space of ambiguity and contradiction, in which the meaning of shamanic healing, Western-style medicine, the village, and bikas remains open to several interpretations.

There is more than one way that local practices such as shamanic healing might stand in relation to Western therapeutics; there is more than one way to imagine what development could represent in a Nepalese village. There is no single, coherent local understanding precisely because villagers' experiences of these relations are themselves contradictory. Local concepts of medical knowledge open one set of possibilities, while the structure of health development presents them with another relationship.

Such contradictions make ritual healing increasingly problematic for people. It is at once necessary within local understandings of affliction and stigmatized within the ideology of modernization as a sign of backwardness and superstition. These are the forms the cultural politics surrounding development take.

Shamans and doctors, as practitioners and as symbolic figures, mark out relations between local ways of life and bikas, offering ways to be a modern villager in Nepal but also reinforcing for people the knowledge that in a modern Nepal, they remain in this class of people known as villagers. The resulting transformations in the way local people understand themselves may well be development's most important effect.

THE EXPANSION OF GORKHA

Among the small hill states struggling for power during the later Malla period was Gorkha, founded in 1559 by Dravya Shah in an area chiefly inhabited by Magars. Legends trace his dynasty to warrior princes who immigrated from Rajputana in India during the fifteenth century.

During its early fight for existence, the House of Gorkha stayed out of the two major confederations in western Nepal. No major expansion of the kingdom occurred until the reign of Ram Shah, from 1606 to 1633, who extended his territories slightly in all directions.

During the seventeenth and early eighteenth centuries, Gorkha continued a slow expansion and appeared increasingly often as an ally of one or more of the three kingdoms in their quarrels with each other, giving the rulers of the hill state experience in the affairs of the Kathmandu Valley. Nar Bhupal Shah (reigned 1716-42) extended his lands toward the Kairang Pass in the north and Nuwakot in the east. He attempted to take Nuwakot and failed, but he did arrange the marriage of his son to the daughter of the raja of Makwanpur.

This son, Prithvi Narayan Shah (reigned 1743-75), made full use of his position to achieve supreme power and was one of the great figures in Nepalese history.

Following in his father's footsteps, he apparently dedicated himself at an early age to the conquest of the valley and the creation of a single state. Before going on the offensive, he traveled to Banaras, or Varanasi, to seek financial assistance and purchase armaments, thus obtaining a personal view of conditions in the outside world, especially the position of the British East India Company.

On his return to Gorkha, he established a number of arsenals and trained his troops to use the more modern weapons he had obtained in India. He arranged alliances with, or bought the neutrality of, neighbouring states.

When King Ranajit of Bhadgaon (reigned 1722-69) quarreled with King Jayaprakasa of Kathmandu (reigned 1735-68), Prithvi Narayan Shah took Nuwakot and laid siege to Kirtipur, which was controlled by the king of Patan, Tej Narasimha (reigned 1765-68).

During the fighting, Prithvi Narayan Shah was almost killed, and when his troops failed to take the town, he withdrew. At this point, he changed direction, as the Gorkhas were to do effectively time and again.

The Gorkhas instituted a blockade of the entire valley, closed off all trade routes, and began executing blockade runners. Gorkha agents remained active in the towns, and the army attempted to starve the valley into submission. When a second siege of Kirtipur also was unsuccessful, Prithvi Narayan Shah turned his attention toward Lamji, one of the Chaubisi principalities, and overran it after several bloody battles.

The Gorkha army reappeared at Kirtipur. After a siege of six months, the town was treacherously delivered to the Gorkhas, and its inhabitants were deliberately mutilated. The Gorkhas moved on to Patan in 1767, but their attention was diverted by the appearance of a 2,400-man expeditionary force sent by the British East India Company to aid the traditional kings of the valley. The British column, ravaged by malaria contracted in the Tarai, had to withdraw quickly without accomplishing anything other than delaying the Gorkhas.

This token opposition by the British, however, was not forgotten by Prithvi Narayan Shah and his successors. With the field again clear, on September 29, 1768, Gorkha troops infiltrated Kathmandu while the population was celebrating a religious festival and took the town without a fight. Jayaprakasa fled to Bhadgaon with Tej Narasimha and Prithvi Narayan Shah was crowned king of Kathmandu. He soon entered Patan unopposed and then moved against villages east of Bhadgaon.

His troops were admitted into Bhadgaon by nobles who had been bought off. Ranajit retired to Banaras, Jayaprakasa retired to die at the shrine of Pashupatinath, and Tej Narasimha died in prison. For the first time, the hill ruler, the raja of Gorkha, had become sole ruler in the Kathmandu Valley. One of his first acts in 1769 was to expel permanently from his territories all foreigners, including traders, Roman Catholic missionaries, and even musicians or artists influenced by northern India's style.

The conquest of the three kingdoms was only the beginning of a remarkable explosion of Gorkha military power throughout the Himalayan region. Prithvi Narayan Shah quickly made a movement toward the Chaubisi states in the west, but after encountering resistance in Tanahu, the Gorkha armies drove east into the Kirata country, overrunning all of eastern Nepal by 1773. They were poised for the invasion of Sikkim, but because its rulers came from Tibet, Sikkim was viewed as a client of Tibet (and thus of the Chinese).

A warning from Tibet and the death of Prithvi Narayan Shah in 1775 stalled hostilities, but a full-scale invasion began in 1779. Resistance was encountered until 1788, when Gorkha forces drove the ruler of Sikkim into exile in Tibet and occupied all of western Sikkim. Guerrilla warfare continued as the Gorkhas constructed a base near Vijaypur to administer the eastern conquests. In the west, a marriage alliance with the rajas of Palpa kept them quiet while General Ram Krishna Rana conquered Tanahu and Lamjung (Gorkha's traditional rival) and advanced to Kaski by 1785. By 1790 all rulers as far as the Kali River had submitted to the Gorkhas or had been replaced.

Even farther to the west lay Kumaon, in the throes of civil strife between two coalitions of *zamindar* (large landowners responsible for tax collection in their jurisdictions), who struggled to control the monarchy. One group invited the intervention of the Gorkhas, who defeated local forces in two battles and occupied the capital, Almora, in 1790. The Gorkhas were poised for greater adventures, but by then they were irritating bigger players and began to encounter resistance to their ambitions.

FEDERAL DEMOCRATIC REPUBLIC

On May 14, 2008 the newly elected Constituent Assembly declared Nepal a Federal Democratic Republic, abolishing the 240-year-old monarchy. The motion for abolition of monarchy was carried by a huge majority; out of 564 members present in the assembly, 560 voted for the motion while 4 members voted against it. Finally, on June 11, 2008 ex-king Gyanendra left the palace. Ram Baran Yadav of the Nepali Congress became the first president of the Federal Democratic Republic of Nepal on July 23, 2008.

Similarly, Pushpa Kamal Dahal, popularly known as Prachanda, of the Communist Party of Nepal (Maoist) was elected as the first Prime Minister on August 15, 2008, defeating Sher Bahadur Deuba of the Nepali Congress Party. On 4 May 2009, Mr. Pushpa Kamal Dahal resigned over on-going conflicts over sacking of the Army chief. Since Dahal's resignation, the country has been in a serious political deadlock – one of the big issues being the proposed integration of the former Maoist combatants, also known as the People's Liberation Army, into the national security forces.

3

India's Responsibility for the Defence and Foreign Policy of Nepal

Nepal, the land of Himalayas and Veda, is today facing a great challenge of ever increasing internal violence by various groups of insurgents. How does it stop the political unrest that cripples Nepal's economy and causes other social problems that could lead to more war and terrorism? Achieving economic success while happily living in perpetual peace is not only an intrinsic desire but also a fervent wish of the citizens of Nepal. Despite advanced technology and the boldness, courage, strength, and intelligence of Nepal's armed forces, the nation still struggles to eliminate violent extremism and to achieve a lasting peace.

Violent extremism is a human problem requiring human solutions. The underlying cause of extremist social violence is accumulated social stress. Therefore, to eliminate such social problems, the military needs to reduce the collective societal stress in Nepal. Is there a way to reduce collective stress and create peace? If so, how could such an ideal goal be achieved in Nepal where tensions are so high? During these dangerous times, Nepal must rely on a scientifically verified approach to quickly reduce the tensions which are fueling violent extremism.

Extensive scientific research indicates that the best way to reduce collective societal stress, eliminate extremism, boost the economy and thereby snuff out war and terrorism is to adopt an ancient Vedic strategy. In modern times this strategy is called Invincible Defence Technology (IDT) and was revived by the late Maharishi Mahesh Yogi in a non-religious manner. It has been quietly and successfully used by members of many faiths worldwide to eliminate conflict in the past.

A Prevention Wing of the Military consisting of 3% of the armed forces of Nepal could achieve this goal. This special unit would be trained in Invincible Defence Technology and would collectively practice its ancient Vedic technologies of consciousness – the Transcendental Meditation (TM) and TM-Sidhi programs – in large groups, twice a day. Extensive research shows that the size of the group needed to reduce social stress in a given population should exceed the square root of 1% of the population size.

To calculate this number, multiply the population size by 0.01, and then take the square root of the result. For instance, the population of Nepal is approximately 27 million: 27,000,000 x 0.01 = 270,000, and the square root of 270,000 is approximately 520, so a group of at least 520 IDT experts is needed. Studies show that when these thresholds are exceeded, crime goes down, quality of life indices go up, and war and terrorism abate. Scientists named this phenomenon "The Maharishi Effect" in honor of Maharishi, who first predicted it.

For instance, a Maharishi Effect intervention was implemented and studied in the US capital of Washington, DC, in 1993. Predictions were lodged in advance with government leaders and newspapers. An independent Project Review Board approved the research protocol. Crime fell 24 percent below expected levels when the group size reached its maximum. Weekend effects, temperature, and previous trends in the data failed to account for changes.

Over 50 studies have shown that IDT works. The causal mechanism has been postulated to be a field effect of consciousness—a spillover effect on the level of the unified field from the peace-creating group into the larger population. Research conducted on the powerful neurotransmitter serotonin shows that it produces feelings of contentment, happiness and even euphoria. Low levels of serotonin, according to research, correlate with violence, aggression, and poor emotional moods.

The IDT study showed that higher numbers of IDT experts correlated with a marked increase in serotonin production among other community members. These results were statistically significant and followed the attendance figures in the IDT group. This finding offers a plausible neurophysiologic mechanism to explain reduced hostility and aggression in society at large. IDT has also been documented worldwide in a study published in the *Journal of Offender Rehabilitation* using data provided by the Rand Corporation.

When large assemblies of IDT experts exceeded the Maharishi Effect threshold for the world during the years 1983–1985, deaths due to terrorism globally decreased 72%, international conflict decreased 32%, and violence was reduced in nations throughout the world without intrusion by other governments. The armed forces of Nepal are responsible for protecting the nation's citizens, and are obligated to thoroughly examine realistic, scientifically validated methods for ending war and terrorism. Nepal's foreign policy and defence policy are largely committed to creating a peaceful world. Therefore, it would be consistent for Nepal to adopt a non-lethal defence system.

Since joining the United Nations in 1955, Nepal has expressed abiding faith in the principles and purposes enshrined in the UN Charter regarding goals of international peace, security, and promoting international cooperation for economic and social development. The Nepal military can play a leading role with its readymade manpower for crisis management with a mostly effortless modification of its ongoing training programs.

Ultimately, it is the duty of the armed forces of Nepal to quickly establish a Prevention Wing of the Military in order to create economic success, peace and stability in Nepal today. India's pursuance of the democracy factor in Bhutan and Sikkim was different from the Nepalese case. Though the security concern emanating out of the communist victory in China was the same, but the pressure of democratic forces was much weaker in Bhutan and Sikkim. The other pressing consideration of the Western intervention, present in Nepal, was almost completely absent in Bhutan and Sikkim.

Nepal's Rana rulers had an active relationship with the UK, US and France, and were keen to exploit that relationship for their political survival as already noted. In view of the absence of the Western concerns and the presence of weak democratic movements, India found it advisable to support and sustain feudal regimes in these two Himalayan countries in the interest of stability. India's policy towards all the Himalayan kingdoms had a similar thrust of retaining the core British strategic framework of keeping these kingdoms as an integral art of India's defence structure, while shedding off its imperial and colonial façade.

Emerging aspirations of people in these countries for democratization were responded to within this framework, i.e., without sacrificing the security interests. This was evident in Nepal as this was also evident in Bhutan and Sikkim. There were also the nuanced differences in the legal status of sovereignty and degree of independence to be exercised by each of them. Nepal was considered a fully sovereign country. Sikkim was treated as a protectorate, slightly higher than the Indian princely states, but lower than Bhutan which gradually evolved into a full sovereign, independent state.

Sikkim was eventually incorporated as an integral part of the Indian Union in 1975. These differences in legal status of the three Himalayan kingdoms were clearly reflected in the

Treaties signed with Bhutan in 1948 and with Nepal and Sikkim (separately) in 1950. The Treaties laid down that while Bhutan was free in its internal affairs, its foreign relations were to be 'guided' by India's advice.

Being an Indian protectorate, Sikkim's foreign affairs were India's responsibility and its internal autonomy was conditioned on 'good governance' to be overlooked by India. Yet another factor that accounted for a more accommodative Treaty with Bhutan as compared to Sikkim as that India's treaty with Bhutan was concluded in 1949, before the victory of communist forces in China and the Chinese assertion in Tibet.

The demand for political liberalization in Sikkim dates back to the victory of India's struggle for independence. Inspired by the Indian example, and with the support and encouragement from the Indian leadership, political parties were organized both in Bhutan and Sikkim. The Sikkim State Congress (SSC) was formed in 1947. It demanded abolition of feudal land holdings, an interim government having representation of popular leaders and eventual merger of Sikkim into India.

The Government of India forded the Sikkim princely ruler (the Maharaja) to introduce land reforms and install a government of popular representatives – two to be the Maharaja's representatives and three nominees of the SSC. India at that time refused to discuss the proposal of Sikkim's merger into India. This is an example of New Delhi siding with the feudal system in the interest of stability and order in Sikkim. Any support to change, if at all, had to be gradual.

The Sikkim ruler promptly introduced some reforms in the legal system and judicial procedures. But he was not forthcoming on the popular representation in the government. The Sikkim Maharaja virtually handed over his power to his son, Palden Thondup who floated a royalist political organization called Sikkim National Party (SNP), on April 30, 1948 with the objective of opposing the SSC. With the help of this party, the feudal ruler of Sikkim tried to consolidate his power provoking the SSC to agitate in 1949eir demands.

The agitators marched to the palace in support of their demands. Under the pressure of the agitators and the Indian Political Officer in Gantok, Mr. Harishwar Dayal, the Maharaja was forced to constitute a new Ministry with popular representation from the SSC. The inherent political contradictions between the Maharaja and the popular representatives, with Crown Prince working the popular ministry all the time, did not allow the compromise devised by India to function. The popular representatives threatened to resign from the government and to resume their agitation for democratization.

The Indian Political Officer interviewed in favour of the Maharaja by dismissing all the popular representatives. To access the situation created by the agitation, Nehru had sent his Deputy Minister of External Affaires to Sikkim. He, it seems, went back with the impression that the Maharaja would be a better ally in strengthening India's security interests in Sikkim than the democratic leaders. That is why, soon after the Minister's departure, the Indian representative in Gantok dismissed the popular government and took the administration in his own hands.

That was the end of struggle for democracy in Sikkim. Subsequently, India continued to strengthen Sikkim Monarchy in the interest of stability until the beginning of the seventies, when again, the larger interests of India's perceived security, democratic movement was encouraged and Sikkim was eventually integrated into the Indian Union.

On the lines of Sikkim, Bhutanese expatriates of Nepali origin inspired by India's independence and struggle of democratization in Sikkim and Nepal, also organized a political party called Bhutan State Congress (BSC) in 1952.

This party called for the grant of citizenship rights and political representation to all the Nepalese settled in Bhutan. Inherent in the party's demands was also the issue of democratization of Bhutan's Monarchical system. In support of these demands, the BSC launched a Satyagraha (non violence residence) in 1954.

This political movement was quickly suppressed by the Bhutan government by mobilizing their militia. There were sections in Indian civil society that lead support to the movement because of the expatriate Nepali population but the Government of India backed the Monarchy and did not let the resistance movement gather any political strength. The Bhutanese government was advised to sort out the citizenship issue which was done in 1958. Subsequently, the Advisory assembly was also setup to perform legislative functions.

An important aspect behind India's support to Monarchies in Sikkim and Bhutan, related to its security interests has been that the resistance movements and forces of democratization in both of these countries had a strong ethnic character. In both Bhutan and Sikkim, democratization demand was raised by the Nepali groups and the Monarchies have been Bhotias and Lepchas in Sikkim and Drukpas in Bhutan; having closer cultural and religious linkages with Tibet.

As a result, supporting democratic movement would have amounted to favoring one side in the ethnic divide and as a consequence, alienating the other one. Indian policy makers did take into account the possibility, howsoever remote, of the ruling Mongoloid ethnic groups in Bhutan and Sikkim seeking China's support in case of India leading its weight with their Nepali protesters. Political instability precipitated in the process would surely have been exploited by China.

A country's foreign policy is "a set of political goals that seeks to outline how that particular country will interact with other countries of the world and, to a lesser extent, non-state actors." Foreign policy is generally designed "to help protect a country's national interests, national security, ideological goals, and economic prosperity." For a small country like Nepal sandwiched between the Asian giants, this can only occur as a result of peaceful cooperation.

Eight months after the introduction of Loktantra (total democracy), Nepal's foreign policy lies in shambles. There can be no doubt that foreign policy lacks direction and that it is not transparent. It is not only uni-dimensional, i.e. only directed towards India or reacting only to impulses from that country. It can even be said that India dictates policy as in the heydays of the Nineteen-Fifties. The Indian Embassy in Kathmandu is the focal and power point for all domestic and (the minimalist) foreign activities.

The Ministry of Foreign Affairs (MoFA) at Shital Niwas could easily be re-named 'the Ministry of Indian Affairs'! Let us set out the instrumental criteria in terms of which we can attempt a dispassionate evaluation of Nepal's foreign relations since the success of the violent political agitation of April and the dismantling of the Royal regime.

In the first instance, we must attempt to analyse the situation arising out of the events leading up to and after the said change of regime. The massive international pressure and funding of the opposition was, no doubt, instrumental in the collapse of the King's administration, which was neither repressive nor dictatorial. India and its strategic partner, the United States played the defining role. India, in fact, brought together the seven opposition parties and the Maoist terrorists (India now denies this characterization).

The Indian Communist parties also interfered in the domestic affairs of the country. In these circumstances, the hands of the new policy-makers were bound tight-they and their Maoist partners had no choice but to toe the Indian line. As one commentator put it, they have been degraded into the 'running dogs of Indian neo-imperialist policy in South Asia.'

Next, let us attempt to assess the flow of information and intelligence that would influence the formation of the perception of the new power elites. Eight months on into the 'new Nepal' the career diplomats in Shital Niwas and former envoys have not been taken into confidence; neither have any think tanks or foreign policy experts. MoFA's own Institute of Foreign Affairs is lying idle since the power take-over.

The foreign minister is a novice in the realm of foreign affairs, and the PM's own advisers are all amateurs (with neither the experience, nor the education and know-how in international affairs). Who has been providing facts and figures is anybody's guess. Whether the sources are in the national interest is another vital question. One of the government negotiators with the Maoists, the minister for Tourism and Civil Aviation, Pradip Gyanwali (who has proven himself most incompetent and out of place in his chosen portfolio) has now gone out of his way to propagate the politics of 'dis-information'.

He lately accused "foreign powers" in attempting to disrupt the elections to the Constituent Assembly" and the United Nations for the delay in promulgating the so-called "Interim Constitution". To divert widespread dissatisfaction with the government's domestic and foreign policies, Gyanwali has been sent to the forefront to intensify the "blame game" (also against the King and the "Monarchists") and to underscore the role of the "foreign hand" (but pointing in the wrong direction!)

The dismal state of affairs is reflected in the indubitable fact that the current government foolishly recalled the ambassadors from nearly a dozen countries and has not yet been able to fill the vacant posts, among them Washington, Tokyo, London, Paris and Brussels (European Union). A significant flow of information has dried up and demonstrates the government's dilettantish conduct of foreign affairs.

Forget about the 'democratic' conduct of external relations; this government is so emasculated that it is unable to reach a consensus on major issues, let alone appoint ambassadors to key countries. Kathmandu is rife with rumours that the main political parties are having a tussle with regard to appointing their own hangers-on and favourites to these lucrative posts. The politics of nepotism is in full swing. In any modern state, it is possible to identify the government units most responsible for handling and managing external relations.

Moreover, the responsibility of coping with the predicaments of foreign affairs, therefore, falls within the jurisdiction of the several units. There exist clear-cut rules, practices and conventions for inter-governmental and interunit arrangements to allow for concerted action. In the case of Nepal, there is a manifest lack of coordination between the PM's office, Shital Niwas, the Defence Ministry, the National Defence Council and the relevant committee(s) of the parliament.

Only a small coterie of power-elites (with little or no knowledge of the conduct of foreign policy) is deciding the fate of the nation. Both the parliament which has in a ridiculous manner declared itself 'sovereign' and the MoFA are only mute spectators in the country's external relations. The principle of checks and balances-a must in any functioning government-is prominent by its absence! So much, too, for 'good governance'.

It stands to reason that when even the major actors are unclear about the nature and conduct of foreign policy, their perceptions of any predicament in our external relations must of necessity be hazy and incomplete. This can only lead to hazardous situations and disgrace. Future repercussions were not thought out when recalling our envoys. This interim government failed to do its home-work when canvassing for the non-permanent Asian seat in the UN Security Council, resulting in a fiasco.

Without considering the history of the problem of Bhutanese refugees and the Indian interests involved, the foreign minister foolishly announced the immanent solution of this cancerous and long drawn-out stumbling block in the multi-lateral relations of South Asia. The government has also failed miserably to set priorities for goals ranging from the imperative, through the desirable to the least-expected, but simply hoped for targets. Its dependence on India has made it muddle-headed and its capacity to act in the national interest circumscribed.

The Indians, on the other hand, have cleverly and diabolically manipulated the Maoist insurgency to further their own interests. To sum up: Nepal has become a prey to the Indo-American grand design of containing China and is on the way to becoming a satellite state in all but name. After a hiatus of five years, India and Nepal have revived their defence ties and will shortly initiate various projects involving procurement of defence and military equipment.

The Chief of the Nepal Army, General Chhattraman Singh Gurung, had made inquiries regarding supply of tanks as well as artillery guns, INSAS rifles, ammunition, troop carriers, bullet-proof jackets and sighting equipment from India. Defence Ministry officials revealed that Nepal has requested for 100 tanks in two phases at concessional rates. Nepal also enquired about Ajeya (T-72) tanks of Russian origin. During the recent three-day joint-secretary level meeting in Nepal, India has agreed in principle to resume non-lethal military supplies to Nepal.

Nepal and India also agreed to share intelligence and to cooperate on constructing an airbase for the Nepalese army in the western part of the country. India also agreed to provide training to Nepalese security personnel to upgrade their capabilities and to share intelligence for improving security. Although India and Nepal have been traditional allies and virtually all of the training and supplies of the Royal Nepal Army were sourced from India, both countries stalled defence cooperation in 2005 after King Gyanenedra took over and Nepal became a republic.

India was skeptical about military cooperation due to the fear of Maoist in the Nepal Army. At this juncture, India is being optimistic and trustworthy about Nepal and has even honored Chief of Nepal Army General Chhattraman Singh Gurung with the title of "Honorary Chief of Army Staff" in India. General Gurung visited various dignitaries and participated in high-level meetings during his Indian visit.

4

Modernization of Nepal

When it became apparent that the *panchayat* system was going to endure, B.P. Koirala and other political exiles began to tone down their revolutionary rhetoric and advocate a reconciliation with the king. On December 30, 1976, Koirala and his close associate, Ganeshman Singh, flew to Kathmandu hoping to "make a fresh attempt." They were arrested for antinational activities and violence, and a tribunal was set up for a trial.

After considerable agitation, Koirala was released in June 1977 because of ill health. He met briefly with the king and then went to the United States for treatment. When he returned to Nepal in November 1977, he was again arrested at the airport. After further public agitations on his behalf, he underwent five treason trials in early 1978 and was ultimately acquitted. Thereafter, despite factional splits, the Nepali Congress resembled other opposition parties in its acceptance of the king's power.

Thus, the pattern of modern Nepalese politics was established—loyalty to the king and opposition to his government. In practice, there were continuing student demonstrations against the *panchayat* system and for human rights in 1977 and 1978. On May 24, 1979, King Birendra announced on Radio Nepal that there would be a national referendum in the near future, during which the people could decide to support or reject the *panchayat* system of government.

This referendum represented the first time in modern history that the monarch had publicly consulted his subjects. Political freedom was allowed to all citizens during the period of preparation for the referendum, and there was intense realignment of political factions inside and outside the *panchayat* system. Finally, on May 2, 1980, out of a potential 7.2 million voters, 4.8 million cast their ballots.

The outcome supported the *panchayat* system, with 54.7 percent for and 45.3 percent against it. Koirala and the Nepali Congress accepted the results. Although the referendum was a victory for the king, its narrow margin clearly indicated the need for change. Accordingly, the king quickly confirmed freedom of speech and political activity and announced the formation of an eleven-member Constitution Reforms Commission. The result, in December 1980, was the Third Amendment of the 1962 constitution, setting up direct elections to the National Panchayat, which would then submit a single candidate for prime minister to the king for approval.

A Council of Ministers would thenceforth be responsible to the National Panchayat, not to the king. In March 1981, the Constitution Reforms Commission announced that elections to the National Panchayat would take place on May 9, 1981. Aside from pro-Moscow factions of the Communist Party of Nepal and a "Group of 38" from the Nepali Congress, political parties rejected the amended constitution and refused to participate in the elections.

The Nepali Congress led by Koirala observed an "election boycott week" from May 1 to 8, but on Election Day a 52 percent turnout of voters chose 111 representatives to the National Panchayat. Surya Bahadur Thapa was returned as prime minister, and the king formed a twenty- eight-member Council of Ministers in June 1981. Opposition politics were in a state of disarray, dominated by the terminal illness of Koirala, who died in July 1982.

The victory of the king was not complete, however. During the elections, more than 70 percent of the candidates favored by the king lost. The *panchayat* system, a major source for local patronage, was becoming the stage for factional fights and shuffling coalitions. On many college campuses, elections for student unions went to communists after violent clashes. The trend toward factionalism in the National Panchayat intensified in 1983, when a serious food crisis and charges of corruption caused the fall of Surya Bahadur Thapa's government.

Lokendra Bahadur Chand took over as prime minister, but two blocs, or *samuha* had emerged in the National Panchayat around Thapa and Chand. The factional fighting did not prevent the celebration in 1986 of the *panchayat* system's twenty-fifth anniversary, which created an opportunity for the second general election to the National Panchayat. The Nepali Congress and most other opposition parties again boycotted the elections, although the communists and a few other small parties did participate.

The elections drew 60 percent of the voters, and 60 percent of the members of the National Panchayat supported Marich Man Singh Shrestha as prime minister. Before elections to the local *panchayat* the following year, the Nepali Congress announced that it would continue its boycott but then changed its strategy and allowed its members to run for local seats, claiming that it could "capture the outposts" of the system and politicize the people.

The poor showing of the Nepali Congress candidates embarrassed the party, however, and revealed its isolation from many rural voters. Despite low growth figures, throughout the 1980s Nepal at least had made some progress in economic development, but it remained in any case one of the poorest countries in the world. The king was achieving a higher profile in international affairs, canvassing widespread support for the declaration of Nepal as a zone of peace and participating in the South Asian Association for Regional Cooperation.

These modest trends encountered a sudden interruption in 1989 when a major international incident with India occurred. On March 1, the Indian embassy announced that trade and transit treaties with Nepal, renewed regularly since the 1950s, would expire twenty-two days later. Both the Indian and Nepalese governments accused each other of delaying negotiations. When March 23 arrived, India declared the treaties had expired and closed all but two border entry points with Nepal.

These closures caused huge backups on the border and delayed or halted the bulk of foreign trade, including crucial shipments of oil and gasoline and the tourist trade, a major source of foreign exchange carefully cultivated under King Birendra. There was a severe decline in agricultural production, layoffs in factories increased, and the inflation rate in 1987-88 rose to 11 percent. The growth rate of the economy, a healthy 9.7 percent in 1987-88, declined to 1.5 percent in 1988-89.

The Nepali Congress, early in its history accused of bowing to Indian opinion, in September organized a National Awakening Week during which 3,500 party members committed nonviolent civil disobedience. Student demonstrations against India began to take on antigovernment tones, and all campuses in Kathmandu closed for two months.

The crisis demonstrated the fragility of the political and economic system in Nepal—an old culture but a young nation— landlocked between two giants and directed by a medieval monarchy. It might be noteworthy to mention the epistemological background on which the consequent presumptions will be constructed.

By ignoring such foundationalist dichotomies, as Marxist dialectics or opposite idealistic bias, the main attention will be concentrated on the shared meanings and structural dispositions of power, regardless of a pseudo objective world. By taking into consideration these premises, seemingly more space will be added to the discourse of cultural globalization, which broadens the milieu of judgment about identity formations. Considering those theoretical premises, we will seek to overcome a daunting gridlock: an analysis of the Asian societies without taking into account global perspectives and various levels of cultural interplay.

In order to avoid the problem of confusing concepts, some of them will be explained briefly throughout the chapter. As "cultural globalization" implies that it has specific sphere of research, at first the term "culture" needs to be emotionally uncharged and defined. We use the term in its conventional sense: "the beliefs, values and lifestyles of people in their everyday existence."

Global power dispositions that constitute the process of globalization and spread of prevailing values across the globe contain certain hierarchies that can be defined by the term "prestige." The widespread use of the English language can be seen as one of the important reflections of current power arrangements. It became lingua franca not for the preponderant value of American or Anglo-Saxon culture, but because of the structural position those two countries, and particularly, the United States occupies in the modern World.

The term "Davos Culture" was coined to refer to those new elites who are scattered all around the world and try to acquire certain, homogeneous type of "habitus" in order to get to the famous economic summit or other events of the same political level. Peter Berger calls them "yuppie internationals" and emphasized the role the American intelligentsia in the formation of their images. He calls it "faculty club culture."

This kind of globalization is carried out by various kinds of agencies: academic networks, foundations, non-governmental organizations, governmental and intergovernmental organizations and multinational corporations. Their agenda is created by the Western (mostly American) intellectuals and it includes: environmental issues, feminism, human rights, multiculturalism, etc.

There is a substantial difference between the nature of economic and cultural globalizations.

The problem is that the former is becoming more decentralized, while the latter still continues to be dominated by the Western cultural or intellectual products. Americans are especially blamed for modern-day "civilizing missions" as they are most actively engaged in spreading American values, by traveling and creating the network of other "globalizers" by not losing their identity (constructing 'ivory castles' around themselves). Sometimes they are genuinely surprised when reactions towards them are hostile.

There are various ways by which the local cultures respond to the pervasive trends of globalization. These efforts range from the complete isolation to what social scientists call "localization." Some scholars even speak about "alternative globalizations," that stem from outside the Western World and have effects on the latter. There is also notable trend of "subglobalization" which involves regional actors spreading global values. Thus, India can have profound cultural impact on surrounding countries, like Nepal, in terms of the popular culture and "global" cultural preferences.

Various interpretations of modernity seek to cut their ties with the West, and transform public discourse in new, favorable conditions. Besides, the West is not homogeneous entity and it helps controversial ideas get new forms and meanings. More serious problem is related to the economic background of cultural globalization as it deteriorates traditional economic structures and raises anti-Western sentiment among lower classes.

Globalization is not operating in a power vacuum. Even not taking into account such social formations and "qualities" as localities and neighborhoods, there is an empowering institution which seeks control over certain territories. Those actors are nation-states that face fundamental problems in a new world. Arjun Appadurai speaks about three main dimensions of the struggle of nation-states: (i) increased effort to control the population and under the sign of its forms of allegiance and affiliation; (ii) the growing disjuncture between territories and collective social movements; (iii) the erosion of the spatial and virtual neighborhoods, due to electronic means of communication.

The nation-state is a project of modernity. It controls neighborhoods and creates its own form of local culture. There is a need in the nation-states to police neighborhoods due to the increased volatility of modernity itself. But media technologies created new ways to transcend the boundaries of the nation-state and function on regional or global level.

Aforementioned class of global intelligentsia can be considered as products of this disjuncture between virtual and actual neighborhoods. But the problem is that, according to Appadurai, it creates the gap between educated high class and common locals.

Nation-states, as we seen, are not passive actors in this process. They create policies how to control the neighborhoods and strengthen national identities. Strategies that countries use in pursuit of these goals include:

(1) Preserving and protecting national and local cultures. States enhance their efforts to strengthen traditional culture by various means, like administrative management and funding.

(2) Resisting global culture.

(3) Globalizing national and local cultures. Countries try to prepare their cultures for global markets. This phenomenon is called "glocazition."

Before starting to analyze the sociopolitical landscape of Nepal, it will be helpful if we draw a larger, regional context of the political developments and pitfalls of democratization. Democratization is a complex process, but one of the indispensable attributes of it, liberalism is intrinsically tied to Western perceptions. It comprises all pertinent liberal values, including civil liberties, potent political parties and developed civil society.

Globalization contributed to the spread of civil NGOs and the rise of new international organizations, which are concerned with such issues as human rights, environment, etc. Authoritative governments appeal to so called "Asian Values" to defend their positions and in this process, they manage to demonize the West. Such attempts lead to the perceptions of collectivist Asian values and their persistence in the global era.

Another interesting observation is made by juxtaposing socialism in Fukuyama's sense and emerging AV ("Asian Values") discourse. Socialism is anti-capitalist and anti-liberal, whereas AV is economic pro-capitalist, while ideologically anti-liberal. Sociopolitical Modernization and effects of Cultural Globalization in Nepal

Before examining an impact of current cultural or political forces on Nepal, it will be appropriate to provide some historical background.

Apparently, Nepal's history throughout the twentieth century is fraught with various modern implications and influences. We will mainly focus on developments on Nepal's political landscape since 1990.

HISTORICAL BACKGROUND

The second half of the twentieth century in Nepal starts with an interesting democratic experiment. In 1958 several parties came to demand elections from the King. As a result of the approved elections, Nepalese Congress was elected and B.P. Koirala became the first prime minister of the country. The king prevailed over the parliament in 1960 and he managed to disband political parties and democratic institutions.

The king proposed new system of mass participation and inclusive democracy, so called Panchayat Raj. Rashtriya Panchayat, the national assembly was the highest body in the Panchayat pyramid. Representatives were elected from lower to higher levels, until they reached the highest positions in the assembly. The Panchayat system also had system of grassroots organizations that were created to express the interests of farmers, students, workers, etc. But these organizations were alien to Nepali society and remained extremely fragile.

The highest assembly was completely controlled by the king. King Mahendra died in 1972, and in 1980 his successors instated the reforms to Panchayat, which led to the creation of the party system and subsequent revolution in 1990. Another major factor that contributed to the changes in Nepalese Panchayat system was the growth of the middle class and socioeconomic transformation.

The country's social structure became more diverse, than it was decades ago. Three developments were essential in unifying the urban class into the solid opposition to the system: 1. Rapid urbanization Nepal had one of the highest urban growth rates in 1980s; 2. The World Bank and other financial institutions demanded an abolition of subsidies and a reduction in welfare programs that reduced the income of the urban poor; 3. The government became more corrupted amid the economic depression.

SOCIOPOLITICAL LANDSCAPE SINCE 1990

Some critics blame traditional rural Nepali society for the lack of the civil values. They argue that despite of the liberal slogans in the 90s patron-client relationships in the society remained intact. In 1990 NC and a coalition of Communist parties organized prodemocracy rallies that led the king to lift the ban on political parties. An interim government drafted a constitution that vested executive power in a prime minister and cabinet responsible to Parliament but retained the monarch as head of state.

After years of instability, the militant Maoist party launched guerrilla war that engulfed much of the countryside. In 2001, government decision to use army against the rebels led to massive killings of an estimated 5000 people. In 2005 once again dismissed the government, assumed executive powers and declared state of emergency. UN's High Commissioner for Human Rights described the issue in a meeting in Harvard University. She said that last January she had visited Nepal and met with the king.

"He assured me of his internal commitment to multiparty democracy and to restraint by constitutional monarchs. ... I thought at last here was an interlocutor who might be amenable to engaging in a peace process," she continued. "For two days, I felt that the commission had been a large success. Then, two days after I left the country, he overthrew the government and put everybody in jail."

Nowadays, Nepalese society is divided into three main parts: Maoists, Royalists and Liberals. Some experts propose a federal model to solve the problems:

"But what people have been demanding prior to and after People's Movement II or 2006-April Uprising is the establishment of the institutions of the secular democracy under the federal democratic republic setup. It has been clear so far that why both Hindu royalists (feudal lords) and the nationalist communists (comrades) are opposing such radical change.

Basically, the republic setup is anti Hindu feudal royalists and the federalism is anti-totalitarian nationalist communists." But where does the liberal model stand? And what is the correlation between liberalism and cultural globalization? Why are royalist and Maoist groups, which are both nationalists (thus, thus, willing to strengthen the nation-state) so popular in Nepalese society? Royalist groups have their roots in the feudal system. They reinforce the dominance of the high caste, Bahun Chhetri, as a part of the traditional Hindu arrangement of society.

Some of these questions are already addressed in the first part of the research, now we will focus on the web site of the Civil Society (liberal) movement in Nepal as a concrete example of our problems.

It says, that "Our first challenge is our own socio-political and cultural mindsets. Whether we are citizens or politicians or intellectuals or professionals we are confronted with our mindsets of two hundred fifty years of feudal socio-political and cultural way of life embedded in your brain cells."

What are these groups, if not the member of "faculty club culture," as Berger calls it? How do they equate social development with the Western concepts of "liberalism" and "civil liberties"? Here is one more example from their web site: "Because we are addicted to live a life by breaching each other's liberty and right under the tread of all mighty and under values and belief of feudal tradition.

As a result, we may be proud of our values and tradition of Nepali society that may be violating our own liberty and our civil rights. Therefore, our first responsibility is to self-educate ourselves to be human being to respect our own civil liberty and human rights before becoming Nepali with all our traditional values and pride; religious beliefs and superstitions."

Will this lead to the further demonization of the West and enhance the process of hybridization that is already on ground in Nepali politics? Maoist groups draw their support from the lower classes that are relatively more vulnerable to the economic changes brought by globalization. Will that lead to the restoration of the traditional economics?

And it is apparently clear that the nation-state in Nepal is undergoing major reforms and recalcitrant nationalist groups still persist to dominate the discourse. Is it a clear sign of the cultural globalization that tends to decentralize power, disunites virtual and actual neighborhoods, and transforms localities? Mark Liechty speaks about the effects of the cultural globalization, how prestige is associated with the West for upper class street "punks" in the street of Kathmandu. Pervasive global culture transforms power dispositions within the society and creates new forms of "prestige."

Glocalization of Nepali tourist image has led to much high awareness of global culture, with an influx of large groups of tourists and development of a new infrastructure. If that was one of the means how nation-state (which was represented by the traditionalist idea of the king) responded to globalization, should we assume that the process of nationalization is becoming contradictory in itself while operating in the global arena?

If authoritarianism is strengthened by the propaganda of the AV, how can liberalism oppose it on its turf of the national, traditionalist discourse? Does that mean that culture globalizations leave no space for structural transformations in the society and the gap is automatically filled by the traditionalist, hybrid ideologies?

Those are open questions as we cannot predict the future, but an observation on the existing identities shows that cultural globalization creates its own autonomous discourse which tends to overlap with the "materialist" changes in the society. It gives us more incentive to ignore any materialist approach (based on Marxist ontology, for example) to the issue and operate within the scope of the symbolic power dispositions.

Nepali civil society which represents the disjuncture between spatial and virtual neighborhoods speaks in the language that might be completely unknown for those Nepali who could enjoy benefits brought by social modernization and urbanization of the society. Nation state finds it difficult to handle with the problems mentioned by Appadurai, but it opposes globalization and westernization vehemently, thus filling the gap with authoritative nationalistic discourse. With respects to this, cultural globalization appears a disruptive force for Nepali freedom seekers and civil society agents.

Can landlocked Nepal resume its historical role of a transit country between China and South Asia? What are its possibilities? What cost does it entail? Transit state entails a country whose functional transaction crosses the frontiers of two countries. The development of a transit state implies the conveyance of people or goods from one country to another, especially on a local public transportation system. Recently, the government of Nepal has constituted a committee to give concrete manifestation to make Nepal a transit country between India and China.

Nepal's nearest seaport is Kolkatta in India which is 1,150 kilometers away. Administrative hassles and time consuming handling of customs often delay in the shipment of goods.

Dependence on a single seaport has made Nepal vulnerable to regular interruption of transit and trade. Economic blockade imposed by India in March 1989 is still vivid in the memory of Nepalese business community and people as to how a lack of perennial transit could inflict problems on a small landlocked country.

Economic growth, export expansion and the utilization of foreign direct investment (FDI) have generated the demand for transport and communication facilities. Mounting costs of transit and transport have increased the costs for import and export and posed additional barrier for Nepal's development. To realize Nepal's potential for a transit state, development disparity between Kathmandu and the periphery and the urban and rural areas has to be bridged by modern transportation and infrastructure developments.

Nepal's northern neighbor, China, has never been a transit state for Nepal for third country trade and the movement of people and goods. High Himalayas in the north of Nepal pose formidable barriers, Tibet is sparsely populated and the great distances between Nepal and China's industrial heartland cities make trade highly costly. In fact, "China's industrial heartland is on its eastern sea-bound, 5,000 km away by train from Tibet".

Just this year China completed a Sanghai-Lhasa railways line and Chinese authorities are trying to expand this rail lines to other Tibetan towns. There are 28 passes on the Nepal-China border but only 3 of them are open and functional throughout the whole year. This has set critical limitation on Nepal's growing commercial interaction with China. Unless Chin develops supermarkets and sound infrastructures in border areas, market integration will not occur very soon. So far, Nepal has not signed any transit agreement with China.

China's national goals of sustaining high economic growth rate, reducing regional inequalities and exploiting the rich resources of western region will probably increase imports and exports in the future which will likely to increase the economic activities of Nepal in the northern region. To expand economic cooperation China-Nepal Non-Governmental Cooperation Forum was set up in 1996. Nepal also serves as a transit country for the Indian and the Chinese trades through land routes. The Raxual-Kathmandu-Khasa road links the three countries. This link road is 390 kilometers.

But the Barhabise-Kodari part of northern road is not well enlarged and well maintained. Therefore, it has created barriers in transport during rainy season. If Syaprubesi section of highway, which is 92 kilometer long and links to Rasuwa, is constructed distance will be shortened and there is every possibility that transit importance of Nepal will be significantly increased.

The Raxual-Trishuli-Rasuwa (265 kilometers) will be the shortest road connecting Nepal's southern with northern borders. The Chinese are helping to build a 22-kilometer road that links Syprubeshi with the Chinese border and is expected to augment growing cooperation between Nepal and China. Nepal-India Transit Treaty was signed in 1971. With the signing of this treaty, Nepal Transit and Warehousing Company Limited (NTWC) have been established by the government to provide transit facilities for Nepalese exports and imports to and from abroad.

This transit agreement with India is periodically renewed. Nepal has only one dry port at Birgunj. It does not have well-equipped storage facilities. The system of tax and revenue collection is not scientifically managed either. An agreement has recently been signed with India to modernize the custom offices and upgrade other facilities of Biratnagar, Birgunj, Bhairahwa and Nepalgunj.

It is equally essential to develop an internet and intranet system to link together industrial and business facilities as a part of efforts to more efficiently manage the transit economy. To make Nepal transit country, it needs to develop good link roads, transportation and communication and storage facilities and develop good neighborly political understanding with both India and China. The completion of railway line in Lhasa by the Chinese government and its possible extension to Nepal's border together with the wide transport connectivity in the south are going to create convenient north-south transport links.

This will also link Nepal to China's industrial cities. Nepal Multi-modal Transit and Trade Facilitation Project (NMTTFP) will facilitate Nepal's economic development in the south as this project is aimed at reducing transport costs with the country's imports and exports as well as rationalizing trade and transit procedures in order to improve the efficiency and organization of transit trade documentation and data exchange. The progress report prepared by the Ministry of Industry, Commerce and Supplies in March 2003 articulates the following objectives for the trade facilitation:

- Improve Nepal's transit transport operations,
- Implement trade facilitation measures,
- Modernize transport-related legislation,
- Prepare an express procedure for transit of containerized cargo by rail,
- Establish a MOC based technical team,
- Promote the benefits of the multi-modal transport concept on the Nepal/Kolkatta corridor, and
- Offer standard carrier insurance policies to the road haulage industry.

Bangladesh has also offered Nepal an access to its seaports Chittagong, Khulna and Chalna. Nepal and Bangladesh are separated by a narrow piece of Indian Territory of about 15 kilometers in the Southeast. To promote trade between Nepal and Bangladesh, Nepal has been given Radhikapur route and importers and exporters have to liaison with Indian authorities. Bangladesh at the request of Nepal, has constructed an Inland Container Depots (ICDs) at Banglaband.

High cost and time-consuming overland transportation across national borders, distance from major world markets and inadequate transport infrastructure have increase costs to trade transactions of landlocked countries. Development of landlocked Nepal as a transit country between India and China holds tremendous potential for Nepal's economic prosperity. Both the neighbors have shown keen interest in developing trade, investments and other cooperation through Nepal are territory.

But, it requires Nepal to fulfill all the preconditions such as freedom of transit, fuller integration of its economy into the regional and multilateral trading system, encouragement of business competition, modernization of roads, communications, upgrading of warehouse facilities, expansion of dry ports, scientific custom handling procedures, security of vehicles, proper banking etc. Infrastructure developments have to be accompanied with political understanding and market integration in tune with regional and global integration processes envisioned in SAFTA, and WTO.

Reducing the costs of transactions is a critical precondition to make trade an engine of economic growth and poverty alleviation. But, Nepal has to see the welfare and well-being of its people and seek political stability through economic development, expansion of production and trade diversification. Otherwise, it would have to face a series of unavoidable problems such as national debt, mounting budgetary deficit, inflation and financial crisis. To address these, it has to approach major financial institutions for loan which are by no means condition free.

This distorts national priorities and might bear serious long term political consequences. This means national priority must take precedence over all other economic and political initiative. Poor governance and weak institutions are at the economic and political initiatives. Poor governance and weak institutions are at the root of Nepal's development problems. Now, it is gearing up and brimming with an idea that works. To be sure, turning Nepal into a transit state holds immense hope and feasible prospect for the modernization of Nepalese state, society and economy and the promotion of good neighbourhood.

5

Perspectives on Nepal-India Relations

Nepal-India relations are once again at the height of talk. The rallying cry by some Indian leaders, joined unfortunately by some ludicrous voices at home for declaring Nepal a Hindu State, the 1950 Treaty, alleged boarder encroachment, and frequent interference into the fluid transitional politics of Nepal are, among others, the main issues. It is not that these issues should not be brought to public debate and discussion. But what appears ominous is the timing and overtone of their being whipped up. One of the influential architects of the Comprehensive Peace Agreement, Girija Prasad Koirala, passed away recently.

The political vacuity his departure has created is further accentuated by the differences, which unfortunately seem increasing rather than decreasing, among the major political parties. Meanwhile, the peace process and a host of issues vital for the meaningful conclusion of it, including the new constitution drafting work remain incomplete, even as the mandated deadline is nearing. The country appears heading fast towards a situation of constitutional vacuum.

If history is any guide, it is in such fluid and turbulent times that Nepal-India relations have often fallen into controversy, with Nepal having to suffer the most damage, whether in the 50s, 60s 90s, and god forbid, not in the distant future. Perhaps, therefore, doing a quick overview on the nature and character of our nearly six decades of bilateral relations and the general public perceptions on these would be appropriate, at this point of time to draw a lesson.

DIFFERING PERCEPTIONS

Two consistent but very dominant perceptions characterize Nepal-India relations. The first one regards that our bilateral relations are rooted, among others, in the similarities in culture, tradition, religion, geography and the way of life. These unique traits of similarities which have helped shape our relations since time immemorial are viewed as strength and virtues of enduring natures. India is held as Nepal's closest of friends, a friend that has always stood by Nepal's side in troubled times.

Occasional bumps in relations are taken as natural because of the intensive and extensive nature of these relations. The underpinnings of relations are believed to be strong enough to withstand occasional ups and downs. It is generally stressed that both countries must continue to strive for the consolidation of the foundation of these relations in light of the changing needs of time and to expand them further into more mutually beneficial areas of cooperation. In other words, reshaping of relations on the basis of mutuality of interest is the leit motif.

Concurrently, counter views held mostly by intellectuals and educated young generations take India as a country still carrying the imperial legacy and haunted by the colonial mindset, always wanting to keep its neighbors under its sphere of influence. Its real intention is neither to see democracy and peace, nor stability and economic prosperity to flourish in its neighborhood. Although it is never tired of repeating the rhetoric of being a true and well-meaning friend of Nepal, its conduct has never matched with its stated commitment of friendship.

It is often wondered whether India is Nepal's true and well-meaning friend as it always professes, or does it merely want to perennially expand its political, social and economic footprints in Nepal, even if it means regime change through creating multiple power centers? These two dominant perceptions which can be termed as" traditional and "radical" do in fact mirror a great deal of truth about our bilateral relations.

Nevertheless, these perceptions do not help us lead to a pragmatic solutions. We can neither afford to bask in the luxury of our traditional friendship alone, nor do our relations can be made more cordial and meaningful if we were to entirely embrace the "radical views". Dwelling on Nepal-India relations in his "Aatmabritanta", late B.P Koirala has very aptly and eloquently explained this point." Our ties shouldn't be interpreted only on the basis of ancient history and culture. This is not an unimportant aspect.

Look at Europe; it may be one culturally, but they were always fighting and killing each other. It was clear good relations cannot be maintained on the basis of cultural affinity alone.

Distrust does not disappear just because there is cultural affinity. Relationships are dependent upon differing perspectives on society and differing expectations we have of the future", says he. Therefore, our quest for answer to the meaningful and productive Nepal-India relations capable of accommodating our aspirations and expectations must be guided by, and premised on, these very two dominant perceptions.

A dispassionate and intellectual enquiry into our relations, therefore, is necessary in the future, keeping in view of our popular aspirations and expectations. Such an informed approach is the only way to redress the past lapses, remove the lurking mistrusts and refashion a long-term model of mutually gainful relationships. Without a shadow of doubt, India's intentions to see democracy, peace and prosperity flourish in Nepal are well-meaning.

The real problem, however, has been the failure on both sides to implement them with sincerity, particularly our economic relations. This is where our bilateral relations seem to have floundered, despite best of intention. We failed to seize the many opportunities that came our way to transform our bilateral friendly relations into an enduring model of Nepal-India economic relations. The development of hydropower was one of the areas that promised so much of economic benefits for both the countries.

We know that if only we were able to harness these abundant resources, we would have helped not only to transform our respective countries' economic profiles, but also to consolidate the emocratization process in Nepal.

It is a sad commentary that our six decades of engagements in this area have failed to yield any tangible benefits. It contributed rather to sow the seeds of mutual suspicions and mistrust. In spite of the tremendous goodwill and enormous amount of assistance poured in Nepal's overall development these well-intentioned Indian overtures have failed to create favorable impressions about India in Nepal?

There is no denying that a lion's share of the blame has to be undoubtedly assumed by our leaders. But India also needs to make serious efforts to remove the deeply entrenched misperceptions. Its actions need to prove that a politically instable and economically underperforming Nepal can never be in its long-term interest.

Its political leaders should refrain from articulating provocative views on our extremely sensitive social, cultural and religious issues at this difficult point of time. It is a truism that India and Nepal, despite their proximity and cultural affinities, have not been able to build up a relationship of mutual trust and confidence, or even partially succeeded in utilising their complementary economic potential for the benefit of their citizens.

Since 1947, when India gained its independence, regimes have changed many times in Kathmandu, as have governments in New Delhi, little has changed in fundamental terms as far as the relationship is concerned. Plus ca change, plus c'est la meme chose (the more things change, the more they remain the same) is a fair description of the story of bilateral relations so far. Nepal is currently experiencing a major, multifaceted crisis.

The constitutional monarchy-multiparty democracy combine is beset with institutional difficulties, and there has been a dramatic erosion of central authority in the face of the eight-year long Maoist insurgency. The failure of governance and absence of leadership are painfully obvious, as is the breakdown in law and order and virtual collapse of the economy.

There are serious questions about the capacity of its fragile Westminster-style democracy to survive not only challenges from the left and right, but popular disillusionment with the democratic experience of twelve years (1990-2002). The institution of monarchy has also been gravely damaged, first by the royal massacre of June 2001 and, since October, 2002, by the ill-advised and misjudged initiatives of King Gyanendra to assume full powers and sideline political parties as well as the Constitution.

The Maoist insurgency is able to demonstrate at will through its tactics of terror and extortion, the impotence of government machinery and its own capacity to shut down factories and empty the roads, but it does not enjoy any real credibility as a democratic alternative to the present arrangement even if the latter is malfunctioning and discredited. The prospect of Nepal as a 'failing State' is a matter of deepest concern not only for the Himalayan kingdom but also for India and, indeed, for many other countries.

In this grim crisis, India and Nepal need to introspect and see how their relationship could measure up to the existing challenges, rather than being held hostage to them. Political and security considerations have usually been the driving force in bilateral ties. Over nearly six decades, India has dealt with every kind of regime in Nepal, tried different tactics and strategies, gone the extra mile in winning friends and influencing leaders — basically guided by its own security perceptions.

Nepalese sensitivities whether at the personal, political level or relating to the Nepalese psyche have not always been fully anticipated or well-managed. Nepalese political elites, for their part, have often exaggerated India's interest or ability to manipulate internal competitions for power in Nepal, and tended to expect political quid pro quos for cooperation even on India's legitimate security concerns.

An inevitable result of such approaches has been the corrosion and devaluation of a relationship whose natural assets and complementarities could well have led it in a very different direction. In the early 1950s, Nehru sought an understanding with the autocratic Rana regime a la British India, while encouraging an end to Nepal's international isolation and modification of its undemocratic polity.

The 1950 Treaty of Peace and Friendship, was a robust imitation of the 1923 Treaty between British India and the Ranas — it could not and did not go down too well with many Nepalese, who felt that the Treaty was unequal, non-credible and un-democratic, and who bristled openly at the suggestion that India's security perimeter legitimately extended up to the Himalayas. India, however, persisted with its efforts with the friendly constitutional monarch (King Tribhuvan) it had helped restore, and the democratic set-up (headed by the Nepali Congress) which it helped to install.

Neither survived for long; but the resentment generated by the excessively visible Indian role in 'guiding' the country's affairs while promoting India's own security interests vis-à-vis China had a lasting impact. In the subsequent decades India switched on and off its active support for friendly democratic forces (especially the Nepali Congress) depending on India's leverage at the given moment and prospects of receiving minimum security-related cooperation from the absolutist monarchs (first King Mahendra, then his son Birendra).

There were many visits and agreements; and much Indian aid which went into building roads, hospitals, communications, irrigation and power projects, and self defence for the Royal Nepalese Army. The result (from an Indian perspective) was only declining levels of gratitude and increased anti-Indian sentiment at the level of the common man in Nepal, and at the level of the government playing the China card, cosying up to Pakistan, systematic non-observance of Nepalese commitments under the 1950 Treaty and other agreements, the campaign to declare Nepal a Zone of Peace, protests on Sikkim's merger with India, much brinksmanship on India's security concerns.

The nationalist Nepali perspective on all this was, of course, quite different and has traditionally been dismissed by the Indian establishment. It is only comparatively recently that Indian experts have, for example, started conceding that the Nepalese sense of grievance on the poor quality of design, inefficient implementation and bad maintenance of Indian executed projects like Kosi and Gandak may not be unjustified; or that if King Mahendra had been handled differently, he would have been as friendly and accommodative of Indian sensitivities as his father; that the misunderstandings between King Birendra and Prime Minister Rajiv Gandhi could have easily been avoided if there had been a little more transparency.

By the end of the 1980s India was pitching in whole-heartedly with the democratic forces while maintaining a cold and formal relationship with the king, foreseeing a popular tide in favour of pro-India groups in any free and fair election. Poor personal chemistry between the monarchy and first Prime Minister Indira Gandhi, and later Rajiv Gandhi, along with other factors, created and sustained mutual suspicions and antipathy ultimately translating into confrontational politics during the government of Rajiv Gandhi.

When Rajiv Gandhi enforced a blockade against Nepal after King Birendra imported Chinese anti-aircraft missiles in contravention of the 1950 Treaty (and also incidentally permitted the Trade and Transit Treaty to lapse) tensions escalated. G. P. Koirala, leader of Nepali Congress, then in the vanguard of the pro-democracy and anti-King movement, is reported to have asked Indian Army ex-servicemen in Nepal's Gurkha districts as to what they would do if there was a war between India and Nepal.

They are said to have insisted, 'India has given us our bread, we will never fight against India!' On the Indian side, the Army Chief of Staff is known to have protested to Rajiv Gandhi that the embargo must be immediately lifted, as it was causing great hardship to the families in Nepal of serving Gurkhas in the Indian Army who were willing to lay down their lives for India's national interests. This is mentioned simply to underline the fact that leaders are sometimes totally out of touch with the sentiments of the people they are supposed to be serving.

When the Panchayat system was replaced by constitutional monarchy and multi-party democracy, after a mass agitation enjoying cross-party political support, there were huge expectations of a new era in Indo-Nepal relations. Indeed, during the first few years, India and Nepal seemed to be making up for the lost time. Visits multiplied, agreements were signed and new vistas of cooperation in trade, economic development and water resources opened up.

But the bold steps taken between the Nepali Congress Government and India in strengthening ties were to some extent undermined by the widespread (if largely unfair) perception that India was putting all its eggs in one 'pro-India' political basket in Nepal in order to promote its own interests. The monarchy was a passive spectator while the opposition (leftist as well as pro-Palace) exploited these sensitivities to create an anti-India vote-bank.

Political infighting within the Nepali Congress brought its government down necessitating mid-term elections, and brought a minority communist (Communist Party of Nepal-UML) government to power (1994) after an election campaign marked by anti-Indian rhetoric. Much to the relief of India, however, the basic direction of bilateral relations was maintained by the communists.

While rejecting the concept of a special relationship with India, and raising 'national' issues like the need for the 1950 Treaty to be updated, the Tanakpur Agreement to be renegotiated and need to solve the Bhutanese refugee problem with greater persistence than its predecessor government, the UML Government of Manmohan Adhikari gave sufficient indication during its brief nine-month tenure, of its serious desire to strengthen relations with India on a long term basis.

For his part, Prime Minister P. V. Narasimha Rao brought home to Adhikari that India would deal with Nepal as a country, irrespective of the political or ideological complexion of the party in power or the (alleged) pro or anti-India leanings of the prime minister of the day. With somewhat uncharacteristic crispness, Narasimha Rao made it clear that while India did not expect reciprocity in an arithmetical sense, there had to be reciprocity at least in spirit, and certainly in core areas of the relationship.

The Adhikari Government fell, after just nine months in office, and was replaced by a coalition of the Nepali Congress (NC), Rashtriya Prajatantra Party (RPP), and Terai-based National Sadbhavana Party (NSP) under Sher Bahadur Deuba. The following years saw political instability assume chronic dimensions. Prime ministers and governments changed with bewildering frequency. Every possible permutation and combination of political parties was forged through temporary alliances in their bid for power.

The result of the general elections of 1999, held despite a threat of disruption by the Maoists, created hope for political stability since it restored a majority Nepali Congress government under K. P. Bhattarai. But history repeated itself; the Nepali Congress squandered away its advantage due to infighting between the Koirala and Bhattarai camps, and the musical chair game helped replace Bhattarai with Koirala and brought Deuba back in power.

The Maoists took full advantage of the political instability. The tragic royal massacre of June 1, 2001, further boosted their prospects. In October 2002, the Constitution itself was derailed when King Gyanendra dismissed the Deuba government, and took one initiative after another, in an unsuccessful bid to find a solution to the Maoist insurgency while consolidating the position of the monarchy at the cost of the multiparty system.

In India too, there was political uncertainty and change. Between 1996 and 2004, the office of the prime minister has seen six changes and there have been four general elections.

Both countries have paid a big price for this political turbulence. Yet initially at least they succeeded in maintaining a certain stability, continuity and direction in bilateral ties, which appeared to vindicate India's long-held conviction that multi-party democracy was not only good for Nepal but offered the best hope for developing bilateral cooperation on a long term basis.

This was partly due to the transparency and public awareness resulting from democratic functioning and a free press, but also due to a consistent approach on India's part not to play favourites in dealing with Nepalese political leaders. A refinement of the Narasimha Rao approach of 'non-arithmetical reciprocity' — as a basis for Nepal-India relations — came in Foreign Minister I. K. Gujral's Chatham House speech of 1996; the now famous 'Gujral Doctrine' of non-expectation of reciprocity in India's dealings with its neighbours (except Pakistan). The 'doctrine' made a huge impact on Nepal, where it generated somewhat unrealistic expectations.

The first test it was subjected to was when the Trade Treaty came up for renewal in December 1996. Commerce Secretary Tejendra Khanna negotiated a far-reaching agreement under Gujral's personal instructions, providing for duty-free access to the Indian market for all goods manufactured in Nepal, irrespective of labour and material content.

The idea was to stimulate Indian investment in export-oriented manufacturing activity in Nepal and thus expand the basket of exportable commodities from Nepal to India — the only way to address Nepal's long-standing grievance of a huge trade deficit and the huge potential for Indian investment in Nepal, which had been largely untapped for decades. The treaty began to show results almost immediately. Over the following five years, Nepalese exports to India increased at the rate of 57 per cent per annum, India's at 14 per cent and a number of Indian companies including Hindustan Lever, Dabur and Colgate invested in joint ventures on the Nepalese side of the border for export to India and third countries.

The Treaty has not had smooth sailing in subsequent years, but the principle of enabling manufacturing industry in Nepal to ride piggy-back on the vast Indian market for the good of both countries has been accepted. The 'Doctrine' came under further scrutiny when I. K. Gujral, on becoming prime minister, visited Nepal in 1997 at the invitation of his counterpart, Prime Minister Lokendra Bahadur Chand.

Apart from other agreements signed, Gujral overruled objections from his bureaucrats and agreed to a long time Nepalese request for an alternative transit route to Bangladesh (the so-called Phulbari route). In order to address the special security concerns posed by the fact that the route passes through the sensitive 'Chicken's Neck' area of West Bengal, it was decided to provide Indian security escort for the Nepal-bound or Nepal-origin cargo — perhaps the most striking example of going the extra mile in accommodating a landlocked neighbour's aspirations in the history of transit agreements.

The fact that this exceptional gesture was being made with a coalition government led by individuals who did not have a particularly 'pro-India' complexion, did not go unnoticed. The message to Nepal that India's cooperation would not be influenced by the political orientation of the government in power in Nepal was further reinforced by the successor government of Prime Minister Atal Behari Vajpayee, when the Indo-Nepal Transit Treaty came up for renewal.

By now three governments had changed in Nepal and Koirala was heading a Congress-communist coalition. In what was possibly a unique concession to a landlocked neighbour, the Treaty was made automatically renewable every seven years, unless either country gave notice to the contrary before its expiry. In other words, Nepal's access to the sea was in principle granted in perpetuity, not something to be renegotiated and renewed every seven years.

To his credit, while other leaders in the ruling party and coalition pulled in different directions on Nepal and relations suffered as a consequence, Prime Minister Vajpayee himself showed the same sensitivity towards Nepal as had his predecessors prime ministers Narasimha Rao and I. K. Gujral, and frequently overruled his advisors in showing accommodation to Nepal's expectations.

The hijacking incident of December, 1999, and the somewhat casual and insensitive way in which even close friends of India like K. P. Bhattarai and G. P. Koirala treated India's requests for cooperation, came as a personal shock to Vajpayee. Subsequently, Vajpayee's personal interest and sympathy for Nepal waned as the inter-ministerial bureaucracy in India took a hard-line position on various issues, often negating concessions earlier accorded to Nepal in the spirit of the Gujral doctrine.

To its credit, the political community in Nepal did make impressive efforts, especially before the hijacking incident vitiated the atmosphere of bilateral relations, to create cross-party consensus for constructive discussions on important bilateral issues. The experience of the Mahakali Treaty was particularly striking. The Treaty was first proposed to the Narasimha Rao government by the Communist Party of Nepal-UML in April, 1995.

It proposed a mega-project at Pancheshwar on the Mahakali River, upstream of Tanakpur on which the CPN-UML, while in opposition, had created a major controversy. The idea was to subsume Tanakpur in a larger project to be jointly designed and implemented (unlike previous river projects in Nepal which had been entirely executed by India, like the Kosi).

Pancheshwar is at a point on the Mahakali where the river forms a boundary stretch, and the proposal was to have two stations of equal capacity on either bank, with power surplus to Nepal's needs being exported to India at mutually agreed tariffs, and additional downstream benefits to be paid for by India. The CPN-UML government fell before the proposal could be discussed.

However, the successor Nepali Congress-RPP-NSP coalition led by Sher Bahadur Deuba, with Water Resources Minister Pashupati Rana and Foreign Minister P. C. Lohani taking the lead, picked up the threads of the same proposal, hoping that the UML, now the main Opposition party, would find it difficult to oppose a draft initiated during its own administration. The Treaty was finalised on the basis of a formal all-party consensus in Nepal, and signed in New Delhi by prime ministers Sher Bahadur Deuba and Narasimha Rao during the former's New Delhi visit in March 1996.

By the time the Treaty was placed before the Nepalese Parliament for ratification the Gujral Government was in office in India; the Nepalese Parliament ratified the Treaty with the requisite 2/3 majority, after a thorough and occasionally divisive national debate.

The Deuba Government fell soon thereafter; its successor was a coalition led by anti-Mahakali dissidents in the RPP and CPN (UML), Prime Minister Lokendra Bahadur Chand and Deputy Prime Minister Bamdev Gautam. The new government opted to honour past international commitments, and the Instruments of Ratification of the Treaty were exchanged during Prime Minister Gujral's official visit to Kathmandu in July 1997.

The Mahakali Treaty attracted attention in a number of countries as an important indication of the ability of India and Nepal as multi-party democracies to reach agreement on cooperation in water resources on the basis of equality, transparency and equitable sharing of costs and benefits.

The Nepalese Constitution requires ratification by two thirds Parliamentary majority for any agreement affecting the country 'extensively, seriously or in the long term'; many had thought that with such a constitutional provision Nepal and India would never be able to reach an understanding on cooperation in such a sensitive area as water, since ratification by Parliament would be next to impossible, given the divisive nature of politics in the subcontinent. Nepal has some 83,000MW of hydropower potential, half of which is feasible for development. It presently has a demand of only 270MW.

With India's energy deficit projected to reach 20,000MW by 2010, the compelling logic of economic complementarity is all too obvious. Also, large-scale export of hydropower is perhaps the only way Nepal can hope to achieve speedy growth and remove poverty within a decade.

The only other resource it has is tourism, which has its limitations. Thus, the fact that despite a hung parliament and considerable political uncertainty, Nepal's main parties could unite to the extent of securing parliamentary ratification for the Treaty was hailed in many quarters as an impressive demonstration of the maturity of Nepal's democracy and the promising prospects now available for investment in the power sector.

That a Power Trade Agreement had already been signed between the two countries during Deuba's visit to India, providing in principle for private sector investment in hydropower projects in Nepal for export to private sector consumers in India, further encouraged interest of prospective investors world-wide. It is unfortunate that the Treaty is being implemented at such a slow pace, mainly because of its over-politicisation in Nepal on the one hand and compartmentalised, overly-technical, poorly coordinated approaches to it in India, on the other.

But for all its shortcomings (no Treaty is probably perfect), it does offer a model for India and Nepal on how to reach important understandings despite the uncertainties of democratic politics and coalition governments. It is waiting to be implemented the moment Nepal's polity can summon the political will, consensus and resolve it once showed, and India the priority it once accorded and sense of accommodation it earlier demonstrated.

It is encouraging to note that meanwhile, India and Nepal are seriously discussing a number of other projects (including Kosi High Dam, Upper Karnali and Budhigandaki); and that at least one private sector hydropower project for export to India (West Seti) has been finalised. During the period between 1990-2001, when King Birendra attempted with some success to play the role of a constitutional monarch, India's relations with the institution of monarchy improved.

The king shed his reserve vis-à-vis India, and in various ways he sent out signals to India as well as his own people that the misunderstandings and bitterness of the 1980s should be forgotten by both countries, and that he was personally a strong supporter of closer India-Nepal relations.

He maintained regular contact with the Indian leadership on all matters of mutual interest, so that to the extent possible, neither country was taken by surprise by developments in the other; graced private and public functions regularly at India House after more than twenty years of avoiding them; made unusual departures from protocol in dealing with the Indian Embassy or visiting Indian dignitaries; paid several private as well as official visits to India, including a pilgrimage to Hardwar, Kedarnath, Badrinath, Dwarika; warmly received President Narayanan on an official visit; and was himself invited to visit India as chief guest on Republic Day, 1999 — the first time a King of Nepal had been accorded this honour in 50 years.

Mutual goodwill and the momentum for strengthening cooperation appeared to have reached unprecedented levels. Speaking in parliament in reply to a no-confidence motion, shortly after the king's visit as chief guest on Republic Day, Prime Minister Vajpayee defended his government's foreign policy achievements by giving the example of Nepal: an election campaign was in progress there, he said, but there was not a hint of anti-Indianism in the air!

Indeed, unlike in previous elections, India-related issues like the 1950 Treaty, Mahakali Treaty or Kalapani border dispute did not figure in the campaign. Tanakpur, which had brought the Koirala government down in 1994 and had once seemed such an intractable issue, was not mentioned even once. The results of the general elections in May, 1999, were widely perceived as a vote for stability, development and apparently also for good relations with India.

Parties and individuals, professing a commitment to the politics of the far left as well as the extreme right, were categorically rejected. India's constant reiteration of its faith in the multiparty democracy-constitutional monarchy arrangement, despite its recent failures, has much to do with its experience of the positive achievements in Nepal and in the bilateral relationship, up to the time of the hijacking incident. Old suspicions and mutual demonisation have, unfortunately, vitiated the atmosphere once again.

As in the past, India's security concerns and Nepal's inability to satisfy them has become the central issue for India, and the ground for reviving anti-Indian sentiments in Nepal has become fertile once more. The Maoist insurgency has, of course, taken full advantage of this in order to enhance its own appeal within Nepal. Until recently, India's formal position on the insurgency was that while it would readily respond to requests for supply of arms, equipment and training, strengthen cooperation on cross-border movement of Maoists and extradite Maoist leaders from India, this should be treated as Nepal's internal matter.

After the visit of Prime Minister Deuba to India in September 2004, both countries have accepted it to be a shared concern. It is expected that Indian support to the Government of Nepal will increase. The latter has been advised at the highest level not to encourage involvement of third parties. What seems to have prompted the change of policy is proliferating cross-border linkages between the Maoist groups on the two sides of the border, the revival of hostile attacks against Indian interests in Nepal, the demonstrated ability of the Nepalese Maoists (e.g., through their recent blockade of Kathmandu and forced closure of dozens of industries all over Nepal) to mock the government's writ in the land, as well as the evolution of new policies on the part of government of India in dealing with its own Maoists.

In India's judgement, the collapse of the constitutional forces in the face of the Maoist threat must be averted at all costs. It is, however, clear that the combination of multiparty democracy and constitutional monarchy in Nepal is saddled with too many inner contradictions and deep mutual distrust, and may not be able, at least in the foreseeable future, to deal effectively with the crisis facing the state. It is far from clear as to how Nepal can be helped in a bilateral framework towards the only viable solution, which is to become an inclusive democracy.

Any inclination on the part of India to be proactive will only attract controversy and become counterproductive. Nor is it clear how complicated issues like the Maoist demand for a Constituent Assembly, future of constitutional monarchy, civilian control over the Royal Nepal Army, disarming Maoist cadres, holding elections, are to be addressed without a facilitation acceptable to all sides if and when a peace process starts.

India and Nepal also need to move beyond the Maoist insurgency and away from traditional concepts of military and strategic consideration. Apart from more effective joint management of the border and improving the infrastructure, the core issue of improvement of the quality of governance on both sides of the border will have to be tackled with a sense of urgency.

Without this, threats to India as well as Nepal, whether from unfriendly third countries or the Maoist insurgency or the drugs-and-arms smuggling network will continue. In this context, India will have to look at the need to respond to the widely held feeling in Nepal that the 1950 Treaty is outdated and unfair to Nepal and needs to be reviewed.

A special relationship — one in which Nepal obtains economic advantages in exchange for dilution of its sovereign space — is less sustainable than a relationship of strategic interdependent economic linkages. Specifically, the two countries need to build on possibilities in the water resources and hydropower sector, and attracting investment and economic growth in the Bihar-Uttar Pradesh-Nepal triangle if the security and economic prospects for the entire sub-region are to be strengthened.

For our political leaders, rather than whipping-up anti-India rhetoric, wisdom lay in their ability to win India's confidence and support at this critical juncture. It is not to be forgotten India's cooperation and goodwill is extremely vital to complete the peace process and the constitution writing works. The underlining need now is for exercising caution and stay united to preempt any possible damage to our bilateral relations, given the extraordinary volatile domestic political environment.

Therefore, learning lesson from history, our leaders need to move together unitedly in such turbulent times, not only to institutionalize peace and democracy but also to prevent Nepal-India relations from degenerating further. Prime Minister Prachanda returned home after paying a five-day state visit to India. He called the visit a success and the visit has opened a new chapter in mutual relations and co-operation between the two countries.

The Indian government welcomed PM Prachanda's visit heartily. Although New Delhi was reeling under the panic after explosions in various parts of the city, nonetheless the Indian media paid significant coverage to the visit. On the second day, PM Prachanda held talks with his Indian counterpart, Prime Minister Manmohan Singh. A joint statement was not the issue in the meeting. However, India agreed to review, readjust, and replace all treaties including the 1950's 'Peace and Friendship Treaty'.

This is a significant achievement for Nepal. Earlier he met with Indian President Mrs. Pratibha Patil, Vice-President

Hamid Ansari, and President of Indian National Congress Sonia Gandhi. PM Prachanda also met the opposition leader Lal Krishna Advani, the leader of the Hindu chauvinist BJP, and who has been critical of the Maoist. Advani congratulated PM Prachanda and welcomed the Federal Democratic Republic of Nepal.

On the third day, he met leaders of several Communist parties in India. Later he addressed journalists at a press conference. He told a large gathering of Indian, Nepali and other international journalists about the agreements made between the two heads of governments.

He said that Nepal and India have agreed to form a joint task force to study and sort out the issues that need revision. He also said that Indian leaders also agreed to help Nepal build infrastructure development and invest in the hydropower sectors.

Talking with the journalists, PM Prachanda said that his party was going to experiment with a new democratic system. He argued that his party was not practising formal parliamentary democracy or one-party communist dictatorship: "We are trying to go ahead with a new democratic system. This policy would strengthen the Proletariat, Dalits and down-trodden communities. We want a people-controlled democracy."

Indian journalists said there had been significant coverage, and especially the print media has given large coverage to the visit and agreements between the two sides in their editorials and analysis. The visit to the southern Indian city of Bangalore, the information technology hub of India, on the fourth day was significant. This was the first time any Nepali Prime Minister has visited the South Indian city during a state visit. Gates welcoming the PM were built in the city and preparation had been made to welcome the Nepali PM. PM Prachanda visited the Indian Space Research Organisation (ISRO), INFOSYS Campus and its BIOCON office. He was quite surprised to see the overwhelming IT development in Bangalore.

Addressing the luncheon meet organised by Confederate of Indian Industry (CII), Prachanda stated that he is:"seeking to bring about a similar change in Nepal." PM Prachanda, the commander of the 10-year long People's War, had always had a keen interest in the information technology sector. He had even encouraged his colleagues and cadres to give emphasis on the information technology during the war. The Chief Minister of Karnataka, Mr.Yeddyurappa, hosted dinner in honour of the Nepal PM at 'The Windsor' Hotel.

The agreements between Nepal and India have been made public. PM Prachanda has called the visit fruitful. Speaking with the media persons at Kathmandu Airport after returning from India, PM Prachanda said that the visit has broken the continuity and started a new chapter. Many are asking; so what was the concrete attainment? In addition, most of them see the Indian grants and promises as the bigger achievement.

The culture of begging from other countries has forced them to think in this way. This was just a courtesy visit to India. The intention was to inform India and the international community about the change in Nepal, the Republic, and to gather their support. PM Prachanda has succeeded in his mission.

Even the BJP leader LK Advani welcomed the Republic and the change in Nepal, although he and his party were supportive of the monarchy earlier. India agreed in reviewing and adjusting the un-mutual treaties. Financial grants and promises are not such big things. We need to build our own country and that is our duty. We should do that and we can. Looking to India and other nations does not make a big difference.

PEOPLE-ORIENTED BUDGET

On the 19th September, the Finance Minister Dr. Baburam Bhattarai unveiled the historic budget of Rs.236 billion for the Fiscal Year 2008/2009. This is the first budget from the Maoist led coalition government and the new Federal Democratic Republic of Nepal. The Finance Minister proposed

Rs.124.19 billion for development, and Rs. 111.82 million for general administration. Further, he has allocated Rs. 16.18 billion for the principal payment, Rs 91.31 billion for capital expenditure, and Rs 128.51 for recurrent expenditure.

The size of the budget of the FDR is about 39.6% more than previous governments. The government has a strategy to build the budget from different sources. One of the sources for the budget is the revenue of about Rs129 billion; foreign assistance Rs 65 billion, foreign grants Rs. 47.09 billion, foreign loans Rs. 18.70 billion and Rs 41.11 million will be the deficit of the budget.

The budget may seem somewhat ambitious, but it is well planned and thought out. Along with the establishment of the Federal Democratic Republic, the budget hopes to address the hopes and aspirations of the people. The Finance Minister has clearly presented the sources and expenditure for the budget, every source is clearly defined. The budget addresses the problems of rural areas as well as the problems of urban areas.

It addresses the marginalised, exploited, neglected peoples and ethnic groups of Nepal. The budget has focussed strongly on education, health, women, hydro electric development, roads, irrigation, and tourism. For socio-economic transformation the government will prioritise infrastructure and industrialisation.

The two pillars of socio-economic transformation will be firstly, cooperatives, and secondly, public private partnership. There is great hope that this budget will be able to change things for the better, and the poor of the country will benefit.

PM Prachanda during his visit in India said that Nepal is going to experiment with a new democratic system. He added- "We have not tried to practice formal parliamentary democracy or a one party communist dictatorship. We have tried to go ahead with a new democratic system in between the two systems."

After Prachanda's comment the NC, some UML leaders and Terai Madhesh Democratic Party (TMDP) leaders openly criticised Prachada's statement. In the meantime, US ambassador to Nepal, Nancy J Powell, met with former Prime Minister Girija Prasad Koirala and UML former General Secretary Madhav Kumar Nepal and discussed Prachanda's remarks. Likewise, British ambassador joined the relay and showed his concern over the remarks of the Prime Minister. He also handed a letter written by the British Prime Minister Gordon Brown to Koirala.

In Nepal, for the past 15 years, the parliamentary leaders have shown enough the real nature the parliamentary system. The CPN-Maoist has never agreed to the parliamentary system. It has only agreed to struggle to achieve its goal through peaceful means. The Nepali people have rejected the failed and infamous parliamentary system and shown their inclination towards socialism. The overwhelming support for the Maoist in the CA election has shown this.

THE EMANCIPATION OF PLOUGHMEN

Along with the abolition of many old feudal customs, the government has declared the emancipation of ploughmen (Haliyas), thus ending an old feudal tradition that dominates in far western Nepal. The government was obliged to take action over the issue when the families oppressed by the Halias tradition arrived in Kathmandu and conducted a hunger strike for their emancipation.

Now they have been declared free citizens of the country. The freed Haliyas are optimistic and they expect much from the government because the government has declared a policy and program of liberty and equality. Before the Haliyas were freed, the Kamaiyas or serfs were freed by the former government of Nepali Congress. After this declaration, however, their lives were actually harder than their previous life in the farms of the land-lords.

The emancipated Kamaiyas and Haliyas did not receive equal rights and possession. The government should have provided land, homes and the opportunity of employment as declared in its policy and programme. Under the rule of the Ranas, Prime Minister Chandra Samsher freed 15,000 slaves from slavery. After their emancipation, the slaves were taken to a place named Amalekhganj (named after the abolition of slavery) in the Terai region. Most of the slaves were freed from the houses of Ranas, Shahs, Thapas, Basnets and the aristocrats of higher ranks, mainly from the capital Kathmandu.

After they were taken to their new place, tmany were struck by malaria and most of the older emancipated slaves and their children died of malaria. Those left alive scattered over different parts of the country. This ended the issue of the emancipation of the slaves. Reviewing the bitter and inhuman experiences of the past, the present government should give its priority on the actual emancipation of those Kamaiyas and Haliys.

Without actually addressing these issues, the issue of the fundamental right of a human being, it is impossible even to think of establishing a new Nepal, a civilized modern Nepal.

JOINT PRESS STATEMENT OF PRIME MINISTERS OF NEPAL AND INDIA

Joint Press Statement on Official visit of Rt. Hon'ble Pushpa Kamal Dahal 'Prachanda', Prime Minister of Nepal to India (14-18 September 2008)

1. The Rt. Hon'ble Pushpa Kamal Dahal 'Prachanda', Prime Minister of Nepal, is on an official visit to India from September 14-18, 2008 at the invitation of H.E. Dr. Manmohan Singh, Prime Minister of India. The Prime Minister of Nepal is accompanied by Hon'ble Mr. Upendra Yadav, Minister for Foreign Affairs, Hon'ble Mr. Krishna Bahadur Mahara, Minister for Information and Communication, Hon'ble Mr. Bishnu Prasad Poudel, Minister for Water Resources and Hon'ble Mr. Rajendra Mahato, Minister for Commerce and Supplies. The delegation includes four members of the Constituent Assembly, senior officials of the Government of Nepal, a business delegation and a delegation of media representatives.
2. During his visit, the Prime Minister of Nepal called on H.E. Smt. Pratibha Devisingh Patil, the President of

India, and on H.E. Shri Mohammad Hamid Ansari, the Vice President of India. The Prime Minister of Nepal had a meeting with the Prime Minister of India, which was followed by delegation level talks, led by the two Prime Ministers, on issues of mutual interest and concern. The Prime Minister of India hosted a banquet in honour of the Prime Minister of Nepal. Shri Pranab Mukherjee, Minister of External Affairs, Prof. Saif-u-Din-Soz, Minister of Water Resources and Shri L.K. Advani, Leader of Opposition in the Lok Sabha called on the Prime Minister of Nepal. The Prime Minister of Nepal had a meeting with Smt. Sonia Gandhi, Chairperson of the United Progressive Alliance (UPA) and the President of Indian National Congress. The Prime Minister of Nepal also visited Rajghat and paid homage to the memory of Mahatma Gandhi. An interaction with the Indian business community was jointly hosted by ASSOCHAM, CII and FICCI in honour of the visiting dignitary. During his stay in India, the Prime Minister is visiting Bangalore from September 17-18, 2008.

3. The Prime Minister of India extended a warm welcome to the Prime Minister of Nepal as the first Prime Minister of Federal Democratic Republic of Nepal. The two Prime Ministers expressed satisfaction at the age-old close, cordial and extensive relationships existing between Nepal and India. Both Prime Ministers expressed their support and cooperation to further consolidate the relationship in the days ahead.

4. The talks were held in an atmosphere of utmost cordiality and warmth. They shared their views and assessment of the situation. The two Prime Ministers acclaimed the importance of peaceful, political, democratic transformation of historic significance in Nepal.

5. The Prime Minister of Nepal appreciated the positive support extended by the people and Government of

India throughout the peaceful political democratic transformation in the country.

6. The Government of India expressed full support to the peaceful, political, democratic transition in Nepal.
7. Both leaders recognized the historic changes that have taken place in Nepal with the elections to the Constituent Assembly and the declaration of the Federal Democratic Republic of Nepal according to the wishes of the people of Nepal.
8. The Prime Minister of Nepal stressed that following the Constituent Assembly elections, bringing the peace process to a logical conclusion, writing a new Constitution and accelerating the pace of economic development are the main priorities of the Government of Nepal in the days ahead.
9. The two sides felt the need to inject new dynamism into the relations between the two countries for a forward looking change in tune with the realities of the time as well as the wishes and aspirations of the people of both the countries.
10. Both sides agreed to reactivate the existing bilateral mechanisms in the evolving context.
11. Both sides noted that the multi-faceted and deep-rooted relationships between the two countries needed further consolidation and expansion in a forward-looking manner to better reflect the current realities. It was in this broader context that the two Prime Ministers agreed to review, adjust and update the 1950 Treaty of Peace and Friendship and other agreements, while giving due recognition to the special features of the bilateral relationship. A High-Level Committee at the level of Foreign Secretaries will be set up for this purpose.
12. The Nepalese side informed that Government of Nepal will take further necessary measures for the promotion of investor friendly, enabling business environment to

encourage Indian public and private sector investments in Nepal.

13. Both sides agreed to enhance cooperation in handling cross-border crime and security concerns. Home Secretaries will meet soon to implement this decision.
14. Government of India will continue to assist the Government and people of Nepal in its peaceful, democratic transition; its economic development and reconstruction. The areas of assistance would include infrastructure, human resource development, health and education.
15. Both sides expressed concern over the large-scale damage caused by the breach of embankment by the river in the Kosi barrage area and decided to launch relief and rehabilitation measures for the victims and the reconstruction of the damaged infrastructure, and other measures as per the agreements, immediately, and take up preventive measures to avoid the recurrence of such events in the long term. They decided to take up preventive measures for the Gandak and other barrages under existing bilateral arrangements. Likewise, the two sides also discussed the problem of inundation in the border areas between Nepal and India and agreed to take up necessary work for its effective prevention on the basis of bilateral consultation.
16. Government of India will provide Rs. 20 crores as immediate flood relief to the people in Nepal. Government of India will also rebuild the segments of the East-West Highway, damaged in the recent Kosi floods.
17. Both sides agreed that Government of India will set up a camp office in Biratnagar for facilitating movement of Nepali vehicular traffic through Bihar for improved access to other parts of Nepal till the Highway is repaired.

18. A three-tier mechanism at the level of Ministerial, Secretary and technical levels will be established to rationalize and raise the efficacy of the existing bilateral mechanisms in order to push forward discussions on the development of water resources in a comprehensive manner, including hydro-power generation, irrigation, flood control and other water related cooperation. The Secretaries will meet in two weeks.
19. The two Prime Ministers directed the Inter-Governmental Committee (IGC) at the level of Commerce Secretaries to meet in one month to initiate a comprehensive review of the existing trade and transit arrangements with a view to promoting industrialization in Nepal, expanding complementarities of bilateral trade on a sustainable basis and removing the barriers to trade.
20. Both sides agreed to further enhance the pace of economic development between the two countries by extending support for the preparation and execution of mega projects, including infrastructure development such as road, rail and hydel-power projects. As a gesture of goodwill of the Government and people of India, Government of India agreed to implement the Naumure Hydro-electric Project on Rapti River.
21. In view of the shortages felt in Nepal for the essential commodities, Government of India will remove bans on the export of rice, wheat, maize, sugar and sucrose for quantities agreed with Nepal. Government of India will also provide a credit of up to Rs. 150 crores to Government of Nepal for the next three months to ensure uninterrupted POL supplies to Nepal.
22. The Prime Minister of Nepal extended an invitation to the Prime Minister of India to pay an official visit to Nepal at an early date. The Prime Minister of India accepted it with pleasure. The date of the visit will be decided through the diplomatic channel.

The government has publicized and ratified its policy and programme for the F/Y (Fiscal year) 2065-66, from the position of an elected national coalition government. The policy and programme has shown a clear path to institutionalize the FDR by creating paths to new possibilities. The government has clearly centralized the main three responsibilities: 1) writing the constitution, 2) bringing the peace process to a logical conclusion and 3) bringing a socio-economic and cultural transformation in the country.

The primary task of the government will be to write the constitution in a fixed time, which will be the most reliable written document of the FDR of Nepal. The government expects help from every section of society to help complete the constitution. The constitution should address the needs, aspirations, hopes, ambitions and dreams of all the Nepalese people who are looking to the government with optimism.

The government and its leadership should be aware that the revival of the monarchy or the imposition of fascism is a possibility because the newly born is always haunted and followed by the past. The constitution should be like a real garden of many flowers, all blooming in the country.

The second task of the government will be to bring the peace process to a logical conclusion. The former rulers and governments could not fulfill their commitment to the people. They fooled the Nepalese people by deceiving them after struggles and movements. Now, hcwever, the government is fully committed to accomplish its promises. The government was formed on the basis of consensus, compromise, agreements and understandings, including the Comprehensive Peace Accord after the decade long People's War and the 19 day Peoples Movement. Only after the formation of the government under the leadership of the CPN-Maoist can this be possible.

The third important task of the government will be to launch progressive socio-economic and cultural transformation programs. It will be necessary to launch the programs in the form of big campaigns in order to end the remnants of feudalism in the country. Only after ending feudalism can the foundation of an independent and self-sufficient new Nepal begin. Long term peace, progress and prosperity are dependant on the strong foundation of the FDR.

CRITICISM

The former Prime Minister Mr. G P Koirala said that the present government has no right to sign any agreement with any friendly country including India. On 4 May 2009, Mr. Pushpa Kamal Dahal resigned over on-going conflicts over sacking of the Army chief. Since Dahal's resignation, the country has been in a serious political deadlock – one of the big issues being the proposed integration of the former Maoist combatants, also known as the People's Liberation Army, into the national security forces.

Regarding the authority of the government in signing an agreement or treaty, there are two aspects: One it is true that the government was not have authority to sign treaties of national significance. Such treaties deserve to be discussed among all the political parties and also in the house of the Constituent Assembly and should be determined by the same body whether such a treaty should be signed or not.

According to them, to achieve good will from a huge country like India is a big victory for Nepal and the rest can be achieved in course of time. It will be premature trying to raise contentious issues like Agreement on Koshi Project, 1950 Treaty, Mahakali Agreement and others at the first visit of a new Prime minister. They go to the extent that even the devastating loss caused by the Koshi dam episode should not be raised at this visit.

We have totally disagreement with these views. We think that this visit is being planned in a specific situation of Nepal in which she is suffering from a calamity caused by the destruction of the Koshi dam. Now it is clear for everybody that the destruction of the dam was not a divine episode, rather it was caused by human mistakes. This dam was constructed by India on the basis of "Agreement of Koshi Project, 1954" signed with the then governments of Nepal and India.

This agreement is also considered to be one of the unequal treaties and agreements signed between the two countries. It was guessed right at the beginning that the dam collapsed because of the overflow of water in the Koshi River. But it was not true. The water swelled in the large river because of two reasons: first, due to the blockade caused by the deposit of sand right around the dam which blocked the flow of water. Second, all the gates of the dam were not opened which caused further swelling of huge amount of water resulting to collapse of about a kilometer long bridge.

According to the terms and conditions of the agreement it is the responsibility of the Indian side to clean the sand deposit and also the opening or closing of the dam gates. Over 50 thousand people have been displaced, over 100 were washed away and about other 100 died after the incident; property worth billions of rupees was lost due to this calamity. The land washed away can be counted in miles and kilometers.

Therefore it is quite natural that the people of Nepal want the various aspects of the Koshi dam issue such as compensation, reconstruction of the dam, and reviewing of the "Agreement on Koshi Project, 1954" to be given prime importance in this visit. There are some hydro power projects such as Upper Karnali and Arun Third signed with the Indian contractors in which there is serious dispute in Nepal.

The border specialists in Nepal have indicated that there are over 60 points in the border which is encroached by the Indian side and amongst them are Susta in Nawalparasi district of Nepal, Dodhara and Chandani in Mahakali, and some points in Jhapa district of Eastern Nepal are the main.

The "1950 Treaty" has constantly become a most contentious issue regarding the treaties and agreements being signed between the various governments of Nepal and India in the past during different periods. It is true that the issue of such dimension cannot be decided and reached to agreement or disagreement at on stroke and this government will not be entitled to exercise its authority to sign such treaty of national importance.

But definitely this issue should come to the agenda in this visit thereby initiating the process of reviewing or making preparation for another treaty which can replace the existing one and can reflect the present reality. Not only the people of Nepal, but many people of the world are carefully watching this visit because of more than one reason. It is being paid by the head of a Maoist led government of Nepal.

It is taking place at a crucial moment in which Nepal is suffering a big shock of devastating Koshi dam episode which relates the host country in many ways. Nepal is facing fuel crisis since quite a long time back. Therefore, the visit of the newly elected Prime minister and his team may likely to be construed as a test case for the new government; whether it will be a good beginning that will inspire the people of Nepal or disappoint them right from the very beginning.

FALL OF KOIRALA DYNASTY

The historical victory of Com. Prachanda to the post of prime minister marks the beginning of a new era in Nepal. Once again, the Nepali people have endorsed the model of Nepali revolution that includes the fusion of both open and underground activities, pen and gun, bullet and ballot, people's war and mass movement. With the election of Chairman Prachanda, our party has become the first ever party in the one-hundred-sixty-year history of international communist movement – with a separate army of proletariat under its command- to make it to the government using these different methods.

Following the demise of Com. Mao in 1976, the CPN (Maoist) is the first ever revolutionary Communist party to lead the government after thirty two years. The new Maoist government in our country is also different in the sense that it is based on the joint dictatorship of both the proletariat and the bourgeois class. There are not any references of such kind of joint dictatorship in any of the Marxist thesis; the Marxist principle that the joint dictatorship of two antagonistic classes in the state is impossible. However, the experience of Nepal has shown it otherwise.

The philosophical and theoretical base of the Nepali experience and experiment will have to be synthesized in the days to come. History has put the onus to justify dual dictatorship of the state on the shoulders of Maoists of the twenty first century. The victory of Chairman Prachanda has another historical facet. This marks the end of five decades of 'Congressocracy' and the Koirala dynasty that has served as the main bulwark for imperialism and expansionism, and has been an embodiment of feudalism and imperialism.

The 30th day of Shrawan has a historical significance in this sense, too. The collapse of Koirala dynasty is a signal of the fall of a pillar of imperialism. This bears no less significance than the fall of monarchy. Truly, the Nepali people were equally suffering from the monarchy and Koirala dynasty. Generally speaking, it was the Koirala dynasty and the 'Congressocracy' that served as the main basis for the existence of Monarchy for half a century.

The fall of Girija is a watershed in Nepali people's fight for nationalism, against imperialism and expansionism. After achieving the goal of republic, the immediate goal of the revolution has also changed and so has been the equation of friends and foes of the revolution. Obviously, hitherto friends have turned into foes and vice versa. Of the two gigantic mountains of feudalism and imperialism, the Nepali people have demolished one huge mountain of feudalism.

As of now, standing in front of the Nepali people is the terrible and gigantic rock of imperialism and expansionism. The conspiracies to prevent the CPN Maoist forming the government during the outcome of this. The Nepali people have, to the large extent, won the struggle of democracy by defeating feudalism, even though it is yet to be institutionalized. However, the fight for absolute nationalism is yet to be started and victory accomplished.

The nature and method of that battle cannot be predicted right at the moment. However, there are no two minds that the fight for nationalism will bear a national character, will be more complicated and a fiercer struggle. The political line of the party, now, must be directed towards that. A lot of reverberation and kind of sensation was caused among the rank and file of revolutionaries by rapidly changing circumstances following the election of Constituent Assembly.

The election of President and Vice-President as well as the collaboration with the UML generated a ripple effect in the party. Most importantly, whether it was correct to join the government has become the central point of debate in the party that has stirred the minds of the rank and file. We must seek out the answers to the above questions in totality, not in fraction, in content, not in the form.

The answer to these questions lies in the strategy formulated by the party, not in the tactics. The revolution never advances in straight line. The revolution moves ahead through many advancements and retreats, victories and defeats, offenses and defenses and so on and so forth. There is no denying that imperialism and expansionism stands in the way of Nepali revolution.

The party has identified this even before the beginning of the PW. Imperialism and expansionism are the two major strategic enemies of the revolution... The success in overthrowing Girija is a major chain in the struggle against imperialism. We are in the transitional phase of negating the old contradiction and the emergence of new contradictions.

This process will take a definite duration to complete. Without the completion of this duration, as well as the process to talk about the movement or uprising or to pull out from the peace process with petit -bourgeoisie impatience will be suicidal. In order to wage the struggle in the days to come, for nationalism along with the total struggle, the need of the hour is broad polarization and forging alliances not only on national level but also in the international level.

This is the stage of forging alliance among patriotic, democratic and left forces. It can be done equally by joining the government or by staying out of the government. It is not the case of something to be 'finished' if the party joins the government or vice versa. Instead of initiating the debate on whether or not to join the government, it is more important and pertinent to start the discussions on whether or not we would be able to mobilize and open multi-dimensional fronts of the revolution in the future.

The question that whether we will be competent to effect sharp polarization between revolutionary and reactionary forces is the most important one, rather than the question of joining or not joining the government. The question of joining or not joining the government cannot be the theoretical one, it is a tactical question. If joining the government helps in the advancement of the future revolution, paves the way to achieve people's democracy, ensures the victory in the struggle for nationalism or pushes the revolution one step forward towards a New Democratic Revolution, then participation in the government is correct, otherwise it is wrong.

If we are unable to chalk out new plans and policies and program of the revolution, to formulate new political and military line in accord with the changed circumstances, we cannot advance the revolution even if we do not join the government. If we are able to sharpen and intensify the class struggle even if we remain in the government, we can advance toward the path of revolution.

NEW ECONOMIC ACHIEVEMENT

For the first time in Nepal's political history, the President of Federal Democratic Nepal, Dr. Ram Baran Yadav, presented a 90-point historic document Policies and Programs of the government at the budget session of the constituent assembly on September 10, 2008. Consequently, the budget session of the CA passed it with a majority vote. The Nepali people were curiously waiting to know how the government allocates the budget funds to achieve those national goals publicized in the policy and programme.

If anyone goes minutely through these policies and programs, s/he will certainly find they are the outcome of ten-year People's War and a nineteen-day People's Peaceful movement that made the people sovereign for the first time.

The program mainly aims to bring the peace process towards logical end, to provide sufficient relief to the people and finally to achieve high economic growth rate.

In order to bring about socio-economic transformation through rapid economic growth, the government has proposed a public private partnership (PPP) economic concept in the policy paper. Under the point 14 of the policy paper, it says the government will give high priority to the bases of common minimum programs prepared by the alliance parties before forming a new national government.

In order to eradicate poverty, according to one report over 31 percent of the total population lives under absolute poverty, unemployment, hunger, no access to education (illiteracy), dependency and inequality, the government will implement transitional economic policy based on PPP concept. The Policy paper forecast a double-digit economic growth is possible in this historic land through the generation of hydropower. Thus, this policy paper says the coming decade of Nepal will be of economic revolutionary decade.

Therefore, the government gives priority to generate different hydroelectric projects i.e. mini, micro, and small and mega projects using unlimited water resources. Almost all human and government economic activities primarily depend on the production of hydropower. If the government supplies targeted amount of electricity, the national will certainly achieve the double-digit economic growth rate. Unfortunately, now our average economic growth rate is 2-4 percent, which is not enough to reduce poverty, hunger, and disease from the nation.

Really, this is the time of using water resources for supplying pure drinking water, irrigation, generating electricity maintaining eco-system rafting etc. Beside these, our biggest rivers have created many troubles in lowland region Terai and the government has to control the flood and manage the water that flows throughout the year. Every Nepali wanted to see a prosperous country. For a long time, different castes, communities and regions were marginalised and they could not contribute anything to nation building.

Now in reverse, the government ought to give them a specific role in a restructured country. After collapsing the feudal autocratic regime, the Karnali people, Dalits, women etc. should go ahead in order to awake their home areas.

For this, the government should bring out a new policy regarding human resources and natural resources like forest, land and water. Hence, emphasis should be on human cooperation, national understanding, government and private investment.

However, domestic investment will not be enough to operate all projects in a confident way. So, foreign investment is required to use these natural resources for the well-being of the Nepali people. Now, the problem of unemployment is a serious issue that forces the Nepal youth to leave the nation and to work taking for a pittance abroad.

First, the government should bring a new industrial policy that strengthens the present industries and encourages the private sectors to invest money to generate jobs, areas written the country. Second, the government has to facilitate the young people to go abroad safely.

Now, different types of training are needed for them to get sound benefit from their labours. More or less, it partly solves the problems of unemployment. This policy paper aims to modernise the agricultural sector through implementation of co-operation. Then, if we establish agro-based small, domestic or medium sized industries, we can generate new jobs and increase the national income of Nepali farmers.

Really, the agricultural sector is a backbone of Nepal's economy. However, Nepal people are dying of hunger. In one side, around 82 percent people are farmers but on the other side, our food production is not sufficient to kill the drought.

The real farmers do not own their own land; they are working on the land of others. Hence, the redistribution of land is necessary to increase the production to solve the problem of unemployment. Then, the main thing is to see how it will be implemented in the days to come.

ART AND LITERATURE

Literature and art are means of struggle in class society. Human sympathy is based on the measurement, norms, values and psychology of class society. Feeling is love between people, appreciation, sorrow and happiness and cooperation to get rid of oppression, be unsatisfied, be agitated, see dreams and be ready for sacrifice. Human sympathy is the source and basis of epics.

So, the people with sentiment are always affected and are in turmoil with the incidents and scenes taking place in the world. A famous Russian poet Pushkin said, "A type of craziness is necessary for poetry". This means that sympathy is necessary in creation. We can say a little more than Pushkin that sympathy is compulsory for every creation. A woman cannot be a mother without menstruation, in that way a creation can not take birth without a continuous waterfall of feeling flowing from the heart of a creator like a heavy rainfall of summer under the cover of cloud.

Sympathy is not a God (Navraj, in Nepali Swasthani epic) born into a pot. It is a sharp and a bitter experience of objective reality. Let's say that it is the pangs of child birth and a quake of the Earth during the time of the crack. The child takes birth if the pang of the child birth is endured. The life and residence perishes at the time of volcano. Precious gems are found after destructive volcano breaks out. A poem can be created if sympathy can reach up to the vast sky.

The trend of the life flows continuously like the Brahmaputra River. If sympathy does not get expressed, the life of a poet comes to meet the fate of the Russian poet Mayakovsky. Sympathy is a uterus where the embryo of intellect develops. Sympathy cannot be without exception to class. It brought humans to the society from the jungle. There is no imagination without love and dream, and no dream without imagination.

Consciousness cannot be without sympathy or idea without consciousness. Human civilization developed in search of consciousness; about the life and the Earth. The glory of human being is in it. It has been said, "Nobody reaches to the climax, without the glory of the self". In this context, sympathy becomes the way of decay and destruction. Human sympathy can take the form of a poem when it is expressed artfully. It is not compulsory that each of the sympathies is expressed in a poetic form.

If fresh water is mixed with gutter water, it becomes dirty and an ugly poem is created. Therefore, sympathy is expressed as a sacrifice against ugly reality. The reality of a great sacrifice created by a new reality creates revolt and revolutionary consciousness against oppression. This is why; human sympathy is the basis of creation and sacrifice. Literature is the expressive form of sympathy, which is artistically and symbolically expressed by the representatives and characters of society. Art is a style, colouring and beautifying.

Mature creators say that a dumb lady becomes beautiful as she is beautified. Ideas are made expressive after they are carried in a beauty parlour of sympathy. Popularity is the expressivity and it is the measurement of value of art. In the sector of art and literature, idealism gives emphasis only in to the form; while dogmatism negates the value of art by giving emphasis only to ideology. Marxist aesthetics has been victorious in the struggle against both.

The idealistic aesthetics of "Art for art's sake" considers the art only for the luxurious means for the rich and forgets the masses. Left sectarianism annihilates the value of art under its priority in ideas. Extreme emphasis in ideology makes lessens sympathy; similarly, the overemphasis on sympathy creates illusion. These both are equally harmful. Lack of sympathy and illusion both create deviation, pessimism, humiliation, slavery, hopelessness and disinterestedness in the creation. Therefore, the literature that can not create sensation can be neither the source of a poem nor the basis for sacrifice.

There is a big development in the expressive forms of human sympathy along with the development of the science and technology. Sympathy can be expressed through sound, wave, song, speech, recitation style, icon (picture), shade, sound, symbol, dance, acting, colour, light, ray, rise-fall of tone and diction. The forms of sympathy created in picture or emotion through the proper mix of rays in camera to attract the readers through the deep emotion with which to touch their heart.

Dialect, folk rhythm, rhyme through the model characters can make sympathy alive. The creation is more alive if it is related with the soil and the labour. Therefore rural sympathy has a natural flow like a fish in the river. Popularity depends on the language of common people, their tongues and their psychology and the level of their consciousness. Capitalism has made the interest of the people corrupt and deformed.

Art and the literature become non-sympathetic if the measurement of the value of the art, talent and appropriateness is money. Death of the art and the literature is inherent in it. Mind reacts according to the sympathy which enters inside the heart of the creator or the people through the form, taste, scent, touch and scene. The intellectual situation of a man is the expression of his physical situation.

The sources of sympathy are the love to another human being, belief in labour and devotion that makes a creator or human sincere to him or her as well as the society. Anthony Queen expresses his bitterness in the way, "We all are renegades; because we have forgotten to love others." There is no feeling without imagination and nihilism has no sympathy. F. Garcia Lorca says, "In the time of shaking the entire world, all the artists are necessary to laugh and weep together." Therefore, the appropriateness of literature must be concerned with society.

6

The Prospects for Democracy in Nepal

Nepal observed the 60th National Democracy Day Friday, 19 February, 2010. At sunrise, the Nepali Army blew bugle from atop the Bhimsen tower situated in the capital Kathmandu and fired salvoes from cannon and guns. The National Democracy Day is celebrated in Nepal to commemorate the day when Nepalese were released from the clutches of 104-year-long Rana autocracy on February 18, 1951.

Among those attending a special ceremony at the Nepal Army Pavilion in Tundikhel, Kathmandu, were President Ram Baran Yadav, Vice President Parmananda Jha, Prime Minister Madhav Kumar Nepal, Chief Justice Anup Raj Sharma, Constituent Assembly chairman Subash Chandra Nembang, ministers and high ranking officials along with foreign mission chiefs. President Ram Baran Yadav in a message issued on the occasion of the National Democracy Day stressed strengthening of national unity in the country.

"The responsibility of drafting the new constitution and establishing peace should be common agenda for all", the President's message says. Addressing the ceremony, Prime Minister Madav Kumar Nepal said that the state of the country would have become different had everyone assimilated the essence of 1951's democracy. "Nepali people have now abolished the autocratic royal regime for good," the Prime Minister added. He urged Nepali people to remain informed and watchful through out the crucial period of transition.

He also emphasized drafting of the new constitution on the stipulated time to institutionalize the federal democratic republic of Nepal. Nepal remarked that federalism does not mean splitting the country into several pieces. "Today, we are able to live proudly as a sovereign and free citizen because of the people's power," said the Prime Minister.

The 2006 Democracy Movement is a name given to the political agitations against the rule of King Gyanendra of Nepal. The movement is also sometimes referred to as Jana Andolan-II ("People's Movement-II"), implying it being a continuation of the 1990 Jana Andolan . The international reaction following King Gyanendra's military coup on 1 February 2005 has been mostly heartening for Nepalis.

Until that date, we felt doomed to be characterised as simple, happy mountain folks inhabiting a Shangri-la, who deserved to be ruled by a deity-king, no matter how unjust. Maoist insurgency tended to be viewed as an anachronism, even fey: trouble in paradise. Meanwhile, Nepal's real story – the decades-long (and continuing) struggle to establish and retain democracy – seemed destined to be overlooked. It was just not picturesque.

But the world's condemnation of King Gyanendra's military coup has made Nepalis feel that we are not being abandoned at this, the most traumatic and transformational era in our history. Still, Nepalis are wary about the international community's trustworthiness, for any vestigial commitment to democracy in Nepal it has shown in the past has proved fickle.

In part this unreliability is because the outside world simply could not understand Nepal after democracy was won in 1990. It has been difficult enough for Nepalis to clarify this chaotic period even to ourselves. We were not prepared for the challenges of democracy. There were no democratic institutions, and very little democratic practice in either public or private spheres in 1990. The caste structure – with the Chettri, Bahun and "high-caste" Newar groups at the top – remained rigidly in place.

It was widely felt that any move in the direction of equal rights for women would destroy Nepali culture. Any mention of ethnic rights could be met with accusations of harbouring separatist, anti-national, even treasonous sentiments. August 15th, 2008, will go down in the history of Nepal as a true red letter day when Pushp Kamal Dahal 'Prachanda' was elected leader of Nepal by its constituent assembly, which met on this historic day to elect a new prime minister.

The victory of the Maoist in Nepal nearly four months ago had clearly indicated that there would be a clear shift in the priorities and policy shift of the new nation. Nepal, which was subjugated for years under the tyranny of a monarch who claimed to be the incarnation of Hindu God Vishnu who was persistently being supported by various regimes in Delhi in the name of Nepal's internal affair despite well known fact how Indian interventions in Nepal's were visible even in those days.

Nepal's election threw unpredictable results in the constituent assembly. Even when the Communist Party of Nepal won a mandate from the people, the way behind the scene activities happened in Kathmandu reflected the growing influence of both India and America in the domestic matters of Nepal. It is alarming that political parties played the same role of their unpredictability till the last vote counted. The first Secular democratic government of Nepal had two new faces as President and Vice President.

While there was nothing much to celebrate once Dr Ram Narayan Yadav took over as president of Nepal but when the vice President Pandey took oath in Hindi, the matter did not remain as fact of choice. Nepal burnt for many days as youths took over the streets, burnt tires and protested against a vice president who they felt was symbol of Hindi imperialism.

Pandey comes from Madesh and Hindi was not his mother tongue, secondly, in the Nepalese constitution, the head of the states and other ministers have to take oath in Nepali.

A petition is already there in the Nepal's Supreme Court, a member of newly elected Constituent Assembly informed me. 'What was the need for a vice president to take oath in Hindi when it is not even his mother tongue, said the Member of Parliament.

It is not that Nepalese have developed hatred to Hindi. Hindi channels, Hindi books sales in large number. Hindi films are hugely popular here but today Hindi is not being seen in terms of a widely understood and spoken language in Nepal but a symbol of Indian imperialism in that country. Nepalese youth are exerting their pride and Hindi simply coming as an obstacle for them. Between English and Hindi imperialism, they would definitely go with the previous one which offer them much greater market and space to develop as latter have treated them in the worst ways.

Unlike his predecessors, Nepal's Prime Minister Prachanda started his 'career' with visiting China. It was a ritual for the every new Nepalese government to pay a curtsy visit to Delhi which enjoyed king's patronage which gave Nepal outdated and unequal water treaties in 1950. Now, the Indian administration is unduly worried. Problem with Delhi's thinking is that any assertion of Kathmandu is taken as anti Indian stand. How can a country so close to India in culture and values turn over night anti Indian.

The dependency of people, their relationship, the close people to people contacts make Nepal India's natural ally but that does not make India to lord over Nepal for every action that it want to take to protect its integrity and interest. It must have a right to decide about the fate of its people and its territory. The members of the new constituent assembly know better about relationship with India. After all, whether it is Maoist or anybody else, close relations with India are part of Nepal's culture but that should be treated on an equal footing and not as another 'Sikkim' as many in Nepal perceive.

This attitude of mini United State in South Asia will make India highly unpopular like the United States under George Bush itself. If the Indian class perceive itself as leader of South Asia it is highly questionable as in today's free world, the days of colonization are over and people will always rise up and revolt against any dominating power. Hence, Indian authorities will have to understand those sensibilities in Nepal. Second, Nepalese people do understand how the Indian authorities made very effort to create confusion till the last date of the election of Prime minister in parliament.

Though, things are not seen in open yet people of Nepal did not like India's overzealousness in what was entirely their internal affair. The irony of the entire situation is that while Indian Ambassador in Nepal was over busy related to political situation there, Indian media discourteously downplayed the entire event. How can media which claim to be a free media ignore such a big event in our neighboring country which has wide ranging implications for our foreign policy?

A country which over threw monarchy and where the new leadership is emerging from the ground can not be ignored. Nepal need kudos from all those who believe in equality of law and secular democratic values that it chose secular democratic constitution. And those who have any doubt should see that in Nepal's Constituent Assembly there are about 55 members hailing from Dalit communities and 22 of them are women.

There are debates on proposed constitutions. The newspaper industry is booming and political debates talks of the town. In the local buses, in schools and colleges, at the FM channels, we find talks of the new constituent assembly and proposed constitution. Unlike our corporate media which is depoliticizing the people, glamorizing Bollywood and cricket as if all other issues of dignity and livelihood have been resolved, Nepal's focus on issue need appreciations from us.

Ofcourse, the new Constituent Assembly can take a few lessons from India. The first and foremost is that India did not abolish right to hold property. There was no big reference in our constituent Assembly as mȧjor members of the assembly were themselves holding huge lands and property. Nepal must constitutionally abolish big properties and put a ceiling law into practice. In India to avoid ceiling, our leaders and religious thugs are doing big business.

They have started acquiring land in the names of mutts, temples, Gurudwaras and churches. Nepal must do away with this. While, it would be futile to say to demolish religious institutions but there should be a clear limit that these religious places need land for worshipping and not for business. Nepal must come out with progressive land laws.

The new Nepalese government must be careful of this international Hindu brotherhood which is taking its wings in Nepal. It is already learnt that former Royal family is not yet a gone case.

They have strong loyalist in Nepal as well as outside Nepal. They will wait for right moment to strike back. And since now Nepal is opting for a secular constitution, the Hindu Right wing supported by India, will take deep root there.

Already, there have been cases of violence in Madhesh and other regions. Nepal must issue stern warning to all such forces which want to disturb peace and brotherhood in the region. It must respect different ethnic groups and give them representation in power structure. The Dalits in Nepal need special protection in the form of not only powerful land reforms but also in terms of representation in government jobs and bureaucracy and judiciary.

It would be advisable that all these areas must have representation from such communities otherwise they will spoil every political action that the new government takes in public interest.

Special provisions like abolition of untouchability and discrimination and provisions for stringent penalties and criminal charges against those who exploits the Dalits in the name of age old traditions. Untouchability is a blot on Nepalese society. India that way had a better record in terms of social revolts like Ambedkar, Phule, Periyar and others.

One does not know fully how much Nepal's Maoist leadership understand the struggles of Dalits and Bahujans in India. They will have to mix up their Maoism with Ambedkarism to fulfill their long cherish desire to bring a complete change in the Nepalese system. A mere change of head of state and government will not change the social structure of Nepal and working of the governance. Nepal needs a social resurgent movement and this is the right moment to do so.

The people of Nepal can not keep quiet because there is a new government. They have to put continuous pressure so that these rebels of yesteryears do not become 'belagam ghoda' i.e. uncontrolled horses, who destroy every institution. Let Secular Socialist Democratic Republic become values of Nepal and be part of its preamble which no authoritarian regime could change.

Also important will be people's right to be secular. While each of our government says we must defend religious freedom, what happen to those who do not believe in these organized religions? India has become a jugular's state where all this 'religious' freedom exist except those who disagree with them. Hence those of who voice our concern and condemnation against religious hatred face the music.

A painting of a painter hurt our religious sentiments, writing of an author make Islam under threat and many more things, one hope that Nepal's secularism will not become a joke like Indian multiculturalism where every thug is enjoying except the common man, in the name of religion. Nepal must allow people a choice to opt for atheism or secularism beyond their conventional religion, a choice already given in Europe and other countries.

Nepal and India need to work together on equal basis. Today, we all are witnessing the fury of river Kosi which has brought a new Tsunami in Bihar which is unprecedented and need emergency help. Though this is no time to discuss the issues of who did it but definitely the government of India can not keep silent on its own follies on those out dated water treaties with Nepal which did not allow efficient functioning of dam as well as made India highly unpopular in Nepal.

Today, we are seen as people who are misusing Nepal's water and other natural resources while thousands of people die every year because of flood fury which originates from Nepal. Hope Prime Minister Prachanda has this in mind. His foreign Minister is expected in Delhi soon and we hope they will discuss all the issues. While differences in democracy will always be there even then a new democratic Secular republic of Nepal will be of greater strength for not only its people but also for India.

A COUNTRY IN CHLOROFORM

This was the legacy of the closed, pre-1990 system. Political parties had been illegal, and could operate only underground. Free speech had been banned, and criticism punishable by law. No one could state their political position openly; communication took place either in tight circles, amid the fear of informers and infiltrators, or via secret messages embedded in public discourse. In this paranoid atmosphere, political activists with liberal, socialist and (various) communist ideologies tended to remain segregated from and mistrustful of one another.

This stifling polity almost guaranteed that when their time came to govern, the parties would stumble. So it proved: when the ruling Nepali Congress Party abandoned socialism for capitalism under pressure from the World Bank and the IMF after 1990, the largest opposition party – the Communist Party of Nepal [United Marxist-Leninist, UML] – awkwardly tacked its old-style communism onto free-market economics without rejecting its strain of totalitarianism, as its Indian equivalents were to do. Nepali political parties did not worry at that stage about a comeback by monarchist and military forces, far less an unimaginable Maoist insurgency.

As a result of this unresolved adaptation to new realities, they muddled endlessly. In the early 1990s, one government after another fell to selfish power grabs, petty infighting and personality-based factionalism; corruption scandals proliferated; parliamentary sessions grew raucous even as street demonstrations, closures and strikes grew. All the major parties eventually split. The accumulated result was to block the progressive social and political reforms that Nepali people desperately needed.

Despite this, the democratic environment did allow lawyers, journalists, businesses and other professional groups to establish themselves. Unions, pressure groups and special interest groups formed. Activism flourished; among the new social movements were those campaigning for the rights of women, *Dalit*, ethnic groups, and gays. Such fragile democratic institutions and practices had barely found their footing when the Communist Party of Nepal (Maoist) went underground and launched their armed insurgency in 1996.

The Maoist demands were for an all-party interim government to be formed, followed by elections to a constituent assembly, and the creation of a new, republican constitution. These demands had their roots in the 1940s, when republicanism had begun to grow and Nepali political parties were expressing aspirations to a new constitutional, democratic order.

Fifty years on, however, the parties chose to be intimidated rather than inspired by the return of these aspirations in a new guise. To debate the demands seriously would require overcoming complacency and genuinely soul-searching for their own ideological commitments. It was so much easier to do what they did: move rightward. As the Maoist insurgency escalated, Congress-UML governments enforced press censorship, suspended civil rights, and imposed a brutal counterinsurgency – eventually deploying the Royal Nepal Army – costing thousands of civilian lives.

These parties passed the Terrorist and Disruptive Acts Ordinance, which made it possible to arrest people based merely on the suspicion that they were Maoists. In 2001 alone, more than 100 journalists were arrested. Amid vicious infighting and factionalism – intensified in the wake of the royal massacre of June 2001 – these parties moved from boycotting an entire session of parliament to eventually dismissing parliament without making the necessary preparations for elections in the war-torn countryside.

The machinations of the political parties caused a constitutional crisis in 2002, leaving King Gyanendra to take advantage. In October 2002 he dismissed the elected prime minister and established his own cabinet of handpicked palace loyalists. His ostensible purpose was to ease the crisis; he even cited Article 127 of the constitution in justification. This convinced very few Nepalis; people and press responded with street protests and strong denunciations against a return to monarchical rule. The king's takeover was dubbed a "royal regression".

But the international community – diplomats, and monetary and aid agencies – was greatly relieved. Political analysts have generally viewed Nepal's travails as a standoff between three major powers: the king/military (or palace), the political parties, and the Maoists. Hari Roka, a political analyst, has added to this troika a fourth power: the international community, whose diplomats and aid industrialists supply more than 60% of the national budget and often hold more sway over Nepal's governance than Nepalis themselves.

These representative individuals were often genuinely disgusted with the ineptitude of the democratic political parties, and concerned about the growing strength of the Maoist insurgency. But unlike Nepalis, they lacked any memory of life under absolute monarchy: somehow, in their minds, the king was a unifying force for Nepal. They threw their considerable weight behind him. India, the United Kingdom and the United States all welcomed his takeover. Aid, including military aid, continued and even grew.

So Nepalis were stuck with a king who had transgressed his constitutional remit. He dismissed cabinet after cabinet, all the while laying the grounds for his final ascendancy to power. This he achieved on 1 February 2005. Before that, he approached the embassies of the three "friendly" countries to gauge their reactions. They – or so they have latterly claimed – unanimously advised the king not to conduct a military coup.

But he did. And only then did it become apparent to the international community that in 2002 it had done no more than help the king buy time, and make the necessary preparations for 1 February 2005. To put it bluntly, the international community funded his military coup. Most complicit were India, the UK and the US, which together had supplied aid to the Royal Nepal Army despite its widespread and systematic human rights abuses.

It should have been an outrage to the taxpayers of these liberal-democratic countries that they were backing this dirty war. But it was not. Nepal was too far away, and its troubles were nebulous, obscure. So what if the king's government did not release any expenditure reports since 2002? So what if the king's salary increased hugely while many of his people were famished? So what if nobody knew how aid money was really being used? Only the Nepalis were outraged. But we did not matter.

This is why, despite the fact that India, the UK and the US all suspended military aid following the February coup, Nepalis remain suspicious of the international community. Aid is, after all, a cynical industry. There are jobs and contracts on the line for donor countries. The donor countries' need to disburse aid is often greater than the recipient countries' need to obtain it.

Democracy, moreover, is not the aid industry's concern; in fact, democracy often deters the aid industry by forcing greater transparency and accountability in public expenditure. An old Nepal hand (who wishes to remain anonymous) voiced a common wariness to me when he said: "If this had been a *competent* fascist coup, they would have backed it. But it's been an incompetent fascist coup. They're embarrassed by how crude it is."

King Gyanendra himself may pay lip service to the notion of democracy, but the army, or at least its top brass, has been openly contemptuous of the idea. It has targeted three groups for the worst repression: democratic political leaders, private media, and human rights activists. The military plan appears to be to silence all potential critics before going after the Maoists. This time, nobody will be able to speak out for the civilians who get in the way.

Nepalis' fear now is that military aid might resume, helping to entrench military rule in Nepal. This is clearly what King Gyanendra hopes. Claiming that cutting off military aid only supports the Maoists, he has been lobbying hard for its resumption – at times begging before India, the UK and the US, at others threatening to ally with China, Pakistan, and even Cuba.

For a few days in late April it appeared that the king would be granted his wish, when the Indian government seemed ready to resume military aid. Indian security concerns over the Maoists were simply too strong, and the country's military was pressing the New Delhi government. But India's government was also opposed by its own left coalition partner and embarrassed by the continuing arrests of political activists in Nepal. Torn between these impulses, it waffled.

Whatever India does, the UK and the US will most likely follow. So far, the UK has generally given non-lethal aid to Nepal's army, while the US has supplied lethal aid as well.

But the supply of helicopters from the UK to Nepal shows how deceptive such categories can be: the Royal Nepal Army has conducted aerial bombing from helicopters for several years, targeting crowds heavily populated by civilians and a few Maoists. "Non-lethal"? What the international community must understand now is that if it resumes military aid, it will be actively helping the king derail Nepal's democracy movement, and in time be held accountable for its betrayal.

If it does so, any appeal by the international community for the restoration of civil liberties, or even of democracy, will mean nothing. For once military rule is entrenched in Nepal, it will be near-impossible to return to developing democratic institutions and practice. Since 1 February, the parties of the democracy movement in Nepal have been scattered and most of their top leaders are imprisoned, under house arrest, or underground. It is extremely hard to regroup under such conditions, but regroup the movement has.

The second- and third-tier cadres of all the parties are coming to the fore in two ways. First, they are voicing the demand for a new constitution via a constituent assembly, thus reclaiming an aspiration their parties had made as early as the 1940s, long before the Maoists appropriated it. Second, they are following the example of student party activists in the past who were often scorned for their advocacy of republicanism.

This move is so far cautious, even nervous – for the monarchy looms larger in the lives and imaginations of older generations. There is some disagreement as to how to form an all-party government. Some parties would prefer to re-establish the parliament that was dismissed in 2002; others prefer to establish a new all-party interim government. But for the most part, the political parties have by a different route reached the same view as the Maoists: Nepal needs a new constitution.

The parties have not overcome their ineptitude and indecision, but they are no longer intimidated by the scare of a return to absolute monarchy, of military rule. This conquest of fear obliges them to scale four new challenges: to throw up good leadership possessed of vision; to move beyond the immaturity that is a legacy of living for so many years underground; to sharpen their governance skills; and – most importantly – to bring the Maoists into a peaceful settlement via a new constitution.

All this can happen, albeit slowly, but only if the international community does not help the king and military to derail democracy before the opportunities can be seized. The king's cautious release from prison of two leading communists, Madhav Kumar Nepal and Amrit Bohara, on 1 May is a small but significant step, reflecting the combination of internal opposition to the coup and external pressure.

Democracy is the only option for Nepal. This has been the main struggle for over seventy years. Nepalis are now regrouping to carry on the democracy movement, defying the severe repression and censorship imposed by the king and the military. They deserve support. The only action that the international community can take in good faith is to make a wager on the Nepali people and their democratic future.

On February 1, 2005 the royal takeover was further advanced as the King appointed a government led by himself and at the same time enforced martial law. The King argued that civil politicians were unfit to handle the Maoist insurgency. Telephone lines were cut and several high-profile political leaders were detained. Other opposition leaders fled to India and regrouped there.

A broad alliance against the royal takeover called the Seven Party Alliance (SPA) was organized, encompassing about 90% of the seats in the old, dissolved parliament. In December SPA signed a 12-point understanding with the Maoists. Within the framework of that understanding, Maoists committed themselves to multiparty democracy and freedom of speech. SPA, for their part, accepted the Maoist demand for elections to a Constituent Assembly.

At the beginning of 2006, the situation became yet more tense as SPA launched agitation programmes around the country. A series of waves of arrests of opposition leaders were conducted. The agitations reached a peak around the February 8 municipal elections, which were boycotted by the SPA and the Maoists. In total, official figures claimed a participation of about 21%. Opposition sources questioned those claims.

APRIL GENERAL STRIKE

SPA called for a 4-day nationwide general strike between April 5–9. The Maoists called for a cease-fire in the Kathmandu valley. The general strike saw numerous protests. A curfew was announced by the government on April 8, with reported orders to shoot protestors on sight. Despite this, small, disorganized protests continued.

On April 9, SPA announced that it intended to continue its protests indefinitely and called for a tax boycott. The government announced plans to step up its enforcement of the curfew and claimed that the Maoists had infiltrated the protests. Prachanda, the leader of the CPN(M), had said that "this is no longer a protest by opposition parties ... it has become a people's movement," and warned that he himself could lead a revolt in the capital.

Protests continued in the following days, with crowds increasing to sizes estimated at 100,000 to 200,000 in Kathmandu in various estimates, more than 10% of the city population. On April 21, opposition sources claim that about half a million took part in the protests in Kathmandu. More conservative estimates talk about 300,000. It is worth noting that a number of the protesters came from outside Kathmandu Valley.

Later the same evening, King Gyanendra announced that he would return political power to the people and called for elections to be held as soon as possible. He called on SPA to nominate a new Prime Minister of Nepal in a speech on a state-owned television station, saying, "We return the executive power of the country to the people. We request the seven-party alliance to recommend a name for the post of prime minister who will have the responsibility to run the government."

The position of Prime Minister has been vacant since 1 February 2005 when King Gyanendra removed Sher Bahadur Deuba from office and dissolved the Nepalese Parliament indefinitely. However, the royal proclamation was rebuffed by the opposition. At 3 p.m. the next day, the leaders of SPA met in the capital, and staked out three demands, namely: reinstitution of the old parliament; formation of an all-party government; and elections to a Constituent Assembly that will draft a new constitution.

REINSTITUTION OF PARLIAMENT

In a nationally televised address, King Gyanendra reinstated the old Nepal House of Representatives on April 24, 2006.

The King called upon the Seven Party Alliance to bear the responsibility of taking the nation on the path to national unity and prosperity, while ensuring permanent peace and safeguarding multiparty democracy. The reinstitution of Parliament was accepted by the SPA. It declared that Girija Prasad Koirala would lead the new government.

The SPA stated that the new parliament will hold elections for a body that would write a new constitution. The move was rejected by the maoists. Baburam Bhattarai stated that merely restoring the parliament was not going to resolve the problems and that the rebels planned to continue fighting against government forces. They still demand the formation of a Constituent Assembly and abolition of the monarchy.

On April 27, however, the Maoist insurgents responded to demands by Girija Prasad Koirala and announced a unilateral three-month truce in the Nepal Civil War. In addition to this, on May 1, Bhattarai announced that if "the elections [to a Constituent Assembly] are free and fair, one has to respect the result of the elections. Then of course we will abide by the verdict of the people." This was seen as a large step forward as it shows the first signs of Maoist acceptance of the democratic process.

On May 2, Koirala announced the new government cabinet including himself and three other ministers from the Nepali Congress: K.P. Sharma Oli from CPN (UML), Gopal Man Shrestha from Nepali Congress (Democratic) and Prabhu Narayan Chaudhari from the United Left Front. This was followed on May 12 by the arrest of four ministers from the ousted royalist government and an investigation into alleged human rights violations by the army during the General Strike.

MAY 18 ACT

The most dramatic move of the post-Loktantra Andolan government came on May 18, 2006 when the Parliament unanimously voted to strip the King of many of his powers. The bill included:

- Putting 90,000 troops in the hands of the parliament
- Placing a tax on the royal family and its assets

- Ending the Raj Parishad, a royal advisory council
- Eliminating royal references from army and government titles
- Declaring Nepal a secular country, not a Hindu Kingdom
- Scrapping the national anthem until a new one is made
- Scrapping the king's position as the Supreme Commander of the Army

The act overrides the 1990 Constitution, written up following the Jana Andolan and has been described as a Nepalese Magna Carta. According to Prime Minister Koirala, "This proclamation represents the feelings of all the people."

May 18 has already been named *Loktantrik Day* (Democracy Day) by some. Although the constitution was accepted, it was always intended to be temporary and on May 29, 2008 a new constitution was voted on by the Nepalese Parliament, which declared that the monarchy would be deposed and a new parliamentary republic would become the Nepalese political framework.

The last time Prachanda was Prime Minister, his government fell because he refused to understand how coalition governments work. He exhibited dictatorial tendencies. In the aftermath he has blamed everyone except himself. Ram Baran Yadav did what he was elected to do: protect the constitution.

Prachanda needed the support of all his coalition partners before he could have sacked the army chief. Even after he had accumulated that support, he needed to go through the president. He did not think it necessary to seek support from his coalition partners, and he totally bypassed the president. Those were two grave mistakes, they were two illegal actions. And that is why his government fell.

It was okay for Prachanda to have led a majority government. But according to Prachanda it was not okay for Madhav Nepal to have led a majority government. Prachanda leading a majority government was a patriotic, nationalist government. But Madhav Nepal leading a majority government was a puppet government run by India. That has been Prachanda's logic.

Someone who does not understand how coalition governments work can not lead a majority, coalition government, let alone a national consensus government. Prachanda's idea of a national consensus government is one where all parties in parliament follow the dictates of the Maoist central committee. He has not learned his lessons. He has not exhibited democratic tendencies.

And that is before the lingering issues of army integration. The idea that 19,000 Maoist soldiers with 3,000 guns will take over a country of 30 million people has always been laughable. Issuing empty threats is generally considered bad politics. Even if the Maoists are okay with Baburam Bhattarai leading a possible national consensus government, there are no guarantees a national consensus government can be formed.

But a willingness on Prachanda's part to be open to that possibility will at least send a signal that the Maoists are now better understanding how coalition governments work. A national consensus government will necessarily have a steering committee representing all participating parties that will take all the key decisions that the government has to take. The parties have been going on the army integration issue exactly the wrong way.

A Nepal Army Bill 2010 has to be worked on by the full parliament, not the party presidents. Bypassing the parliament has been the reason the army integration issue has gone nowhere. The bill has to go through a full debate. That bill would decide the future size and composition and modality of the future Nepal Army.

7

Nepal China Relations and its Effects

The keystone of Nepal's China policy was maintaining equal friendships with China and India while simultaneously seeking to decrease India's influence in Nepal and Nepal's dependence on India. Further, Kathmandu felt that the competition between its two giant neighbors—China and India—would benefit its own economic development. The first recorded official relations with China and Tibet occurred near the middle of the seventh century.

By the eighteenth century, Nepalese adventurism in Tibet led to Chinese intervention in favor of Tibet. The resultant Sino-Nepalese Treaty of 1792 provided for tribute-bearing missions from Nepal to China every five years as a symbol of Chinese political and cultural supremacy in the region. In the Anglo-Nepalese War of 1814-16, China refused Nepal's requests for military assistance and, by default, surrendered its dominant position in Nepal to the growing British influence.

However, it appeared to be expedient for Nepal to retain the fiction of a tributary relationship with China in order to balance China against Britain. Nepal invaded Tibet in 1854. Hostilities were quickly terminated when China intervened, and the Treaty of Thapathali was concluded in March 1856. The treaty recognized the special status of China, and Nepal agreed to assist Tibet in the event of foreign aggression.

Relations between Nepal and China and Tibet continued without critical incident until 1904, when British India sent an armed expedition to Tibet and Nepal rejected Tibet's request for aid to avoid risking its good relations with Britain. Beginning in 1908, Nepal stopped paying tribute to China. By 1910, apprehensive of British activity in Tibet, China had reasserted its claim to sovereign rights in Tibet and feudatory missions from Nepal.

In 1912 Nepal warned the Chinese representative at Lhasa that Nepal would help Tibet attain independent status as long as it was consistent with British interests. Nepal broke relations with China when the Tibetans, taking advantage of the Chinese revolution of 1911, drove the Chinese out. When the Chinese communists invaded Tibet in 1950, Nepal's relations with China began to undergo drastic changes.

Although annual Tibetan tribute missions appeared regularly in Nepal as late as 1953, Beijing had started to ignore the provisions of the 1856 treaty by curtailing the privileges and rights it accorded to Nepalese traders, by imposing restrictions on Nepalese pilgrims, and by stopping the Tibetan tributary missions. The break between Kathmandu and Beijing continued until 1955, when relations were reestablished with China. The two countries established resident ambassadors in their respective capitals in July 1960.

In 1956 the Treaty of Thapathali was replaced by a new treaty under which Nepal recognized China's sovereignty over Tibet and agreed to surrender all privileges and rights granted by the old treaty. In 1962 Nepal withdrew its ambassador from Tibet and substituted a consul general. An agreement on locating and demarcating the Nepal-Tibet boundary was signed in March 1960. Within a month, another Treaty of Peace and Friendship was signed in Kathmandu.

The Sino-Nepal Boundary Treaty was signed in Beijing in October 1961. The treaty provided for a Sino-Nepal Joint

Commission to agree on questions regarding alignment, location, and maintenance of the seventy-nine demarcation markers. The commission's findings were attached to the original treaty in a protocol signed in January 1963. During the Sino-Indian conflict of 1962, Nepal reasserted its neutrality and warned that it would not submit to aggression from any state.

Although the warning was directed at China, Nepal continued to support China's application for membership in the United Nations. A potential source of irritation in Sino-Nepalese relations was relieved in January 1964 when China agreed to release the frozen funds of Nepalese traders from Tibetan banks.

An agreement to construct an all-weather highway linking Kathmandu with Tibet was signed in October 1961—a time when neither Kathmandu nor Beijing had cordial relations with New Delhi.

The Kathmandu-Kodari road opened in May 1967 but did not yield any commercial or trade benefits for Nepal. Because of the severe restrictions imposed by Beijing even before the road was opened, Kathmandu had closed its trade agencies in Tibet by January 1966.

Although the highway had no economic or commercial value and was not viable as an alternate transit route, it was of strategic military importance to China. The highway established direct links between two major Chinese army bases within 100 kilometers of Kathmandu to forward bases at Gyirong in Tibet. Throughout the latter half of the 1960s, Nepal's relations with China remained fairly steady.

One exception was the belligerent activities of the Chinese officials in Nepal who eulogized and extolled the successes of the Cultural Revolution (1966-76) during the summer of 1967. The emergence of a strident and confident India in the early 1970s introduced some new dimensions in Nepal's China policy. King Birendra did not abandon the policy of equal friendship between China and India but wanted to woo China to counter India's growing influence in the region.

China had implicitly recognized India's predominance in the region, however, and was willing to oblige Nepal only to the extent of pledging support in safeguarding its national independence and preventing foreign interference. In an open challenge to India's primacy in Nepal, Nepal negotiated a deal for the purchase of Chinese weapons in mid-1988. According to India, this deal contravened an earlier agreement that obliged Nepal to secure all defense supplies from India.

Nepal's overtures to China also had economic implications. Ever since an economic aid agreement between China and Nepal had been concluded in 1956, China's steadily increasing economic and technical assistance was being used to build up Nepal's industrial infrastructure and implement economic planning.

According to a 1990 report, an estimated 750 Chinese workers were in Nepal, most of them working on road-building crews and small-scale development projects. The foreign trade balance also was in Nepal's favor. China reportedly has ceded some territory to Nepal to facilitate boundary demarcation and has endorsed Nepal as a zone of peace.

The bilateral relations between the Federal Democratic Republic of Nepal and the People's Republic of China have been friendly and defined by Nepal's policy of balancing the competing influence of China and Nepal's southern neighbour India, the only two neighbors of the Himalayan state Nepal, Tibet and China.

Nepal's historical relations with China (and Tibet) have been shaped by conflicts over territory and the control of Tibet. In 1792, Nepal was forced to sign a treaty stipulating the payment of tribute to China after the latter defeated Nepalese forces in Tibet. China refused Nepal's request for assistance during Anglo-Nepalese War (1814-16), and the latter's defeat led to the establishment of the British Empire as the dominant power in the region.

Having retained its independence, Nepal continued to try to balance the influence of China and British India. Nepal invaded Tibet in 1854, but hostilities ended soon after China intervened,; the Treaty of Thapathali, concluded in March 1856, recognised the special status of China and Nepal's commitment to help Tibet in the event of foreign aggression. In the 19th century, Nepal aligned itself with the British Raj in India and supported its invasion of Tibet in 1908.

When China sought to claim Tibet in 1910, Nepal sided with Tibet and Britain and broke relations with China after Tibet drove Chinese forces out in 1911. Maoist leader Prachanda, who has recently been engaged in a bitter attack on India, has said he wants a "new level of understanding" to be developed with the "big neighbour" with which Nepal enjoys "distinct" ties, unlike China.

The chairman of Unified Communist Party of Nepal (Maoist) emphasised that India and China cannot have an equal role in the affairs of Nepal as India's ties with Nepal have a "specific" character "dictated" by aspects like open border andhistorical, geographical and cultural linkages. "We are never ignoring our distinct historical, geographical and cultural relationship with India.

We cannot ignore it. Only we can develop a new level of understanding to strengthen our relations," the 56-year-old former prime minister told in an interview on Sunday, January 24, 2010. He said the new understanding with India needed to be developed on the basis of "changed scenario" in Nepal and after addressing all outstanding issues, like revision of the 1950 Friendship Treaty and resolving Kalapani and Susta border disputes.

Insisting that the impression about his being anti-India is wrong, Prachanda said, "The fact is that we want to develop a new basis and new level of understanding (with India) to strengthen the relationship and to have economic development in this country."

Prachanda, who led a decade-long armed struggle against the monarchy before joining the mainstream in 2005, regretted that his demands for revising the Friendship Treaty and solving other issues were being misconstrued as an attempt to create some difficulties."We are not against good relations with India," he said.

"But to have good relations, we should focus on some issues of history, we should have to address old treaties, the (1950 Friendship) Treaty of (former King) Rana regime, solve border issues Susta and Kalapani," he said, adding he wanted these issues, as also the trade imbalance, to be addressed once and for all. Prachanda, whose original name is Pushpa Kamal Dahal, has recently been engaged in a vitriolic attack on India, alleging that it has been interfering in Nepal's affairs and "dictating" to its leadership. This prompted a sharp reaction from New Delhi.

"If we are able to convey our concerns to Indian leadership, it will be very easy to develop newer basis, to have a good relations with India," he contended.

Prachanda, who is seen as pro-China, observed that both India and China have fast growing economies and "We want to benefit from our big neighbours."

Asked whether India and China had the equal role in Nepal, Prachanda said, "There is no comparison... We cannot compare. There is no confusion in our mind."

Maintaining that he favoured "good neighbourly relations with these big neighbours", he said, "obviously there is a major role for India because of open border, history, culture, geography. All these things dictate the policy.""We have distinct relations with India, specific feature of relationship with India, dictated by history, geography, culture," Prachanda said.

To reinforce the special character of Indo-Nepal relations, he noted that his two daughters are married in India, making it a "roti, beti ka samband (a relationship of bread and daughter)."

When pointed out that he is seen to have pro-China tilt, the Maoist leader said, "This is baseless. People have some sort of prejudice and some sorts of illusion."

"We want to build good neighbourly relations with both the countries. But there is no comparison. India is

India, China is China. We don't want to be pro-China or pro-India. We will be pro-Nepalese."

Asked what then explains his six visits to China over the last two years, he sought to underline that he had travelled to India and stayed there much more regularly, even dating back to his underground days in 1990s.

"I visited India hundreds and hundreds of time, even during war. Even after becoming PM, I visited India three times," he said. He said he wanted Nepal to benefit from India's economic growth which would be good for India itself. "If Nepal remains poor and unstable, it will have impact mainly on India. It will have impact also on China but because of historical, geographical and cultural and economic relations, there will be serious impact between Nepal and India," he said.

DIPLOMATIC RELATIONS AND NEPALESE NEUTRALITY

The 1950–1951 Invasion of Tibet by the People's Liberation Army raised significant concerns of security and territorial integrity in Nepal and India, drawing both nations into a close relationship with extensive economic and military ties. China ordered restrictions on the entry of Nepalese pilgrims and contacts with Tibet, and increased its support for the Communist Party of Nepal, which was opposed to the Nepalese monarchy.

The 1950 Indo-Nepal Treaty of Peace and Friendship that had established a close Indo-Nepalese relationship on commerce, defence and foreign relations, was increasingly resented in Nepal, which began seeing it as an encroachment of its sovereignty and an unwelcome extension of Indian influence; the deployment of an Indian military mission in Nepal in the 1950s increased these concerns.

In 1955, Nepal established diplomatic relations with the People's Republic of China and exchanged resident ambassadors by 1960. In 1956, both nations signed a new treaty terminating the Treaty of Thapathali of 1856 and Nepal recognised Tibet as a part of China.

In 1960, Nepal and China signed a boundary settlement agreement and a separate treaty of peace and friendship. Nepal also began supporting the change of China's seat in the United Nations. In 1961, Nepal and China agreed to build an all-weather road connecting the Nepalese capital Kathmandu with Tibet. During the Sino-Indian War of 1962, Nepal maintained neutrality.

ECONOMIC AND STRATEGIC RELATIONS

In the 1970s King Birendra of Nepal proposed Nepal as a "zone of peace" between India and China and in the 1980s, Nepal began importing Chinese weaponry in contravention of its 1950 treaty with India and has since sought to establish extensive military cooperation in a move to reduce perceived Indian influence.

When the United States, United Kingdom and India refused to supply arms to the regime of King Gyanendra of Nepal, who had assumed direct rule to suppress the Maoist insurgency during the Nepalese civil war (1996 - 2006), China responded by dispatching arms to Nepal, in spite of the ideological affinity of the Maoists with China.

After the peace process and national elections in Nepal in 2008, the new Maoist-led government announced its intentions to scrap Nepal's 1950 treaty with India, indicating a stronger move towards closer ties with China. In 2007-08, China began construction of a 770-kilometre railway connecting the Tibetan capital of Lhasa with the Nepalese border town of Khasa, connecting Nepal to China's wider national railway network.

NEPAL-CHINA-INDIA

There are five landlocked states (LLS) in Asia: Mongolia, Afghanistan, Bhutan, Laos and Nepal. Nepal has two neighbors, China and India. A triangle can be sketched to promote friendship in-between our neighbours. We all Nepalese have entered into a new era, thrashing feudalism; adjacent to our victory is the great opportunity to review our foreign affairs with both the countries from new phase. Being focused on our own national interests, we should build common outlook.

On the Basis of Infrastructure: It is certain that low income and lack of infrastructure are the major added handicaps of the LLS.

But, our country is endowed of natural resources. Protecting and utilizing these sources, we can give a face-lift to our motherland. We can overcome the lack of infrastructure. If we utilize our infrastructures in a right approach, then our business services will be of advanced quality and it will not be costlier. Our LLS can thus face the inflation phase.

Our south neighboring country has again woken up in search of raw materials from other countries. Perhaps, it might be to execute Version 2.0 of Booming India. "India's economy is jogging along, despite the media hype about a slowdown.

But India Inc. needs crucial raw materials that are available only in other countries. Rather belatedly, the Government of India is waking up to the economic potential of diplomacy."

While our cooperative friend in the north; has advanced its infrastructures. "China is emerging as a major financer of infrastructure projects in Africa.....".

With this regard, Nepal can play as a transit route for India and China, enormously. Most often think-tank and Asian Track Diplomats have their own prophecy. According to their notion, another Suez Canal and Panama Canal is possible via Koshi River Route in an enormous effort of Nepalese people and peoples Government.

The economic-architects of our glorious party need to sketch an equilateral triangle that formulates equidistant policy and utilize both the friendly countries to advance our infrastructure.

UNCERTAINTY WITH THE PRO-INDIAN AND SOUTH

The truth is on the surface. Persons do not reveal themselves to be pro-Indian but in core, they act in such a way, people ultimately define them as their puppets. In a program run by

BBC World Service Trust, Minister of Foreign Affairs initially declared PM's India Visit will just to make a good-will. No revision over the issue of unequal treaties will execute, as per his address via saajha sawal. Pro-Indian, are purposefully sympathetic with the south-block and seek for good-will.

Instead, we hope peoples' Prime Minister precisely broach over the particularly criticized issue. The Indian ruling class has its own haughtiness. South block is always worried with the penetration of Himalayan Frontiers as prescribed by the architect of foreign policy. Our Nepalese leaders have no essential to bow down before Indian rulers. Beloved Government of Nepalese people need to review the foreign policy and new treaties will be made based on equality.

Moreover, Chairman Comrade has already made amply clear in his recent address to nation as First Prime Minister of FDR Nepal. He committed his Government to conduct the traditional foreign policy based on Panchasheel- the five principle of co-existence. India being a transit state for Nepal, sometime, it uses its strategic position as an economic or political lever against LLS. We had also passed through such incident once with India. It was India's irrational role to lure Nepalese leaders to adopt special bilateral relationship with them.

We can take the illustration of South African Countries, Uganda and Kenya. Uganda had also faced such relation with Kenya, the transit point. When Uganda's Minister of Labor announced a policy of replacing unskilled Kenya-workers' with Uganda nationals in 1970, the Government of Kenya threatened to refuse handling Uganda's goods at the important port of Mombasa.

But there are still a lot of queries in an Indian's role. Do they really like to see developed Nepal? Will they stop their double platform policy? Will they act as a good transit-neighbor state? Do they accept Nepal as an independent, sovereign country with its own identity from their inner core of their heart?

DIPLOMATIC ROLE OF NEPAL FOR PEACE, PROGRESS AND PROSPERITY

Nepalese ruler P.N Shah and popular Essayist and Poet L P Devkota comparison is still incomplete as per the demand of time in the context of 21st Centaury. Other if tends to violate peace and seize Peoples' Rights will certainly adopt the definition of Comrade Badal. Nepal and Nepalese people can also play crucial role as an intermediary in-between China and India.

In other word, Nepal can act as a Cultural Diplomat. Only then, equidistant policy could come into practice. A tripartite association of Nepal, China and India could be formed to discuss over the regional peace, progress and prosperity. According to Nepalese Government Policies and Programs, survey will be carried out to construct Lhasa-Kathmandu-Pokhara-Chitwan Route and Raxaul-Amlekhgunj petro-pipeline project was to be completed.

This type of balanced co-operation between Nepal - India and Nepal - China will certainly promote equidistant policy. Moreover, to introduce Nepal as a Universal Zone of Peace, Progress and Prosperity and to Buddha (a traditional socialist) as a Light of Universe are genuinely important matters. South Block needs not to be worry with the penetration of Himalayan frontiers. Hence, there is a possibility of mutual friendship. Previously, demolishing "big-brother" arrogance with the south is the prior. Promotion of continuing mutual friendship with Peking is not a great deal. Finally, tripartite friendship exists.

8

Maoist Problems and its Impact on India: Nepal Relations

India's External Affairs Minister SM Krishna undertook a three-day official visit to Kathmandu from January 15, 2010. According to the Indian Embassy in Kathmandu, at least five memorandums of understanding signed during Krishna's visit. The MoUs include construction of a National Police Academy at Panauti in Kavre district, Indian assistance for the Nepal Stock Exchange, construction of roads in the Terai, establishment of a science learning centre and a solar electrification project. Krishna will also take up issues related to Indian security and counterfeit currency issues.

Though the visit is timely and significant, uncertainties over the future of the peace process continue due to differences between the political parties on contentious issues like federalism, rehabilitation of Maoist combatants, and the nature of Constitution. The UCPN-Maoist leader Prachanda has accused the ruling parties of being puppets of the Indian ruling class, accused the Indian establishment of intervening in Nepal's internal affairs and trying to derail the peace process.

He also said that the UCPN-Maoist should hold direct talks with New Delhi since the ruling parties are guided by remote control and talks with them to establish civilian supremacy have been failing. The Maoists have made elaborate arrangements to express displeasure during Krishna's visit. Recently, they declared the fourth phase of their nationwide agitation demanding restoration of civilian supremacy and formation of a Maoist-led national government.

As part of the fourth round of protest programmes, senior party leaders will visit those locations along the open border with India where India has reportedly occupied Nepal's territories. The Maoists will organise mass rallies at several bordering regions 'encroached' by India and torch the copies of the various treaties with India. They will hold demonstrations outside the Indian Embassy and Singha Durbar on January 19.

Krishna's visit is taking place at a time when the Maoist sponsored anti-India feeling is at an all time high in Nepal. Maoists have been consistently branding the 1950 treaty as unequal, raising issues such as illegal encroachment and the recruitment of Nepalse Gurkhas into the Indian Army. But none of these demands are genuine and valid. The Maoists, in fact, do not want to resolve these issues since these give them huge political dividends to retain public support.

Pushpa Kamal Dahal alias Prachanda, during his nine month tenure as prime minister, did not take any steps to withdraw from the 1950 treaty though clause 10 of the agreement cleanly mentions that the "Treaty shall remain in force until it is terminated by either party by giving one year's notice." The issue figured prominently during his visit to New Delhi in September 2008.

On this occasion, Prachanda had agreed with India's Prime Minister to "review, adjust and update" the 1950 Treaty of Peace and Friendship and other agreements, while giving due recognition to the special features of the bilateral relationship. Why did Prachanda not use clause 10 of the treaty and agreed to review the same during his visit? Regarding the Gurkha recruitment issue, Pracahnda preferred to remain tightlipped during his visit to India.

On the eve of the visit, Deepak Bahadur Gurung, chairman of the Nepal Ex-Servicemen's Association, warned that his organisation would start a new 'People's War' if the Maoist government stopped the recruitment. Most importantly, Maoists' argument about Gurkaha recruitment being colonial is illogical because Gurkha Nepalese have been joining the Indian Army purely on a voluntary basis. This is not forced recruitment or conscription by the Indian Army.

Given the geographical dynamics in the border region, "encroachment" is more a natural phenomenon than man-made. Rivers flowing from Nepal to India frequently shift their course during the monsoons. As a result, certain portions of the border region either come to Nepal or to India depending on the shifting of the river course. Since farmers from both countries find that part of the land fertile, they encroach upon it for agricultural purposes.

In fact, Prachanda during his last visit to India acknowledged the problem of inundation in the border areas and agreed to take up necessary work for its effective prevention on the basis of bilateral consultation. Both countries have already (unofficially) agreed that 98 per cent of the border is demarcated except two disputed areas in Kalapani and Susta. India's former external affairs minister Pranab Mukhrjee during his official visit to Kathmandu in November 2008 talked about it before the media.

Interestingly, then the Maoist-led government in Kathmandu did not contradict his view on border demarcation. The issue rose to prominence again only after Prachanda's resignation. The Maoists have accused encroachment of Nepalese territory by Indian security forces in the Dang district. The problem is not only with the Maoists. India has consistently given space to the Maoists to take advantage of the faultlines in India-Nepal relations.

Till date, India has hardly clarified its stand on these controversial bilateral issues in a public forum. All discussions have taken place only at the official level, which have been tampered with and then highlighted by the pro-Maoist or Royalist Nepalese media. One such faultline is the absence of high-level political engagements from the Indian side while Nepal is passing through political turbulence. In the last 13 years, seven Prime Ministers of Nepal have visited India in return for one Prime Ministerial visit from India to Nepal.

Prime Minister I. K. Gujaral visited Kathmandu in June 1997. The political imbalance in the relationship has been gradually eroding India's traditional leverages in Nepal. If the vacuum continues, other countries including China may consolidate in near future.

Another major faultline is unnecessary statements from various agencies of India about internal developments in Nepal. Third, India has a very good relationship with many leaders of Nepal cutting across party lines. But it is yet to introduce a comprehensive policy towards Nepal.

India's options in Nepal:

1. Stability in Nepal is extremely important for India. It has to acknowledge that the present political stalemate is an internal matter of Nepal and encourage the stakeholders to hammer out their differences. India should strike a neutral stance and play the role of an honest negotiator to bring the various factions together.
2. Existing controversial treaties, border disputes, encroachment issues and the Indian Embassy's alleged support to certain groups in the Terai region and personal level support to Nepali Congress leaders are major irritants in India-Nepal relations. These issues have been generating huge anti-India feelings and thus need immediate attention. This will help prevent the growing Chinese role in Nepal. India needs to come out with a clear policy on these issues and express positive views to resolve them.
3. India should focus more on socio-economic and development programmes. India's assistance to Nepal

should be enhanced and directed towards projects which benefit the Nepalese people directly.

4. Hydro-projects and dams situated on the Indo-Nepal border should be maintained and managed by the Union Government under the Ministry of External affairs.
5. Border crossing should be mechanized. People crossing the border should be treated with dignity.
6. India should realize that the monarchy is gone for ever although the pro-monarchy sentiment remains. India needs to acknowledge the emergence of new forces in Nepal and learn to deal with them.
7. India should enhance and upgrade co-operation with Nepalese agencies to patrol and manage the border.

Anti-India feeling is a permanent phenomenon in India's neighbourhood including in Nepal. India should not deterred by these activities. This visit is a golden opportunity for India to reactivate its relationship and reassure both the ruling and opposition parties about India's positive contribution to the peace process. During the visit, India should come out with some official statements that India is interested more in people to people relations and the prosperity of Nepal.

If possible, India should seriously engage and talk to the Maoists. They may have their own ideology which may not be comfortable to India. But there is no harm in talking to them and learn about their concerns. Similarly, India should make its concerns in Nepal clear to the Maoists. It should clarify through actions and declare that India has no intention to interfere in Nepal, that it respects Nepal's sovereignty and that it is ready to work with any dispensation in Nepal for furthering mutual security and economic concerns.

Even after India had achieved independence from Britain in 1947, Nepalese-Indian relations continued to be based on the second Treaty of Sagauli, which had been signed with the government of British India in 1925. Beginning in 1950, however, relations were based on two treaties. Under the

Treaty of Peace and Friendship, ratified in July 1950, each government agreed to acknowledge and respect the other's sovereignty, territorial integrity, and independence; to continue diplomatic relations; and, on matters pertaining to industrial and economic development, to grant rights equal to those of its own citizens to the nationals of the other residing in its territory.

Agreements on all subjects in this treaty superseded those on similar matters dealt with in the previous treaties between Nepal and Britain. In the Treaty of Trade and Commerce, ratified in October 1950, India recognized Nepal's right to import and export commodities through Indian Territory and ports. Customs could not be levied on commodities in transit through India.

India's influence over Nepal increased throughout the 1950s. The Citizenship Act of 1952 allowed Indians to immigrate to Nepal and acquire Nepalese citizenship with ease—a source of some resentment in Nepal. And, Nepalese were allowed to migrate freely to India—a source of resentment there. (This policy was not changed until 1962 when several restrictive clauses were added to the Nepalese constitution.)

Also in 1952, an Indian military mission was established in Nepal. In 1954 a memorandum provided for the joint coordination of foreign policy, and Indian security posts were established in Nepal's northern frontier. At the same time, Nepal's dissatisfaction with India's growing influence began to emerge, and overtures to China were initiated as a counterweight to India.

King Mahendra continued to pursue a nonaligned policy begun during the reign of Prithvi Narayan Shah in the mid-eighteenth century. In the late 1950s and 1960s, Nepal voted differently from India in the UN unless India's basic interests were involved. The two countries consistently remained at odds over the rights of landlocked states to transit facilities and access to the sea.

Following the 1962 Sino-Indian border war, the relationship between Kathmandu and New Delhi thawed significantly. India suspended its support to India-based Nepalese opposition forces. Nepal extracted several concessions, including transit rights with other countries through India and access to Indian markets. In exchange, through a secret accord concluded in 1965, similar to an arrangement that had been suspended in 1963, India won a monopoly on arms sales to Nepal.

In 1969 relations again became stressful as Nepal challenged the existing mutual security arrangement and asked that the Indian security checkposts and liaison group be withdrawn. Resentment also was expressed against the Treaty of Peace and Friendship of 1950. India grudgingly withdrew its military checkposts and liaison group, although the treaty was not abrogated.

Further changes in Nepalese-Indian relations occurred in the 1970s. India's credibility as a regional power was increased—and Nepal's vulnerability was reinforced—by the 1971 Indo-Soviet Treaty of Peace, Friendship, and Cooperation; the 1971 IndoPakistani War, which led to the emergence of an independent Bangladesh; the absorption of Sikkim into India in 1974; increased unofficial support of the Nepali Congress Party leadership in India; rebellions fomented by pro-Beijing Naxalite elements in 1973-74 in West Bengal State bordering Nepal; and India's nuclear explosion in 1974.

Nepal adopted a cautious policy of appeasement of India, and in his 1975 coronation address King Birendra called for the recognition of Nepal as a zone of peace where military competition would be off-limits. India showed some flexibility in placating Nepal by distancing, if not disassociating, itself from the Nepalese opposition forces based in India, agreeing to a favourable trade and transit arrangement in 1978, and entering into another agreement on joint industrial ventures between Indian and Nepalese firms.

The latter agreement, by opening the possibilities of India's investment, indirectly furthered India's domination of Nepal's economy. India also continued to maintain a high level of economic assistance to Nepal. In the mid-1970s, Nepal pressed for substantial amendments to the 1971 trade and transit treaty, which was due to expire in 1976. India ultimately backed down from its initial position to terminate the 1971 treaty even before a new treaty could be negotiated.

The 1978 agreements incorporated Nepal's demand for separate treaties for trade and transit. The relationship between the two nations improved over the next decade, but not steadily. India continued to support the Nepalese opposition and refused to endorse Nepal as a zone of peace. In 1987 India urged expulsion of Nepalese settlers from neighboring Indian states, and Nepal retaliated by introducing a work permit system for Indians working in Nepal.

That same year, the two countries signed an agreement setting up a joint commission to increase economic cooperation in trade and transit, industry, and water resources. Relations between the two countries sank to a low point in 1988 when Kathmandu signed an agreement with Beijing to purchase weapons soon after a report that China had won a contract for constructing a road in the western sector to connect China with Nepal.

India perceived these developments as deliberately jeopardizing its security. India also was annoyed with the high volume of unauthorized trade across the Nepalese border, the issuance of work permits to the estimated 150,000 Indians residing in Nepal, and the imposition of a 55 percent tariff on Indian goods entering Nepal. In retaliation for these developments, India put Nepal under a virtual trade siege.

In March 1989, upon the expiration of the 1978 treaties on trade and transit rights, India insisted on negotiating a single unified treaty in addition to an agreement on unauthorized trade, which Nepal saw as a flagrant attempt to strangle its economy. On March 23, 1989, India declared that both treaties had expired and closed all but two border entry points. The economic consequences of the trade and transit deadlock were enormous.

Shortages of Indian imports such as fuel, salt, cooking oil, food, and other essential commodities soon occurred. The lucrative tourist industry went into recession. Nepal also claimed that the blockade caused ecological havoc since people were compelled to use already dwindling forest resources for energy in lieu of gasoline and kerosene, which came mostly via India. To withstand the renewed Indian pressure, Nepal undertook a major diplomatic initiative to present its case on trade and transit matters to the world community.

The relationship with India was further strained in 1989 when Nepal decoupled its rupee from the Indian rupee which previously had circulated freely in Nepal. India retaliated by denying port facilities in Calcutta to Nepal, thereby preventing delivery of oil supplies from Singapore and other sources. A swift turn in relations followed the success of the Movement for the Restoration of Democracy in early 1990. In June 1990, a joint Kathmandu-New Delhi communiqué was issued pending the finalization of a comprehensive arrangement covering all aspects of bilateral relations, restoring trade relations, reopening transit routes for Nepal's imports, and formalizing respect of each other's security concerns.

Essentially, the communiqué announced the restoration of the status quo ante and the reopening of all border points, and Nepal agreed to various concessions regarding India's commercial privileges. Kathmandu also announced that lower cost was the decisive factor in its purchasing arms and personnel carriers from China and that Nepal was advising China to withhold delivery of the last shipment.

The communiqué declared that Kathmandu and New Delhi would cooperate in industrial development, in harnessing the waters of their common rivers for mutual benefit, and in protecting and managing the environment. There has been much fast and loose talk In Kathmandu these past weeks, as analysts try to come to terms with the Communist Party of Nepal (Maoist)'s victory in the constitutional-assembly election on 10 April 2008.

The Indian government might understandably be worried that it will be blamed - or, by Maoist sympathisers, credited - for the Maoist victory, as it has driven Nepal's peace process, operating through the leadership of Nepal's established political parties: the Nepali Congress and the Communist Party of Nepal (Unified Marxist-Leninist / UML).

India has always been influential in Nepal, but its involvement increased dramatically when it took a lead role in persuading the Maoists to enter peace talks with the Congress and the UML. This came after King Gyanendra's military coup in 2005. Until the coup, India had unfailingly backed the unpopular monarch - by granting him recognition as a legitimate head of state even as he usurped extra-constitutional powers; and offering aid to the Royal Nepal Army in support of its atrocity-ridden counterinsurgency against the Maoists.

New Delhi backed a "twin-pillar" system of constitutional monarchy and parliamentary democracy in Nepal. India was therefore deeply embarrassed when the king effected his military coup. (Just one day before, when the Indian envoy had asked the king point-blank about the possibility, the monarch had denied having any such design). This breach provoked New Delhi to sever ties with King Gyanendra, and to suspend military aid.

India, urged on by Nepalis as well as by the international community in Nepal, went on to host talks between the seven-party political alliance and the Maoists in New Delhi in November 2005, talks which eventually led to a Maoist ceasefire and the signing of a twelve-point agreement. This in turn paved the way for the joint democratic-Maoist "people's movement" of April 2006 to end the king's absolute rule; and for the subsequent launch of a complex, multi-layered peace process, of which the 10 April election to the constituent assembly was but one component.

This trend of events meant that India had recovered from the setback of the coup to restore its position in its pesky northern neighbour. Now, however, the sweeping Maoist victory has caught it off-guard. True, officials in New Delhi tried to appear sanguine as the Kathmandu election results trickled. Siddharth Varadarajan of India's The Hindu could even write of senior officials "(seeking) to dispel the impression that India was worried or shaken"by the Maoist triumph and saying"that the government not only accepted the electoral verdict in its northern neighbour but also welcomed it."

Pranab Mukherjee, India's foreign-affairs minister was quoted extensively as deeming the Maoist victory a positive development. Some Indian analysts did express concerns that the Maoists' ascendance in Nepal might strengthen India's own Maoists. But most went on to dismiss suggestions that anything even vaguely negative might come of the result in Kathmandu, and even to mock claims by Nepali analysts that the Maoists had benefited, in part, from fear and intimidation. In New Delhi, it seemed, everything was coming up roses.

PK Hormis Tharakan, a former head of India's intelligence agency, the Research and Analysis Wing (RAW), summed up the mood: "Obviously, the common man in Nepal has made all the difference. For those who know and care for Nepal, the shape of things emerging from these polls could not have been better. It would be an understatement to call it a historic event".

All this cheering was not a little disingenuous, for it was open knowledge that on the eve of the Nepali election, India had fully expected the Congress to emerge as the largest party, with the UML in second place. It anticipated being able to continue working through its proxy figure Girija Prasad Koirala - the Congress's elderly and infirm president - or his dynasty (most members of which were, in the event, defeated in the election).

Thus, India's truer reaction was captured by Bharat Bhushan of India's Mail Today: "The Maoist sweep in Nepal elections has taken the international community, including India, by a complete surprise. The shock is all the more in New Delhi because the Foreign Office mandarins had hoped that no single party would get a majority and the tried and tested Nepali Congress (NC) as the single largest entity would be the pivot of future developments in the country."

Bhushan went on: "In short, it would be back to the predictable old days of backroom manipulation, with those in charge in Kathmandu looking over their shoulder for Delhi's approval. Alas, such hopes have been dashed." A closer look at the Maoists' victory makes it clear that Indian policy has harmed the very force it sought to promote in Nepal - the Nepali Congress Party - and with it, Nepal's peace process.

POLICIES OVERT AND COVERT

This is a large claim, and to amplify it requires a quick review of India's policies throughout the peace process. India's overt policies have mainly focused on re-establishing democracy in Nepal by bringing the Maoists out of war and into the realm of politics: judicious and selfless, as befitting a country positioning itself to be a global as well as regional superpower.

India does have other interests in Nepal - especially hydropower and trade and transit treaties - but these are lesser issues: after all, it cannot force exploitative agreements on a small neighbour, nor can Nepal itself hold out on grounds of stubborn patriotism. There is, then, no real disagreement on India's overt policies in Nepal.

It is the covert policies that cause worry. They (as many Indian analysts will admit) often lack transparency and are not subject to scrutiny. It is also true that India is not a monolith, and its policies are not unitary. Both elements - secrecy and confusion - are a challenge to clear discussion. Indeed, most reporting of Indian involvement in Nepal (in Nepal as well as India) is characterised by quotes from well-placed if anonymous sources and vague, if knowing, allusions.

For many reasons, those "in the know" or regarded as such simply cannot, or will not, go on record about what precisely India is doing in Nepal. This shroud of secrecy allows the commentariat in both countries to indulge in gossip, speculation, and conspiracy theorising. Within the Indian government, the ministry of defence is extremely influential in shaping policy towards Nepal. The Indian military has a Gurkha contingent, and close professional ties to the Nepal army, which it has equipped and trained over the years.

This is relevant to an understanding of how Nepal's peace process has unfolded. The process had three proposed components:

- the now-complete constituent-assembly election
- the integration of the Maoists' People's Liberation Army into the Nepal army
- truth and reconciliation - including the prosecution of war crimes committed by both the Maoists and the military, in the war of 1996-2006 that took approximately 13,000 lives.

In principle, the components affecting military matters should have been completed before the election of 10 April 2008. (Indeed, in hindsight the Congress and the Unified Marxist-Leninists deeply regret having gone into the fray against a party that still had an army and a militia intact).

It was, naturally, their own decision to do so; but there is little doubt that they were listening to India in this matter. The problem is that India has been overconfident of its reach within Nepal. In India, ministry of defence and military lobbies have backed the open (and illegal) refusal of Nepal's chief of army staff, General Rukmangat Katwal (or Katuwal), to integrate the People's Liberation Army into the Nepal army.

The thinking in India has been that the Maoist military should eventually be converted into either a border-security force (as has been done in settling insurgencies in India's northeast) or into an industrial- security force. India has also vociferously denied to the United Nations Mission to Nepal (Unmin) the opportunity to do much more towards the process of army integration than housing the People's Liberation Army in cantonments, and storing its weapons (as well as a corresponding number of weapons of the Nepal army).

Indeed, India's basic response to Unmin has been: "not in my backyard". Unmin has again and again requested a larger mandate, but India has again and again blocked such a possibility. This has now resulted in Nepal having a ruling party with its own army of 20,000-plus, and a militia called the Youth Communist League.

When Nepali analysts point out that the Maoist victory in the constituent-assembly election was aided by fear, they do not necessarily mean that the Maoists directly bullied voters into voting Maoist; they mean that the Maoists' threat to return to war in case they lost in the polls was rendered extremely credible by their having an army.

The reasons why many Nepalis voted for the Maoists are varied, and desperation at the failure to fulfil the other conditions of the peace process must take its place alongside open-hearted endorsement. India's delaying of army integration, and refusal to allow Unmin a greater role, carries a great deal of responsibility here.

The matter of truth and reconciliation is as potent as that of demilitarisation and army integration. Nobody in Nepal - save for the victims' families, and a handful of human-rights activists - has been sincere about the prosecution of war crimes committed by the Maoists or the military. India itself has a surprisingly poor record on human rights - as witnessed in Kashmir, Gujarat, the northeast and its other conflict-zones.

It has never pushed truth and reconciliation in Nepal because it does not quite see the value of such a mission. Now, both the Maoists and the Nepal army are likely to compromise on the prosecution of the other's war crimes for the sake of attaining a "larger good", i.e., army integration. Victims' demands for legal redress are very likely to be ignored, and the moral standing of the new, integrated military force will remain compromised. Again, India's undervaluing of this component of the peace process bears a vital responsibility here.

POLITICS, ONLY POLITICS

In short, the peace process was already failing before the constituent-assembly election. This failure was caused, in great measure, by the prevailing feeling within the leaders of the Nepali political parties that the peace process was but an empty, mechanical ritual - one that allowed the Congress and the UML to regroup with India's help, while the rest of the international community served as donors.

The focus here has been exclusively on politics, only politics. Yet in this, too, India - like the Congress and the UML - badly miscalculated. What the Nepali people had expected, after the success of the April 2006 movement and the launch of the peace process, was new leadership. Instead, the discredited old leadership - the Koirala clan in the Congress, and the "politics of punditry" mafia in the UML - returned resurgent, with the backing of India.

Still, Nepalis were willing to give the establishment politicians a chance. But instead of reforming their parties and making way for fresh new ideas, all they did was to consolidate their hold. The April 2006 - April 2008 period saw dire nonsense-politics: monarchists floating the idea of crowning a "baby king" to save the monarchy; right-wingers in the parties suggesting that the Congress and UML ally with the Nepal army to effect an oxymoronic "democratic coup" against the Maoists.

India did more than tolerate this nonsense: it enabled it by patronising the parties' old leadership. Then India went on to defeat this leadership by supporting the political parties newly emerging in the Madhesi (or Terai/Tarai, the southeastern region of Nepal).

This is the site of India's most covert involvement in Nepal. Some analysts in New Delhi claim that India's intelligence branches were acting independently, rather than through the ministry of foreign affairs, in funding the establishment of the Terai Madhes Loktantrik Party (TMLP) and the Madhesi Janadikhar Forum (MJF, generally called the Forum). Others say that this was part of a foreign-ministry "master-plan". In either case, the Indian government's help towards the founding of these parties is widely acknowledged.

Bharat Bhushan points out in Mail Today: that: "New Delhi contributed to the rout of the centrist Nepali Congress by promoting a regional breakaway group consisting of Madhesis who are of Indian ethnic origin from the Terai region. The Terai National Democratic Party, which was created at India's insistence, managed to win a few seats but it cut into the traditional vote bank of the Nepali Congress contributing to an overwhelming Maoist victory in the region."

The establishment of the TMLP and the Forum is not, by itself, a negative thing. Like the three other civil-rights movements currently on their way in Nepal (the Janajati, Dalit, and women's-rights movements), the Madhesi-rights movement enjoys very wide grassroots appeal.

Its calls - for increased representation through proportional elections, for quotas and reservations, and for federalisation and regional autonomy - all resonate deeply with ordinary Nepalis, who experience Kathmandu as a faraway, and often near-colonial, presence.

What differentiates the Madhesi rights movement from the other three is the oppositional strategy it has chosen. Dalits and women remain vastly under-represented both before and after the constituent-assembly election. But the Janajatis (or ethnic nationalities) have gained considerable ground afterwards, as have the Madhesis. (Overall, the Janajatis remain under-represented, upper-caste Madhesis are now over-represented, while lower-caste Madhesis remain under-represented).

The crucial difference between these two groups is that while Janajati activists have sought space within the (extremely exclusivist) Congress and UML, the Madhesis have chosen to break away, and to form new parties (the TMLP and the Forum). It remains to be seen which strategy will prove more effective in furthering civil-rights agendas.

But this much is sure: the TMLP and Forum will have to reckon with India's involvement in their establishment, and in their future course - just as India will have to reckon with their fierce independence. For there is no guaranteeing that these parties will follow India's dictates in the coming weeks, months and years. These are revolutionary times in Nepal; and it is extremely difficult - for Nepal, let alone for India - to decipher the motivations of the Nepali people, and to anticipate their actions ahead.

INDIA'S FUTURE COURSE

Indeed, India's tendency to treat Nepal casually, as one of its far-flung states, one that it - above the rest of the international community - should have patronage rights over, is unhelpful. In the post-election climate, with the question of India-Nepal relations on the agenda (including the matter of renegotiation of the 1950 peace-and-friendship treaty between the two countries) it is also unsustainable. India now faces three urgent questions.

The first is: having helped to land Nepal's peace process in a ditch (by leaving army integration and truth and reconciliation until after the constituent-assembly election), will India now help to salvage it? Even if the answer is positive, who does India envision overseeing army integration? In the days immediately following the 10 April election, India was unequivocal that Unmin should leave now that the election had been held.

Yet it looks increasingly unlikely that a range of political forces - the victorious Maoists, the defeated (and wounded) Congress and UML, and the inexperienced new parties of the Madhesh - will, between them, amicably manage such a potentially explosive task, one with far-reaching implications for the future of peace in Nepal. India's own direct involvement in this will be completely unpalatable.

It may, as a result, find itself having to reverse its stance on Unmin, which has already laid the groundwork for the kind of meticulous, apolitical bureaucratising that might neutralise the many dangers that come with such an integration. India will also have to reconsider its undervaluing of truth and reconciliation in Nepal.

This - including the prosecution of war crimes - is essential to establish the legitimacy of any new military force that might ensue. In this, India may be best served by supporting the Office of the High Commissioner for Human Rights in its work in Nepal. The second urgent question facing India is: having (inadvertently) helped the Maoists to their electoral triumph, will India now help them transform into a democratic party?

So far, New Delhi has shown perfect willingness to engage with the Maoists. But what will happen if the Congress or the UML, or a faction of them (the defeated Congress leadership, say) refuses to cooperate? A lobby around Girija Prasad Koirala is already challenging Maoist chairman Prachanda's claim to high office. What will happen if forces ally, instead, with the king or the Nepal army (in the oxymoronic "democratic coup"). What will India do then?

The third urgent question facing India is: having already engaged in covert politics in Nepal, will India continue to engage in shadowy, behind-the-scenes meddling in the coming weeks, months and years? If India is the new United States, will Nepal be its new Central America? These are dark questions. For now, the mood in Kathmandu is a bit dark. Behind a façade of normalcy, the national elite is deeply anxious about the Maoists' victory.

The king - due to be deposed in less than a month - is desperate. The Nepal army's top brass remains defiant. The business community is jittery, and liberals feel endangered. A fightback may be in the offing, a fightback that may amount to nothing much - or may mire the country further in political gridlock, armed conflict, or even a dirty war. Is India prepared to avert these worst-case scenarios, or to help resolve them constructively if they do come to pass? There is still time to rectify past mistakes, and to avert future mistakes. That process might begin with greater transparency, accountability and open discussion.

9

Nepali Citizens as Part of Indian Armed Forces: Impact on Relations

The Tripartite Agreement between the United Kingdom, India and Nepal was a treaty signed in 1947 concerning the rights of Gurkhas in military service. From the first quarter of the 19th century, Gurkhas from Nepal had served under the British, first in the armies of the East India Company, and then the British Indian Army. The terms and conditions of service for the Gurkhas were solely a matter for the British Indian authorities, without reference to the British Government in London.

As a part of this arrangement, it was agreed that Gurkhas in British and Indian service should enjoy broadly the same conditions of service, to ensure that there was no unfair advantage to serving in one or other, thus maintaining economic stability and social harmony in the Gurkha recruiting areas. Thus, the governments of the United Kingdom, India and Nepal came to sign the Tripartite Agreement (TPA).

From the end of the Indian Rebellion of 1857 until the start of the First World War the Gurkha Regiments saw active service in Burma, Afghanistan, the North-East and the North-West Frontiers of India, Malta (the Russo-Turkish War, 1877–78), Cyprus, Malaya, China (the Boxer Rebellion of 1900) and Tibet (Younghusband's Expedition of 1905). Between 1901 and 1906, the Gurkha regiments were renumbered from the 1st to the 10th and redesignated as the Gurkha Rifles.

In this time, the Brigade of Gurkhas, as the regiments came to be collectively known, was expanded to twenty battalions within the ten regiments. During World War I (1914–18), more than 200,000 Gurkhas served in the British Army, suffering approximately 20,000 casualties, and receiving almost 2,000 gallantry awards. The number of Gurkha battalions was increased to thirty-three, and Gurkha units were placed at the disposal of the British high command by the Nepalese government for service on all fronts.

Many Nepalese volunteers served in noncombat roles, serving in units such as the Army Bearer Corps and the labour battalions, but there were also large numbers that served in combat in France, Turkey, Palestine, and Mesopotamia. They served on the battlefields of France in the Loos, Givenchy, Neuve Chapelle and Ypres; in Mesopotamia, Persia, Suez Canal and Palestine against Turkish advance, Gallipoli and Salonika.

One detachment served with Lawrence of Arabia, while during the Battle of Loos (June-December 1915) a battalion of the 8th Gurkhas fought to the last man, hurling themselves time after time against the weight of the German defences, and in the words of the Indian Corps commander, Lieutenant-General Sir James Willcocks, "... found its Valhalla".

During the ultimately unsuccessful Gallipoli campaign in 1915, the Gurkhas were among the first to arrive and the last to leave. The 1st/6th Gurkhas, having landed at Cape Helles, led the assault during the first major operation to take out a Turkish high point, and in doing so captured a feature that later became known as "Gurkha Bluff".

At Sari Bair they were the only troops in the whole campaign to reach and hold the crest line and look down on the Straits, which was the ultimate objective. The 2nd Battalion of the

3rd Gurkha Rifles (2nd/3rd Gurkha Rifles) was involved in the conquest of Baghdad.

Following the end of the war, the Gurkhas were returned to India and during the interwar years, they were largely kept away from the internal strife and urban conflicts of the subcontinent, instead being employed largely on the frontiers and in the hills where fiercely independent tribesmen were a constant source of troubles..

As such, between the World Wars, the Gurkha regiments fought in the Third Afghan War in 1919 and then participated in numerous campaigns on the North-West Frontier, mainly in Waziristan, where they were employed as garrison troops defending the frontier, keeping the peace amongst the local populace and keeping the lawless and often openly hostile Pathan tribesmen in check. During this time the North-West Frontier was the scene of considerable political and civil unrest and the troops stationed at Razmak, Bannu and Wanna saw an extensive amount of action.

During World War II (1939–45), there were ten Gurkha regiments, with two battalions each making a total of twenty pre-war battalions. Following the evacuation of the BEF from Dunkirk in 1940, the Nepalese government offered to increase recruitment to increase the total number of Gurkha battalions in British service to thirty-five.

This would eventually rise to forty-five battalions and in order to achieve this, third and fourth battalions were raised for all ten regiments, with fifth battalions also being raised for 1 GR, 2 GR and 9 GR. This expansion required ten training centres to be established for basic training and regimental records across India. In addition five training battalions were raised, while other units were raised as garrison battalions for keeping the peace in India and defending rear areas.

Large numbers of Gurkha men were also recruited for non-Gurkha units, and other specialised functions such as paratroops, signals, engineers, and military police. A total of 250,280 Gurkhas served during the war, in almost all theatres. In addition to keeping peace in India, Gurkhas fought in Syria,

North Africa, Italy, Greece and against the Japanese in the jungles of Burma, northeast India and also Singapore. They did so with considerable distinction, earning 2,734 bravery awards in the process and suffering around 32,000 casualties in all theatres.

GURKHA MILITARY RANK SYSTEM IN THE BRITISH INDIAN ARMY

Gurkha ranks in the British Indian Army followed the same pattern as those used throughout the rest of the Indian Army at that time. As in the British Army itself, there were three distinct levels: private soldiers, non-commissioned officers and commissioned officers.

Commissioned officers within the Gurkha regiments held a *Viceroy's Commission*, which was distinct from the King's or Queen's Commission that British officers serving with a Gurkha regiment held. Any Gurkha holding a commission was technically subordinate to any British officer, regardless of rank.

MAIN TERMS

The main points of the agreement are:

- The Gurkha soldier must be recruited as a Nepali citizen, must serve as a Nepali citizen, and must be resettled as a Nepali citizen.
- All religious and cultural observances must be preserved in accordance with the demands of the Hindu faith.
- Gurkha soldiers in both the Indian and British Armies should receive the same basic rates of pay, although allowances may be paid to reflect differences in the costs of living between countries where Gurkha soldiers might serve outside Nepal.
- Subject to satisfactory performance and conduct, all soldiers should be allowed to serve for sufficient time in order to qualify for a pension

- All Gurkha soldiers should be allowed an extended period of leave in Nepal every three years.
- Gurkha soldiers recruited into the respective armies are liable for service worldwide.
- Gurkhas are fully integrated into the Army to which they are recruited and under no circumstances are they to be considered mercenaries.

The agreement applies to the 3,500 Gurkhas serving in the British Army, and close to 40,000 Gurkhas in the Indian Army. It does not apply to Gurkhas in the Royal Nepal Army. The TPA underpins the unique terms and conditions of service of the Gurkha soldier which in a number of key areas differ markedly from those of his British or Commonwealth counterpart.

Such differences arise because of the need to maintain broad comparability with certain Indian Army conditions of service, to protect the Gurkha national, religious, cultural and domicile status and the need for Gurkhas to maintain close links with Nepal throughout their service. It is against this background that the UK Government has continued to maintain separate terms and conditions of service for Gurkhas.

NEW GURKHA CONDITIONS AND TERMS OF SERVICE

The maintenance of different terms and conditions for Gurkha soldiers as opposed to their British counterparts has been a source of friction in recent years, particularly in regard to pension provision.

While Gurkha pensions provide a high standard of living in Nepal, they were calculated at a fraction of the pensions provided to British soldiers. As a consequence, in January 2005, the British Government announced a review of Gurkha terms and conditions to attempt to rectify these inequalities.

In May 2007, a new set of proposals was adopted, with a number of points in different areas:

- Nationality and Status
  - Gurkhas should be recruited as Nepalese subjects, and should remain so throughout their service

- — Gurkhas should only be recruited to units of the Brigade of Gurkhas, and these should remain predominantly Gurkha manned
- Recruitment and Selection
  - — Recruitment should remain in Nepal
  - — Recruitment should become the responsibility of the Army Recruitment and Training Division
  - — Nepalese women should be recruited into the Brigade of Gurkhas
- Pay, Pensions and Allowances
  - — Gurkha pay should be brought into line with UK pay rates based on employment qualifications
  - — All Gurkhas recruited after a specific date will join the standard Armed Forces Pension Scheme. Those recruited before that date will be given the option of remaining in the Gurkha Pension Scheme or transferring to the AFPS

A major proposal is the drawing up of a bilateral memorandum of understanding between the governments of Britain and Nepal, and allowing the TPA to lie. It is unclear how this would affect the recruitment of Gurkhas in the Indian Army. Gurkhas have been part of the British Army for almost 200 years. The Gurkhas who have fought since the times of Queen Victoria till Queen Elizabeth II, there´s no noteworthy memorial in Britain. The Gurkhas are now based at Shorncliffe near Folkestone.

In a landmark ruling on 30 September 2008 the High Court in London decided that Gurkhas who left the Army before 1997 did have an automatic right of residency in the United Kingdom. In line with the ruling of the High Court the Home Office is to review all cases affected by this decision.

On the 29 April 2009 a motion in the British House of Commons by the Liberal Democrats that all Gurkhas be offered an equal right of residence resulted in a defeat for the Government by 267 votes to 246, the first, first day motion defeat for a government since 1978. Nick Clegg, the Liberal

Democrat leader, stated that "This is an immense victory for the rights of Gurkhas who have been waiting so long for justice, a victory for Parliament, a victory for decency." He added that it was "the kind of thing people want this country to do".

On 21 May 2009, the Home Secretary Jacqui Smith announced that all Gurkha veterans who retired before 1997 with at least four years service would be allowed to settle in the UK. The actress and daughter of Gurkha corps major James Lumley, Joanna Lumley, who had highlighted the treatment of the Gurkhas and campaigned for their rights, commented: "This is the welcome we have always longed to give".

The number of the Nepalese Gurkhas, serving in the British army has been sharply reduced from a World War II peak of 112,000 men, and now stands at about 3,500. During the two World Wars, 43,000 young men lost their lives. Gurkha, also spelled as Gorkha , are people from Nepal, who take their name from the eighth century Hindu warrior-saint Guru Gorakhnath and from the hill town of Gorkha from which the Nepal had expanded.

"Better to die than be a coward" is the motto of the world-famous Nepalese Gurkha soldiers who are an integral part of the British Army. They still carry into battle their traditional weapon - an 18-inch long curved knife known as the kukri. Gurkhas are best known for their history of bravery and strength in the Indian Army's Gorkha regiments and the British Army's Brigade of Gurkhas.

The Gurkhas were designated by British officials as a "Martial Race", which means thought to be naturally warlike and aggressive in battle, and to possess qualities of courage, loyalty, self sufficiency, physical strength, resilience, orderliness, the ability to work hard for long periods of time, fighting tenacity and military strategy.

Prince Harry lived with a Gurkha battalion during his 10 weeks in Afghanistan. Historian Tony Gould said Gurkhas have brought an excellent combination of qualities from a military point of view. He said: "They are tough, they are brave, they are durable, they are amenable to discipline.

Former Chief of staff of the Indian Army, Field Marshal Sam Manekshaw once famously said about Gurkhas: If a man says he is not afraid of dying, he is either lying or he is a Gurkha. Professor Sir Ralph Turner, MC, who served with the 3rd Queen Alexandra's Own Gurkha Rifles in the First World War, wrote of Gurkhas:

> "As I write these last words, my thoughts return to you who were my comrades, the stubborn and indomitable peasants of Nepal. Once more I hear the laughter with which you greeted every hardship. Once more I see you in your bivouacs or about your fires, on forced march or in the trenches, now shivering with wet and cold, now scorched by a pitiless and burning sun. Uncomplaining you endure hunger and thirst and wounds; and at the last your unwavering lines disappear into the smoke and wrath of battle. Bravest of the brave, most generous of the generous, never had country more faithful friends than you."

The Gurkha war cry is "Jai Mahakali, Ayo Gorkhali" which literally translates to "Glory be to the Goddess of War, here come the Gorkhas!" The word Gorkha is derived from the prakrit words "go rakkha" (Sanskrit gau-raksa, literally "cow-protector"). This was used by Guru Gorakhnath, the spiritual leader of the Gorkhas, the name given to his disciples.

During World War I (1914–18), more than 200,000 Gurkhas served in the British Army, suffering approximately 20,000 casualties, and receiving almost 2,000 gallantry awards. The number of Gurkha battalions was increased to thirty-three, and Gurkha units were placed at the disposal of the British high command by the Nepalese government for service on all fronts.

During World War II (1939–45), there were ten Gurkha regiments, with two battalions each making a total of twenty pre-war battalions. Following the evacuation of the BEF from Dunkirk in 1940, the Nepalese government offered to increase recruitment to increase the total number of Gurkha battalions in British service to thirty-five.

10

Trafficking of Nepali Women in India

At least hundreds of thousands, and probably more than a million women and children are employed in Indian brothels. Many are victims of the increasingly widespread practice of trafficking in persons across international borders. In India, a large percentage of the victims are women and girls from Nepal. This report focuses on the trafficking of girls and women from Nepal to brothels in Mumbai, where nongovernmental organizations say they comprise up to half of the city's estimated 100,000 brothel workers.

Twenty percent of Mumbai's brothel population is thought to be girls under the age of eighteen, and half of that population may be infected with the human immunodeficiency virus (HIV). Trafficking victims in India are subjected to conditions tantamount to slavery and to serious physical abuse. Held in debt bondage for years at a time, they are raped and subjected to other forms of torture, to severe beatings, exposure to AIDS, and arbitrary imprisonment.

Many are young women from remote hill villages and poor border communities of Nepal who are lured from their villages by local recruiters, relatives or neighbors promising jobs or marriage, and sold for amounts as small as Nepali Rs.200 [$4.00] to brokers who deliver them to brothel owners in India for anywhere from Rs.15,000 to Rs.40,000 [$500-$1,333].

This purchase price, plus interest (reported to be ten percent of the total), becomes the "debt" that the women must work to pay off — a process that can stretch on indefinitely. Only the brothel owner knows the terms of the debt, and most women have no idea how much they owe or the terms for repayment. Brothels are tightly controlled, and the girls are under constant surveillance. Escape is virtually impossible. Owners use threats and severe beatings to keep inmates in line. In addition, women fear capture by other brothel agents and arrest by the police if they are found on the streets; some of these police are the brothel owner's best clients. Many of the girls and women are brought to India as virgins; many return to Nepal with the HIV virus.

Both the Indian and Nepali governments are complicit in the abuses suffered by trafficking victims. These abuses are not only violations of internationally recognized human rights but are specifically prohibited under the domestic laws of both countries. The willingness of Indian and Nepali government officials to tolerate, and, in some cases, participate in the burgeoning flesh trade exacerbates abuse.

Although human rights organizations in Nepal have reported extensively on the forced trafficking of Nepali girls to Indian brothels, and sensationalist coverage of trafficking issues is a regular feature of the local press, the great majority of cases is never publicized, and even when traffickers have been identified, there have been few arrests and fewer prosecutions.

In India, police and local officials patronize brothels and protect brothel owners and traffickers. Brothel owners pay protection money and bribes to the police to prevent raids and to bail out under-age girls who are arrested. Police who frequent brothels as clients sometimes seek out under-age girls and return later to arrest them — a way of extorting bigger bribes.

Girls and women who complain to the police about rape or abduction, or those who are arrested in raids or for vagrancy, are held in "protective custody" — a form of detention. Corrupt authorities reportedly allow brothel owners to buy back detainees. In Nepal, border police are also bribed to allow traffickers to transport girls to India. In many districts, traffickers exploit political connections to avoid arrest and prosecution.

On return to Nepal, the few women who escape the brothels and appeal to the police for help, or who are returned by the Indian police, are shuttled from one police station to another as they make their way back to their home districts. Some remain in police detention for weeks until their guardians come and collect them. Women who have managed to survive the system of debt bondage frequently become recruiters to fulfill their owners' requirement that they find another girl to take their place.

If women who return home have managed to earn money, they are more easily accepted back into their communities, and may eventually marry. Those who escape the brothels before they have paid off their debts, who return without money, or who are sick and cannot work, are shunned by their families and communities. Many will return to India.

Existing laws in both countries have had virtually no effect on curbing trafficking. Poor training, corruption and the lack of political will among senior government officials on both sides of the border means that the laws go unenforced. Officials also try to evade responsibility for the problem by categorizing trafficking as purely a social problem.

Lack of transborder cooperation between India and Nepal compounds the problem. Apathy on the part of both governments, the highly organized nature of trafficking networks, police corruption and the patronage of influential government officials means virtual impunity for traffickers.

This report is based on interviews conducted with trafficking victims, most of them Nepali women in their twenties who were trafficked to India as teenagers or older women in Mumbai who were still involved in the industry. The interviews are supplemented with case material and interview transcripts provided by social workers, human rights activists and representatives of other nongovernmental organizations who work on trafficking and AIDS-related issues, and interviews with government officials and police officers in Nepal and India between March and September 1994.

In Nepal, researchers visited the capital city of Kathmandu, villages in Nuwakot district and in the Pokhara valley, and the border towns of Birganj, Butwal and Bhairahawa. Human Rights Watch/Asia conducted interviews with police officers, activists and with seven women who had returned from India, all but one of whom stated that they had been forcibly trafficked for the purposes of prostitution. Methods of coercion ranged from false job or marriage offers to drugging and kidnapping.

Four of these women were alleged to be HIV positive by neighbors or aid workers. Of the interviews, four are detailed accounts by women who had returned to Nepal within the last year. These four testified to the methods of force and coercion used by traffickers and provided information about areas of origin of victims and routes travelled, conditions in the brothels, the role of the Indian police, methods of escape and return, and treatment upon return, both by the authorities and by relatives.

In India, Human Rights Watch/Asia interviewed Nepali women still working in brothels, brothel owners, local doctors, activists, and lawyers in both Mumbai and Delhi. We found that the nature of the business of forced prostitution directly affects research. The red-light districts in Mumbai are the locus of a wide range of organized criminality, including smuggling, drugs, extortion, and trafficking.

The network of underworld activities with their hierarchies of "dons"and their agents pervades the business of forced prostitution. In the brothels, fear of madams and pimps makes women reluctant to talk substantively with outsiders for any length of time. It is extremely difficult for researchers to speak to women alone, without the presence of a senior member of the brothel.

Local activists who have spent years building up trust told Human Rights Watch/Asia that the information they receive appears to be amended as time passes and greater levels of trust are attained. We found many women were wary of requests for personal information. Ages were routinely masked by girls who were under the legal age of consent for sexual activity.

Women who had escaped the industry reported having been coached by brothel owners to give set responses to questions about their ages, homes, villages and queries about how they ended up in prostitution. In addition to fear of retaliation from brothel management, a sense of shame and the sense that they lack any alternative to prostitution may also lead women to give misleading information about their route to this life.

While Nepalis are trafficked into many Indian cities, Human Rights Watch/Asia chose to focus on Mumbai because it appears to have the highest concentration of Nepali girls and women in prostitution. In Mumbai, according to the calculations of an organization of Nepali brothel staff, there are about 20,000 Nepalis in the city's flesh trade — other agencies estimate that the actual number is closer to 50,000.

Most of these women and girls work for Nepali *gharwalis* (madams), and almost all are illiterate. Seventy percent are thought to belong to ethnic minority groups such as the Tamang, Gurung, Magar, and Sherpa. Women and girls from Nepal's Hindu majority communities comprise about ten to fifteen percent. Sixty percent of these girls and women are thought to have contracted HIV.

In both Nepal and India, women who were or had been sex workers were hesitant to speak with researchers and reluctant to discuss their experiences except in the most general of terms, fearing reprisals from pimps, police and brothel owners, and the social stigma surrounding prostitution.

Although most women with whom we spoke had some idea that forcible trafficking was illegal, and some had even attempted to make complaints against their traffickers after they returned to Nepal, few knew much about the legal process, or had been kept informed about the progress of their cases. Women who are trafficked into forced prostitutionquickly learn to see police as their enemies, and to accept society's judgment that they themselves are criminals because they have engaged in prostitution, even if they have been beaten and raped into compliance.

While there has been some acknowledgement by government officials in both countries about the magnitude of the problem and the need for action, neither India nor Nepal has taken serious measures to stop trafficking. Despite a plethora of national and international legal instruments that address trafficking and abuses common in the industry, the trade continues to prosper.

The burden of responsibility rests with India to stem the demand for new victims, and to protect the women and girls whose rights are violated on its territory. It must investigate and prosecute all those involved in trafficking and brothel operations, including police and other government agents who profit from the abuse. Nepal and India together should cooperate in police training for border operations. All reports of border police involvement in trafficking should be investigated and those responsible punished.

The international community also has a responsibility to see that both India and Nepal uphold their international obligations to prevent trafficking. Unfortunately, few governments have recognized this as a government responsibility, preferring to view the flesh trade as an unfortunate social evil with its roots in poverty. Trafficking in women and children has become an enormously profitable industry — one that will not be stopped without international scrutiny and pressure.

POLITICAL AND ECONOMIC BACKGROUND

Nepal's extreme poverty and its economic and political relationship with India have facilitated the trafficking of Nepali women and girls to brothels in India. Nepal is a small, landlocked country that shares borders with two powerful nations — China and India — and depends on them for development assistance and trade; it also borders the tiny kingdom of Bhutan, approximately one sixth of whose population of some 600,000 currently reside as refugees in eastern Nepal.

Nepal is mountainous, with little infrastructure or industry. Ninety percent of its population of some nineteen million people resides in rural areas, dependent on subsistence agriculture. Nepal's large ethnic variety reflects its geography and includes people from the subtropical lowlands of the Terai on the Indian border, who have much in common with the people of northern India. The central hill dwellers share a mixture of Indian and Tibeto-Burman roots, and mountain people trace their origins to Central Asia and Tibet.

For decades, members of these largely Buddhist communities like the Tamangs (the preponderant majority), Sherpas, Lamas and Gurungs have been targeted by brokers who supply women and girls to Indian brothels, children of both sexes for work in carpet and garment factories in Nepal and India, and people of all ages for road building and construction.

The Tamangs live in large numbers in the remote hill villages of Nuwakot, Sindhupalchowk, Kavre and Dhading districts, but the search for jobs has scattered them in small numbers throughout the country. Trafficking of women from Nepal's hill communities began in the nineteenth century, when the feudal Rana family, a line of prime ministers who ruled Nepal from 1846 to 1951, began recruiting Tamang girls from the Helambu (Yolmo) region of Sindhupalchowk, northeast of Kathmandu, to serve as concubines for the ruler and his family.

Owning concubines, or "Helambu girls," became a mark of high social status. The oligarchical Rana regime was overthrown by the hereditary monarchy in 1951, but the recruitment of women and girls continued, only now they were sold to brothel owners in India's red-light districts. The internationalization of trafficking in girls and women was due in part to a political alliance forged between Nepal and India in the last days of the Rana regime that opened the border between the two countries for travel and trade.

Nuwakot, Sindhupalchok and other hill districts in the Bagmati Zone around Kathmandu became particularly notorious for trafficking. But as Indian demand for Nepali prostitutes grew, and the threat of AIDS increased the demand for new girls, girls from many castes and communities and from other regions of Nepal was recruited for sale in Indian brothels. Today, instances of forced trafficking of women and girls for prostitution in India have been reported in virtually every district of Nepal and from all castes and ethnic groups.

POLITICAL STRUCTURE

Despite Nepal's transition to multi-party democracy in 1990, its towns and villages remain tightly controlled by powerful local leaders, many of them members of wealthy families who have traditionally dominated village life. Under the previous single-party system, termed "*panchayat* democracy," these local bosses gained political influence beyond their home districts, nurturing the growth of a complex network of political patronage.

The panchayat system, which was established by King Mahendra in 1962, was a four-tiered system which provided for popular elections only at the local level, where the electorate was easily controlled by local landowners. The 1962Constitution also provided for a prime minister, nominated by the king, and prohibited political parties. Nepal was declared an "independent, indivisible, and sovereign Hindu state" with the king as the ultimate source of executive, legislative and judicial powers.

From the start, the power of the panchayat was land and caste-based and plagued by local rivalries and factionalism. Poor and landless villagers were compelled by necessity to choose sides, allying themselves with a patron who could provide them with work. This created an ideal environment for the development of trafficking networks and criminal gangs. According to one scholar:

> Once in power, group leaders...traditionally used political positions to strengthen private networks by dispensing patronage, in addition to enriching themselves.
>
> These patron-client hierarchies were also reflected in the ties between *Rastriya* [National] *Panchayat* ... members and their local factions. The absence of political parties exacerbated the formation of personality-based coalitions among members of the *Rastriya Panchayat.* These nation-level factions were generally geographically oriented, centered on assembly members with large government-run facilities or projects in their districts.

At every level, politics under the Partyless *Panchayat* System was characterized by intra-elite struggles for control of government resources. In 1972 King Mahendra was succeeded by his son, King Birendra. The panchayat system, altered in 1980 to provide for the direct election of the *Rastriya Panchayat* based on universal adult suffrage, remained in force until April 1990, when a massive pro-democracy movement led to the adoption of a multi-party system.

Since then, other political forces have begun to make inroads into local administration. The government of Prime Minister Girija Prasad Koirala, of the Nepali Congress Party, was elected by popular vote in May 1991. On July 10, 1994, Koirala resigned after his government lost an important parliamentary vote.Elections was held November 13, 1994, two years ahead of schedule, and a Communist government under Manmohan Adhikary took power.

But former panchayat members still wield substantial power locally and allegations of corruption and political patronage of criminal gangs — traffickers of human beings, drugs, and precious metals in particular — persist and are apparently well-founded. Politicians who have gained power through the electoral process are also now accused of engaging in similar activities.

Under the 1990 constitution, the king retains executive power, and appoints the leader of the parliamentary party commanding an elected majority in the House of Representatives as his prime minister. The political relationship between royalists (largely former panchayat members), who still wield significant power at the local level, and the elected leadership remains uneasy. The government appears to have insufficient control over the police force, the principal violator of human rights in Nepal.

ECONOMIC FACTORS

The flourishing trade in Nepali women and girls in India must be understood in the context of economic conditions in both countries. Nepal's extreme poverty makes recruiting in its rural villages easy and profitable. Because of its economic dependence on India and the political ties between the powerful Nepali Congress Party and the Indian government the previous government of Nepal was inhibited from regulating the border or actively combating cross-border crime unless the Indian government also committed itself to stemming demand by enforcing anti-trafficking laws.

In the past decade Nepal has undergone increased industrialization in urban areas such as Kathmandu and in towns in the Terai, the lowland area along Nepal's southern border with India. This growth was made possible by trade agreements between India and Nepal and reflects much Indian investment. Many new businesses in Nepal are Indian-owned or employ Indian workers. Indianindustries south of the border recruit large numbers of Nepali workers who bring currency back into Nepal. Import of Indian products and export of Nepali resources, including timber, is growing rapidly.

Despite this growth in urban areas, there has been little change in Nepal's rural economy, which remains largely dependent on subsistence agriculture. Many rural villages are very far from urban markets where crops could be sold if a surplus existed. In most cases there is little surplus and hill villages suffer lean periods at the end of each growing season — hence the attraction of work in the city.

In addition, despite government efforts at land reform, most tillable land in rural Nepal is owned by a few influential, often high caste families. Members of lower castes and poorer ethnic groups have difficulty sustaining themselves on their meager landholdings and are engaged in a continuous search for new ways to generate income. Tamang peasants are among Nepal's most impoverished minority groups.

Today, according to Jyothi Sanghera, an activist who presented her findings to the U.N. Working Group on Contemporary Forms of Slavery in 1991, an average Tamang family owns less than one hectare of unirrigated land. Most were already tenants before Nepal implemented a series of land reform acts in the 1950s, at which time the vast majority were evicted — left landless or with small plots of arid land on steep hill slopes.

No longer able to survive on subsistence farming, and with virtually no access to education or other means of entry into a cash-based economy, the Tamang were forced to migrate in search of other means of support. They found it in low-paying seasonal work as porters or manual laborers in the lowlands, or on road construction sites in India.

Tamang men were also recruited for the Gurkha regiments of the British and Indian armies. But these communities soon found there was another, more lucrative way to earn money. "A commodity... has been created that sells, and sell[s] very well at that, in the labour market of the sex industry: the body and sexual labour of the Tamang woman..."

Border towns on both sides are bustling markets, catering to residents from both countries seeking jobs and bargains. They also provide a natural market for smuggling and prostitution, serving as a nexus for brokers and agents who take advantage of the crowds of anonymous travellers, the guest lodges, and the easy access to transportation.

A 1950 treaty with Nepal provided for free passage and trade across the Nepal/India border. Article 7 of the treaty reads:

The Government of India and Nepal agree to grant, on a reciprocal basis, to the nationals of one country in the territories of the other the same privileges in the matters of residence, ownership of property, participation in trade and commerce, movement and other privileges of a similar nature.

Successive governments of Nepal expressed dissatisfaction with the treaty several times, but although either country could terminate the treaty with a year's notice, India has not wished to lose the privileges it enjoys, and Nepal cannotafford the consequences of a deterioration in its trade relationship with India. On February 9, 1995, India announced that it was ready to hold talks with Nepal's new government on amending the forty-five-year-old treaty.

The effect of the open border policy on the prevention of trafficking of women is clear. No passports, visas or residence permits are required for nationals traveling between India and Nepal. Because people pass freely between the two countries for work, shopping and business (according to Nepali police, up to 100,000 people per day through one popular border post), it is extremely difficult for border police to check illegal activity.

Traffickers and their victims move easily across the border, and the onus is on individual police officers to stop and question suspicious-looking travellers. The problem is compounded by consistent reports of police corruption on both sides of the border. In India's red-light districts, the demand for Nepali girls, especially virgins with fair skin and Mongolian features, continues to increase. It is impossible to say how many girls and women are employed in the sex industry in India or what percentage of the total is from Nepal.

Estimates have been based largely on the numbers of women employed by brothels in urban areas, but prostitution exists in every city and town in India and in many villages, and statistics vary enormously. Dr. I.S. Gilada, general secretary of the Indian Health Organization (IHO), estimated in various studies conducted between 1985 and 1994 that there were between 70,000 and 100,000 prostitutes in Mumbai, 100,000 in Calcutta, 40,000 in Delhi, 40,000 in Pune and 13,000 in Nagpur.

Based on his statistics, Nepali social workers estimate the number of Nepali girls and women now working in Indian brothels at about 200,000 and believe that between 5,000 and 7,000 new Nepalis end up in Indian brothels every year. The Indian Council of MedicalResearch estimates the total number of prostitutes in India at about one million. By contrast, the Bharatiya Patita Udhar Sabha (Indian Association for the Rescue of Fallen Women), a voluntary organization dedicated to the welfare of the country's sex workers, estimates that in 1992 there were more than 8 million brothel workers in India and another 7.5 million call girls.

There is simply no way to verify these statistics, but it is clear the percentage of Nepali girls in Indian brothels is very high, that their numbers appear to be increasing, and that the average age at which they are recruited is significantly lower than it was ten years ago, dropping from fourteen to sixteen years in the 1980s to ten to fourteen years in 1994. Dr. Gilada of IHO told our researcher that the youngest girl he had seen in a Mumbai brothel was nine years old.

While Human Rights Watch/Asia has chosen to focus on Mumbai because it is the city which appears to have the highest percentage of Nepali prostitutes, Nepali women are trafficked into many other Indian cities. Of the roughly 3,500 women in prostitution in Delhi's red-light district of G.B. Road, activists estimate that about 150 are from Nepal. In Calcutta, various studies conducted by the All India Institute of Hygiene and Public Health (AIIHPH) in 1993 estimate that 20 percent of the 5,000 sex workers in the Sonagachi red-light area are Nepali. According to one AIIHPH expert, over 500 Nepali girls arrived in Sonagachi in 1993 alone.

In the state of Gujarat, which borders Maharashtra, a survey undertaken by the International Society for Research on Civilisation Diseases and Environment estimates that of the total number of persons in prostitution in Suratcity, 80 percent were from outside the state, with 10 percent of these persons from Nepal. The voluntary organization also found that many persons in prostitution in Mumbai periodically visited Surat because of the market for prostitution there.

Although tourism is an important industry in both countries, and sex tourism appears to be on the increase in India, tourism is less a factor in the sex industry than local demand. All of the women Human Rights Watch/Asia interviewed reported that most of their customers were Indian. Some were also Nepali, although in at least one case Nepali customers were discouraged, for fear they would help Nepali girls escape.

Brothels are big business. Despite expenses incurred in employing a network of agents to recruit new workers in Nepal (some procurers are reportedly paid up to Indian Rs.6,000 [about $200] per trip) and protection money that is paid weekly to police and local crime bosses (said to total Rs.200 [$6.60] per brothel inmate per week), even the cheapest of brothels can turn a substantial profit, generally collecting from Rs.50-Rs.100 [$1.66-$3.33] per client, with much more for special services.

A brothel may employ anywhere from four to fifty workers, and an inmate may serve more than fifteen clients a day, on an average of twenty-six to twenty-eight days a month. The brothel owners generally provide no more than two meals a day and most workers are allowed to keep only the tips from their clients, Rs 2 to 5 (fifteen cents or less) per man.

With these meager resources, they must cover their own expenses for food, clothing, and personal effects. The cost of medical care is typically paid by the owner, and then added to a inmate's "debt" –sometimes with interest. The owner, who frequently owns more than one brothel, clearly stands to make a profit, but agents, local police and others involved in the industry also benefit. As one former prostitute told Human Rights Watch/Asia, "Police, doctors, *dalals* (pimps), they are all fed by the brothels."

PATTERNS OF ABUSE

There are two distinct patterns to the trafficking of girls and women from Nepal. The best known and oldest involves the enticement of mainly Tamang girls from hill districts where the flesh trade has become an almost traditional source of income. But the incidence of forced trafficking from other parts of Nepal is also on the rise. Poor migrant women and children whose families have moved to Nepal's urban areas in search of employment are the principal victims. These girls and women come from all castes and ethnic groups.

Human Rights Watch/Asia visited Nepal and interviewed women from several areas of Nepal who had been trafficked to India and had returned. In all cases, families, neighbors and friends play an active role in forced trafficking by concocting fictitious marriage and job offers, contacting recruiters and brokers, or simply luring girls away from home on outings or errands, kidnapping and selling them. Regardless of the victims' origins, their reports of abuse in Indian brothels are remarkably consistent.

The average age of the thousands of Nepali girls recruited every year for prostitution in brothels in India has reportedly dropped in the past decade 0from fourteen to sixteen years in the 1980s, to ten to fourteen in 1991, despite new laws promulgated in both countries in 1986 designed to stem trafficking and child prostitution.

Police in areas with a high incidence of trafficking state that the average age of new trafficking victims is about thirteen. However, trafficking victims are frequently coached by captors to conceal their true ages. Girls forced into prostitution in Mumbai's brothels may remain trapped in the brothel system formore than ten years, during which time they may be sold from one brothel to another many times.

CASE HISTORIES

The following cases, based on interviews conducted by Human Rights Watch/Asia in March 1994 with young women in Nepal who had returned from Mumbai, and in July 1994 with women still employed in Mumbai's brothels, describe some of the patterns typical of trafficking between Nepal and India. The first, "Maya" represents a case of simple abduction. Although she filed a complaint against her traffickers, no one was ever prosecuted.

MAYA

"Maya" is from a small village in Nuwakot district. She is twenty-three, but looks much older. She has dark circles under her eyes; her skin is dry and lined. A local health worker thinks she was ejected from a brothel in Mumbai after testing positive for HIV, a story Maya denies.

Maya said she first left her village when she was eighteen and returned to her village in July 1993, after spending three years in an Indian brothel.

Maya was married to a man from a nearby village when she was around thirteen. Soon after, her husband began seeing someone else. He moved out when Maya was sixteen, married a second wife and took her to Kathmandu. Maya had lived alone for two years when her father-in-law told her she should follow her husband to Kathmandu. He took her there. At her husband's house she was beaten and treated very badly.

In 1990 a fellow villager began visiting the house. The second time he came to visit, he brought another man along. They invited Maya and her husband to come out to see a movie. Maya's husband told her to go ahead without him. The three of them boarded a bus, which Maya said kept going farther and farther from Kathmandu. Eventually, they went through the border at Kakarbhitta. They were never stopped or questioned by the police.

After two days traveling by bus, they reached Mumbai and the men left Maya at a house and told her they would pick her up the next day. They never came back. Maya realized she was in a brothel when she saw that the house was occupied by about twenty-five women, all but three of whom were from Nepal. Two or three were girls she had known from her own village.

The brothel where Maya worked was called a "pillow house," lowest in the brothel hierarchy where most new girls start out. It was a large building, with several rooms where thewomen lived, slept and worked. There were eight beds in each room and curtains dividing the beds. All of the girls' and women's earnings were turned over to the brothel owner, a woman named Renu Tamang from Urleni in Nuwakot district.

The women worked from noon to 1:00 a.m. They were given no days off. After a year, the owner told Maya that the broker had been paid for her and that she was responsible for paying back her purchase price, but she was never told how much she owed. The owner told her she could go home only after she paid off her debt. Maya noted that another brothel inmate, a woman from Trisuli, had worked there for thirteen years and had never managed to pay off her debt.

Maya was beaten severely for the first four or five days she was held in the brothel because she refused to have sex with customers. They continued to beat her until she submitted. Later on, she was beaten with bottles and thick sticks because she was not earning enough. She said that all the brothel inmates were beaten if they did not earn enough. Her customers included Indians and foreigners — Germans, Singaporeans, Filipinos and Saudi Arabians.

The customers would select the women they wanted, and the women could not refuse, or they would be beaten. In the three years Maya was held in the brothel, she never received any form of contraception. Girls who became pregnant would be given abortions. The brothel did not provide condoms, but occasionally customers brought their own.

Maya said that she never asked clients to use condoms because she did not know they could prevent AIDS. She said she had heard about AIDS, but did not know anything about it. Because she stayed in the brothel only a short time, she did not know the symptoms. After one year in Mumbai, Maya began to get sick. She developed a high fever and was taken to the doctor who gave her an injection, but she did not know what it was. She then returned to work.

Maya told Human Rights Watch/Asia that she and two other girls, one from Sindhupalchok who was sick, and one from Gorkha, decided to escape from the brothel. All of them had been beaten often and thought they should flee to save their lives. Maya said that while some police officers often came as clients to the brothel, one branch of the police force frequently raided the brothel looking for child prostitutes.

The three women appealed to these police to help them escape, and the police took them to the border and handed them over to the Hanuman Dhoka police station in Kathmandu. Maya was sent on to the police in Ranipowa and then Trisuli, where she was held in detention for ten days. From there it took her six days to reach Nuwakot. As Maya understood the police policy on returnees, the police inform the girl's family by letter and then hold her until relatives come to collect her.

Maya and the two other women filed complaints at the Hanuman Dhoka police station in Kathmandu, and the police told them that they would be informed once the traffickers were found, but as far as she knows, no one was ever arrested. Maya's health deteriorated after her return. She lost weight and suffered from diarrhea, high fevers and stomach aches. Since returning to the village, her health has improved slightly. In January 1994, she was treated with traditional medicine and feels that she has been cured, although she remains very tired and weak and cannot work. Local health workers suspect Maya may not have escaped but was ejected from the brothel in India because she had contracted HIV.

TARA

At thirty-four or thirty-five years old, "Tara" is a senior woman in a brothel in Mumbai. She was described as the "in-charge" of the younger brothel inmates by a local activist. Senior women like Tara are frequently used by gharwalis to keep track of newer inmates. They watch for escape attempts, listen for forbidden conversations with customers, and accompany younger girls when they leave the premises for medical treatment.

The interview with Tara was instructive because it reflected both her experiences as a young trafficking victim, and her attitudes now which are closer to those of brothel management. Tara arrived in Mumbai eighteen or nineteen years ago when she was sixteen years old. She told Human Rights Watch/ Asia that she grew up in Nuwakot jilla [district] and got trapped into prostitution when she went with two girlfriends to see the cigarette factories at Janakpur, on the Nepal/India border.

We fell into the clutches of a dalali [procuress] — a Nepali dalali at that. We were three girls together, in the beginning. We spent two years together, but then we were separated. I don't know what happened to the other two girls. I often wonder what happened to them. When I was captured, I could not escape or return to my home: they would have caught me for sure. If I had known what was to happen to me, I would have killed myself halfway.

[But] leaving this life is not an option for me, I simply cannot think about it. My purity was violated, so I thought: why go back, go back to what? I may as well just stay here. If I ever catch that damn dalali, I don't know what I would do to her. If I ever catch her, you have simply no idea what I will do to her.

Tara described her bewilderment upon arrival in Mumbai: When they brought me here, it was in a taxi. I kept looking around, wondering what kind of work was going on in this area of this big city. Everywhere I looked, I saw curtained doorways and rooms in this area.

Men would go and come through these curtained entrances. People on the street would be calling out, "Two rupees, two rupees." I asked the other Nepali women if these were offices; it seemed the logical explanation. In two days I knew everything. I cried.

The building in Mumbai where Tara lives and works has two floors, and probably houses about fifty women. There are two "maliks" [bosses] for the building. Tara said there were four rooms on her floor, and four Nepali girls and two Indian in her room. She said that when she first came, there were mostly Nepali girls working there, and a Nepali gharwali. Now both Indian and Nepalis work together. She said that like her, these younger Nepali girls came from the mountain areas of Nepal.

Despite the fact that Tara was herself an unwilling victim of the industry, she remained caught in the system for nearly twenty years and is now a senior inmate with management responsibilities. Her testimony, bitter when referring to the past or to women who have managed to escape, was generally sympathetic to her gharwali — with whom she probably shares a similar history.

The fact that she has not attempted to return to Nepal or to open her own establishment suggests that she has not escaped the cycle of debt.

Many girls return to their home area, build houses. Money is everything. It gets you acceptance in the village. There is no one in Nepal who does not know about Mumbai, and this business, not one person in Nepal. The gharwali is good to the girls and does not harm them. She makes the food arrangements, takes care of their needs. It is when a girl falls into the clutches of bad men, thugs, *goondas* [thugs], that she is defiled by them, and ill-treated in many ways.

Tara's testimony reflects some of the most persistent myths of the trafficking industry — that all prostitution is voluntary and driven by economic hardship, and that many prostitutes become rich and return home. Brothel inmates report being coached to give stock answers to questions from investigators andcurious customers, and oft-repeated success stories help keep inmates striving to earn.

"Santhi," a woman whose case is described below, told Human Rights Watch/Asia "In the brothels we were told by the owner to tell the police we came by ourselves because we didn't have food. We were told to say we were twenty-five years old. If we didn't say that we would be beaten." A relief worker who had done research in Mumbai and knows Santhi says brothel inmates she interviewed gave her similar answers when she questioned them about their past.

THE PATH TO MUMBAI

The Nepali girls and women who were interviewed by Human Rights Watch/Asia were forcibly trafficked into India. They did not work as prostitutes voluntarily but were held in conditions tantamount to slavery.

Promises of jobs and marriage are common techniques by which recruiters entice their victims to leave home. But other, more overtly coercive tactics such as kidnapping are also reported. Girls who are already in debt bondage in other industries, particularly carpet factories, are particularly vulnerable.

THE TRAFFICKERS

Traffickers are most typically men in their twenties or thirties or women in their thirties and forties who have travelled the route to the city several times and know the hotels to stay in and the brokers to contact. Traffickers frequently work in groups of two or more. Male and female traffickers are sometimes referred to as *dalals and dalalis*, (commission agents) who are either employed by a brothel owner directly, or operate more or less independently.

Professional agents who recruit for the bigger brothels reportedly may be paid up to Rs.6,000 [$200] per girl. But most traffickers are small-time, local recruiters who earn considerably less. In either case, to stay in business they need the patronage of local bosses and the protection afforded by bribes to the police.

Female traffickers are referred to as *didi* or *phupu didi* (literally, paternal aunt). In Nuwakot district, according to local activists, the majority of *didis* are returned prostitutes from five or six Village Development Committees (VDCs) ineastern Nuwakot.

The peak trafficking months in Nuwakot and Sindhupalchowk are between June and late August or early September when the *didis* return to the villages to participate in local festivals and to recruit girls to bring back to the cities.

These months precede the harvest, when poverty is felt most acutely, making it easy to recruit. People become especially vulnerable every year from June to August, which are known as the "hungry months."

At this time, every mountain village of Nepal suffers from more than the usual level of poverty, while they wait for the new harvests. Villagers have depleted their store of grains, and their hunger drives them to the local moneylender and feudal lord. This impossible situation has forced many young people from the mountain villages to urban centres, where they search for employment and a better future. Most young men work in factories, transportation, and construction, whereas the young girls and women work in garment and carpet factories, and in domestic service. A proportion of the young women will disappear to India.

Family members — uncles, cousins, stepfathers — also act as trafficking agents. Of seven trafficking victims interviewed by Human Rights Watch/Asia in March 1994, six were trafficked to India with the help of close family friends or relatives. In each case, the victim complained of deception. Girls are recruited in a number of ways. Village girls and their families are often deceived by smartly dressed young men who arrive in the village claiming to have come from Kathmandu and offering marriage and all the comforts of modern urban life.

They go through a local ceremony and leave the village never to be seen again. The girls end up in Indian brothels. Sometimes older men promise the girls employment in the city. Another avenue is through distant relatives or friends who pretend to arrange a marriage with relatives or friends in another village, but instead abduct the girl and send her to India. Sometimes a trusted individual abducts the girl on the pretext of educating her in India.

Trafficking appears to be on the increase throughout Nepal and to be growing most rapidly in areas where it has so far received the least attention –towns and villages along the east-west highway, border towns, tourist centers and, according to some reports, the camps that house Bhutanese refugees in

Jhapa district in eastern Nepal. Local women who have returned from India are also employed as recruiters. These women are exceptionally well-placed to identify potential trafficking victims because they already know the local girls and their families.

Women who are already in the sex trade and have graduated to the level of brothel keepers, managers or even owners travel through the villages of their own and neighboring districts in search of young girls. Though not very typical, the following story encapsulates the essence of the dream of success and glamour that these women symbolize to the simple village girls.

Only a short time before my visit, a madam had alighted upon this remote hill village in Sindhupalchowk in a helicopter rented from Kathmandu, for which she must have had to pay a sum of about $1,000. She descended like a celestial fairy mother in the midst of these poor village folk, in all her resplendent finery, and doled out little gifts of baubles and cosmetics to the starry-eyed adolescent girls....When this madam left the village, seven young girls disappeared with her.

The typical agent is far less glamorous, and the number of Nepali prostitutes who manage to become wealthy in India is minuscule. Most recruiters are women desperately trying to escape the abuse and debt bondage of the brothel system themselves. Perhaps the most pernicious and lamentable examples in this category are those women who are themselves forced into prostitution and who have been told by their brothelkeepers that the only way they can procure their release is by furnishing a substitute.

At any given time, several of these women travel to their villages in the hope of cajoling a younger female relative, a friend or just another village woman to accompany them. Most often they are successful...and return with another victim, in lieu of themselves. However, once free they do not make an exit from the prostitution market, they merely end up working as... [independent] prostitutes and finally hope to set up their own little shop with five women working under them...

These local agents buy girls from their families, sometimes for as little as Nepali Rs.200 [$4], or tempt them with promises of future earnings, and take them to the Indian border where they are sold to a broker or for anything from IndianRs.1,000-Rs.8,000 [$22-$266]. These middlemen then sell them to brothel owners in Mumbai and elsewhere for Rs.15,000-Rs.50,000 [$500 - $1,666], depending on the girl's age and beauty. Virgins command higher prices.

PADMA

"Padma" is the *gharwali* of a small brothel in Mumbai. She told Human Rights Watch/Asia that like many others, she came to India as a young girl, from a remote village in the mountains of Nepal. After twenty years in the profession she now runs a brothel which employs between three and six girls.

It took us six days of trekking to get to Kathmandu. Nowadays there is a bus service, so it is not so bad. Can you imagine: Six days! That was really bad. I don't know anyone else in the profession from my own village, but I know others, a couple of others, from neighboring villages. In my house ['ghar'], there are usually three or four girls. Sometimes there are six, but that is the maximum. There is no fixed number. In fact, there really is no telling from moment to moment.

CARPET FACTORIES

Carpets are Nepal's most important export and, along with tourism, one of its most essential industries. Besides being notorious in their own right for appalling working conditions, the pervasive use of child labor and debt bondage, Kathmandu carpet factories have been important recruitment centers for Indian brothels. In 1994 it was estimated that half of all Nepal's carpet workers arechildren.

Girls and boys from poor rural hill families, 47 percent of them Tamang, are recruited from their villages and sold or apprenticed to factory owners. Brokers working within the carpet factories select likely girls and entice them into leaving the factory with offers of better jobs elsewhere — a relatively easy task since many carpet workers are themselves caught in a state of debt bondage where they receive no wages. The brokers then arrange for their transport to India, frequently with the complicity of friends and family members.

Child Workers in Nepal Concerned Centre (CWIN), a Kathmandu-based organization dedicated to the rights of children, reported in 1994 that of 300 Nepali prostitutes interviewed in Mumbai, 40 percent had been trafficked from carpet factories. In March 1994, A.R. Panday, the chief district officer of Nuwakot confirmed that the trafficking network that operates in Nuwakot district used the carpet industry in Kathmandu as a secondary point of recruitment.

Guardians will send girls to Kathmandu as labourers. There they learn a more sophisticated life, and then will be tempted by a broker who takes them up to the border. The carpet industry employs backward castes — Danuwar, Himal, Tamang.... Girls are attracted by idea of work in the city, they are ambitious. The broker works from inside the factory, selects a girl and convinces her to go with him and then takes her to the border and sells her.

Sexual abuse of girls in carpet factories is commonplace. Almost half of the more than twelve hundred girls under sixteen working in carpet factories in 1992 who were interviewed by CWIN complained of frequent sexual abuse, including rape by adult co-workers, managers and brokers for the factories. According to children's rights advocates, underground brothels operate out of some of Nepal's carpet factories.

[S]ome carpet factory brokers...roam in the villages to lure young girls to work in the carpet factories of Kathmandu where many of them are forced into prostitution and even trafficked to Mumbai. These girls are abused and exploited by storekeepers, loom masters and checkers before they give up and agree to do the "night shifts." And they sell themselves for Rs.20-50 [0.40-$1.00] per trick. The customers are arranged by the pimps in the factory who take commissions from the girls. In Kathmandu's many garment factories, too, the girls do one kind of work during the day and another kind at night. The following cases of women interviewed:

NEELA

In 1989, when she was fourteen, "Neela's" stepfather took her from their village in Sindhupalchowk to Bhaktapur, a suburb of Kathmandu, where a friend of his got her a job in a carpet factory. A few months later, in January 1990, a young male co-worker who had been introduced to Neela as her "cousin" suggested that they leave the Bhaktapur factory and go to Kakarbhitta, a town on the Indian border, where, he claimed, working conditions were better and they could earn more money.

Neela agreed, and was taken out of the factory by her stepfather, her stepfather's friend and this young man. After six days, traveling by bus and by train, they arrived in Mumbai. There, Neela was taken to the grounds of a temple where the men introduced her to two women. She was told to go home with the women; the men would join them later. Neela was taken to a house that she later discovered was the home of the brothel manager.

She stayed there overnight, and at 6:00 the next morning she was taken to another house where sixteen or seventeen girls were asleep on the floor. Because she was so young, Neela was taken to a separate"training" room where she was kept for three months, after which she was told she had been sold for Rs.15,000 [$500] and would have to work there until she paid off her debt. Her first customer was a middle-aged man who paid Rs.5,000 [$166] for her because she was a virgin. Neela said the manager always charged more money for new girls, but she was never told how much the regular customerspaid; all the money was given directly to the owner. Nor was she told how long it would take to repay her debt.

As the youngest in the brothel, Neela's treatment was better than for many of the girls and women working there. She was not beaten, even when she was caught trying to escape one night by pretending to go to the toilet which was outside behind the brothel. However, she was insulted and threatened, and saw others who worked there frequently beaten severely, "until blood came from their mouths," for trying to escape and for fighting.

Many other girls in the brothel were under-age and all were Nepali. Neela told Human Rights Watch/Asia that the brothel was frequently raided by police in search of underage girls and that when the police came, the brothel owners would try to hide the newcomers, because "not all police were the same." Sometimes police who came in civilian dress as paying customers and sought her out specifically would raid the brothel later.

Neela said condoms were not available in the brothel where she worked although customers sometimes brought their own. She never asked a customer to use a condom. After about a year in the brothel Neela was picked up in a police raid and taken to an ashram, a shelter, for children because she was underage. In the ashram she tested positive for HIV.

After two years there, when Neela was eighteen, the police asked her if she wanted to go home. She said she did, and the Indian police informed the Nepali police and she was taken to Kathmandu. She was brought first to Hanuman Dhoka police station in Kathmandu, then to Bhaktapur police station. She was held for eight days in Bhaktapur police detention.

During that time the police took her to Teku Hospital for an HIV test. She was not told the reason for the test; the police only told her that they were taking her for a check-up because she was returning from Mumbai. Afterwards she was told she had tested positive for HIV. Neela said a journalist interviewed her just two days after she arrived in Kathmandu — while she was still in police custody — and her photo and story were published in a local paper, but she did not know which one. Because of this she decided not to try to locate her family. She now lives in a shelter.

SANUMAYA CHAUDHARY

Sanumaya (Sanu) Chaudhary, age fifteen, was trafficked to India in 1991, also by a co-worker in a carpet factory, and rescued in January 1992. Her case was first published by the *Independent*, a Kathmandu-based English-language newspaper, in September 1992, soon after she lodged a complaint with the policeagainst a twenty-year-old woman who had taken her to India. Since then, Sanu's story has been reprinted by several organizations who worked with her.

Sanu's parents were migrants from Bara district in south-central Nepal who had come to Kathmandu to work in a carpet factory. Sanu's parents placed her in a small boarding school for destitute girls near the factory, but she was expelled for her suspected romantic involvement with the factory manager.

Back in the carpet factory, Sanu, who had just turned fifteen, became friendly with an older girl who told her there were better paying jobs available in a carpet factory in Raxaul, just across the Indian border. The two girls talked it over with Sanu's parents and decided to go to Raxaul. Sanu took a only a change of clothes. She borrowed bus fare from her new friend.

After three days of traveling by bus and by train, the two girls arrived in a city Sanu thought was Raxaul. It turned out to be Mumbai. The girls went directly to a building Sanu's companion said was the carpet factory and met the manager.

Sanu was told she could have a bath; when she finished bathing, she found her friend had disappeared. Sanu was taken to a large room with five beds separated by curtains. She was given a nightgown and her clothes were taken away. Several older girls wearing thick make-up came into the room with men and drew the curtains behind them.

The noise the couples made frightened Sanu. Then one of the men she had seen at the entrance to the building came into the room and ordered Sanu to go to bed with him. When she refused, he raped her and beat her for resisting.

For the next week, Sanu was subjected to repeated rapes and beatings by brothel guards — a "breaking in" period that is routine in many brothels. After a week of this abuse, she stopped fighting and began taking customers. Sanu was told she could leave the brothel when she repaid the Rs.50,000 [$1,666] the proprietor claimed had been paid to her parents.

SANTHI

In addition to actual recruitment from the factories, false offers of employment in Nepal's carpet factories are a common ruse used to entice potential recruits. In an interview with Human Rights Watch/Asia in March 1994, "Santhi", age twenty-nine, told interviewers that after she was tricked into going to India by traffickers who offered her work in a carpet factory, she spent more than ten years in Mumbai brothels before finally making her way back to Nepal. In Mumbai, she contracted HIV.

Santhi, who returned to Nepal in 1991 after more than ten years in a series of brothels in Mumbai, ran away from her home in Sindhupalchowk when she wasa teenager. She went to Kathmandu where she first found work as a domestic servant. A male cousin came to Kathmandu to visit her and offered to help her get a job in a carpet factory in Birganj, a town on the Indian border. He told her that if she worked in the factory for two months she would begin earning a salary.

Santhi left the house where she had been working and went with him. They travelled by bus, and then by train and then by taxi, going from Kathmandu to Birganj to Mumbai. Midway, they were joined by an older man whom Santhi did not know. When they reached Mumbai they stopped in a park. Santhi was told to wait with her cousin.

The older man left them in the park, and returned with a woman he introduced as his sister and said that they should go with her. They all got in a taxi and went to a house. Santhi was put in one room and the men were given another. That was the last time she saw them. Santhi found out later that a month after she arrived in Mumbai, her cousin took her sister from their village and brought her to Mumbai as well. Her sister and she were bought by the same person, but were kept in different brothels.

Marriage Offers

Fraudulent marriage offers are another common ruse employed by recruiters. In some cases, the traffickers actually go through a marriage ceremony. In others, the marriage offer itself is enough to lure a woman away from home.

A police officer in Butwal told Human Rights Watch/Asia that in 1989 he arrested a very handsome youth in Jhapa district in eastern Nepal who had trafficked nine girls to Mumbai by marrying them. He took each to Mumbai and abandoned them in a crowd. An accomplice would then approach them, offer to help them find the missing young man and lead them to a brothel. The following case is typical of this kind of deception.

SITA

"Sita", thirty-one, returned from India in October 1993 after working for ten years in a Mumbai brothel. She is a high-caste Hindu from a small village in Tanahu District, near Pokhara. Sita was married when she was fourteen. After two years of marriage, she became pregnant and her husband went to India in search of work. Her in-laws mistreated her so Sita returned to her parents' home.

In 1983, when she was twenty and her son was four, a neighbor (who was also a relative and a close friend of Sita's) commented that Sita's husband had been gone a long timeand probably was not coming back. She asked Sita if she would be willing to remarry, because there was a man from India who wanted to marry her.

Soon after, the neighbor came to the house and told Sita that the man from India was waiting for her on the bridge at the main road and that he wanted to elope. It was around noon; Sita told her family she was going to the fields to work and went instead to the bridge, perhaps ten minutes away. She brought her son with her.

The man was waiting for Sita as the neighbor had said. They caught a bus to Pokhara, the nearest town. In Pokhara he offered Sita a cigarette. Sita said she had learned to smoke from a friend in the village and so she took it. After smoking the cigarette, she remembers very little and thinks she may have passed out. Sita said she remembers boarding another bus and then waking up in a large cement room with a ceiling fan and three beds with curtains around them.

The door was closed. There were six or seven other women in the room and she asked them where she was, but they spoke to her in a language she did not understand. The man who brought her there took Sita's son and said he would show him around town. They never returned. Sita was frantic. She wanted to go out and search for them, but the owner, a woman from eastern Nepal, told her she had been sold to a brothel and could not leave. Sita never saw her son again.

Sita escaped to Nepal in October 1993 with the help of a Nepali vegetable seller she befriended in the brothel. Everyone in her village thought she was dead. When Sita returned to Nepal, she was afraid to go directly home — worried her family would not accept her — so she sent a message from Pokhara saying she had returned. It was the time of the Teej festival, when married daughters return to their home villages to visit their families.

Everyone in the village came to the place where she was staying and hugged her and cried. Sita lives in her parents' home, where we were able to interview her. She says her family treats her well, because they know she was taken to India against her will. According to a lawyer familiar with her case, her brothers are less welcoming, and Sita may face problems when her elderly parents die.

Abductions

Simple abductions also occur, although they are less common than cases of fraud. Several women mentioned that they, or other women in the brothels where they worked, had been drugged by their abductors.

DEVI

"Devi," age twenty-seven, lives with her parents in a small house in a village on the outskirts of Pokhara. She is a high-caste Hindu. Devi is married, but her estranged husband is said to be working in Korea, and she has not heard from him in years. Devi was trafficked to India in early June 1993. She returned to Nepal in December 1993.

During that time, she was sold to three different brothels in less than four months because she refused customers and repeatedly tried to escape. When she finally did escape she worked in a textile factory for three months before the owner of the factory brought her home.

Devi was taken to India by neighbors, a mother and daughter, whom she knew quite well. They told her that they had to go to a market far from their village to pick up something and asked her to come along. Devi often went places with them, but usually they travelled by bus.

That day there was a taxi waiting for them. They travelled a long way, and it was very late when they finally arrived in Badi Bazaar. They got in another taxi and arrived at a village house like her own. She was put in a room and the door was locked. Devi had no idea where she was.

A woman called Nithu told Devi that the woman she came with had gone out and would be back later, but she never came back. After three nights, Nithu made Devi travel with her by taxi and then train to another town. When Devi pleaded with her to let her go, she was told "No, you have been sold and have to work. All Nepali girls have to work."

Devi was taken to a room where she saw five girls from Pokhara whom she knew and four others. She asked the other girls there to help her escape, and eight days later when the brothel owner found out, Devi was sold to another brothel. After three or four days she attempted to escape again, this time by appealing to a Nepali client for help. She was overheard by another girl in the brothel who informed the owner.

Devi was sold late that night to a third brothel. There were underage girls in all the brothels in which she worked. In the first two the average age was fifteen or sixteen. In the third brothel there were fifty girls and women of all ages; the two youngest were fourteen. Devi was never told how much the first two owners paid for her. The last owner told her she had paid Rs.40,000 [$1,333] for her and that she would have to work it off.

KAMALA

"Kamala", age twenty-six, returned to Nepal in September 1993 after spending nine years in India. She was drugged and abducted by her stepfather's elder brother and his son and trafficked to India when she was seventeen. Kamala had been visiting her uncle and his three children, who lived in Biratnager, a town very near the Indian border. Once when she was visiting he suggested that theymake a trip to Jogvani.

The uncle, his wife and eldest son went along. Along the way they stopped for tea. Kamala was given milk. The milk smelled bad, but she drank it anyway. The next thing she remembers is waking up slightly on a train and then perhaps again in a taxi. When she really woke up she was in a big hall with a lot of lights, which turned out to be a hotel lobby, but she does not know the name of the hotel.

Her cousin and uncle were with her. They told her that they needed to go to the bank and left her alone in the hotel lobby. While they were gone Kamala overheard two men speaking Hindi; they were talking about taking someone to a brothel. She asked the men what they were talking about and who they were taking to a brothel. She asked where her relatives had gone.

The men told her she had been sold. She started to cry and said that it was impossible, she did not believe it. They asked her if she could read and when she said she could (she had studied up to the seventh standard), they showed her a receipt for Rs.40,000. The hotel owner told her that this was not the first time her uncle and cousin had brought girls there. They had brought two other girls previously — one was Nepali, one looked Indian and was from the Terai.

The men tried to put her in a taxi. She said she had to go to the toilet first and a small boy showed her where it was. She locked herself in and would not come out. She said she was able to lock herself in because the hotel owner did not know she was there and there were a number of stalls, so she hid. That was at about 9:00 p.m. She hid in the toilet until about 4:00 a.m.

By then she was sure the men had given up. She slipped out of the hotel and escaped. She was taken in by a woman who lived in a nearby slum who got her a job as a domestic servant in the home of a couple who worked at a hospital. But as is the case with many domestic workers, her employers "held" her salary for her so that when she left their service, she had no money. It took Kamala nine years working as a domestic servant in two different households to make her way back to Nepal.

The Routes

The trafficking industry in Nepal is remarkable not only because it represents the work of large and well-organized criminal gangs and preys on very young victims, but also because the villages from which girls and women are trafficked are so remote. Most are far from the nearest road. Much of the journey from the hill villages to Kathmandu, which can take more than two days, must be covered on foot over rugged mountain paths.

Villagers say that despite this, it is not uncommon for traffickers to travel these paths on nights with full moon withseveral girls in tow. Police intervention is extremely rare.

From their villages, girls are first taken to Kathmandu, either to guest houses or carpet factories, or from there to border towns like Birganj, Kakarbhitta, Bhairawaha or Biratnagar where they are sold to brokers. The going rate is said to be about one thousand Nepali rupees [$20].

Girls abducted from the Terai and eastern Nepal are usually taken directly to the border. The brokers then travel by bus or by train to India — to Mumbai, Calcutta, Delhi or to smaller cities — and sell these girls to a brothel owner or madam for up to Rs.50,000 [$1,666]. According to researchers in

Kathmandu, most brokers travel by local bus to Delhi, and then by bus or train to Mumbai. Buses, they say, are preferred because they are less obvious than trains.

Local police in Birganj told Human Rights Watch/Asia that although their town was a well-known border crossing for traffickers, the routes change frequently: Lately, the girls have changed their route. Now they go through Gaur and Thori (to the east and west of Birganj respectively), two places with minimal Nepali customs and some Indian customs police who are not very vigilant.

Activists note that trafficking routes also appear to be changing with migration to the Terai. While there is still much trafficking from the hills of the Bagmati zone, as families migrate in search of work, more girls are being sold from urban areas and villages along the highways.

IN THE BROTHELS

Nepali women in India's red-light areas remain largely segregated in brothels located in what are known to their Indian counterparts and their customers as "Nepali *kothas*" or compounds. The concentrations of Nepalis vary from city to city, but appear to be highest in the Mumbai neighborhood of Kamathipura. Brothels vary by size, physical configuration, ethnicity of sex workers, and price. But in all cases, movement outside the brothels is strictly controlled, and inmates are subjected to both psychological and physical abuse.

The cheapest brothels, nothing more than dark, claustrophobic rooms with cloth dividers hung between the beds, are known among Nepalis as "pillow houses." About one-fifth of all Mumbai's brothel workers, or approximately 20,000 women, work in squalid brothels like these on numbered lanes (or *gallis*) in Kamathipura. Certain lanes, likethe 11th and the 13th, are known particularly as Nepali gallis. Many customers seek out Nepali prostitutes specifically, because of their looks and their exotic reputations.

The segregation of Nepali girls and women in these gallis exposes them to a wider range of clients, and a wider and more unpredictable range of sexual expectations, treatment, and disease. Nepalis are sought out by customers who think their "golden" skin make them more attractive. Brothel owners say Nepalis' faces and bodies stay youthful longer.

The Nepalis also suffer from a reputation of sexual compliance among both Indian sex workers and customers, who say Nepalis engage in higher-risk sexual acts, such as anal intercourse and sado-masochistic sex, than their Indian counterparts, who may have more control over the terms of sexual contact. Consequently, kotha managers and their clients view Nepali women in prostitution as a special case, and madams routinely receive special requests for Nepalis.

Foreigners from outside India, particularly the Middle East, are also said to view Nepalis as special within the sex industry. Most girls and women start out in these cheap brothels where they are "broken in" through a process of rapes and beatings. They are frequently then resold to other brothels where they can bring in more money for the owner. Some women are also resold as punishment for escape attempts.

An activist in Nepal who has counselled many returned prostitutes related what he knew of the Indian brothel system. There are several grades of prostitutes, based on beauty, hard work, "talent." The top are call girls. Then comes "bungalow," which is a higher grade of regular brothel, then comes "pillow house," which is the lowest. Most girls start out in pillow house and work up if they do well....Some girls receive training, how to approach customers, languages.

During training girls are beaten and locked in a room like a jail, but a very small one, until they stop fighting. At first a girl gets two or three clients a day, then it escalates.... In pillow house girls can have as many as forty customers a day. But they earn no money until they havepaid off their debt. After they have paid off their debt, one part of their earnings goes to gharwali, one part to "local taxes," and one part to herself.

It is one or two years before a girl is allowed out of the brothel and then, after they have confidence she won't try to escape, she is allowed to go to the cinema or shopping with a guard from the brothel....If a girl manages to escape, she is illiterate, she knows nothing about the city. She will fall victim to local people or the police. Both psychological and physical means are used to "break in" new girls purchased for the brothels.

Indian activist Preeti Pai Patkar of the organization *Prerana* (inspiration), which works for Mumbai sex workers' rights, told Human Rights Watch/Asia that there were special interior lanes in areas like Falkland Road in Mumbai where rooms and even whole buildings were maintained especially for torturing newly-procured women. Younger girls and children are reportedly hidden in attic spaces in these buildings.

Psychological abuse, threats and intimidation are an integral part of the process and are used exclusively with girls who are purchased as virgins and can therefore be sold for higher prices if their "training" does not include rape. This psychological abuse continues well beyond the first customer, however, with brothel staff using conflicting messages to break down the victim's resistance and build dependency.

A common tactic involves certain brothel staff treating the victim abusively, telling her repeatedly that she is dirty or defiled, for example, while another — often the gharwali herself — consoles her and tells her that she is among family. When the psychological approach does not work, the brothel staff resorts to physical abuse, or allows customers to do so. This abuse can include beatings, gang rapes, and torture with burning cigarettes.

DEBT BONDAGE

Debt bondage, prohibited under The Supplementary Convention on the Abolition of Slavery, the Slave Trade and Institutions and Practices Similar to Slavery, is defined as a situation in which debtors pledge their personal services against a debt they owe, but the person to whom they owe it fails to deduct the value of their services from the debt, or the length and nature of those services are not respectively limited and defined.

The debt bondage which supports the trafficking nexus is also tantamount to forced labor, defined by the ILO as, "All work or service which is exacted from any person under the menace of any penalty and for which the said person has not offered himself voluntarily." Slavery and forced labor are prohibited by other international law and under Nepali and Indian laws.

India enacted the Bonded Labour System (Abolition) Act in 1976 which outlaws all forms of bonded and slave labor. In addition, article 374 of the Indian Penal Code makes it a crime to compel unlawfully any person to labor against his or her will. Every Nepali girl or woman with whom we spoke said that the brothel owner or manager forced her to work by invoking her indebtedness.

This supposed debt, and the threats and beatings that accompanied it, were the major obstacles between her and the possibility of freedom. For most of the women interviewed, the debt was the amount of money the brothel owner said she paid a broker when the girl was purchased, plus the costs of medical care and protection money or payoffs to police and local thugs. Men interviewed in Nepal who were familiar with the brothel system said the girls were also charged 10 percent interest on their purchase price.

The Delhi-based welfare organization, Bharatiya Patita Udhar Sabha, charged in a 1993 letter to the Home Minister that some madams in Delhi even compelled girls to sign forms stating that they were voluntarily working as maid servants and also as bonded laborers until they repaid the loans they had purportedly undertaken. Although occasionally the gharwali may pay for food, clothes and medicine, these costs are frequently added to the debts.

In any case, a girl's indebtedness to the gharwali is based on the gharwali's own expenses. For example, a gharwali who has paid Rs.15,000 [$500] to purchase a girl, plus an additional Rs.5,000 [$166] to the police so she will not be arrested under theImmoral Traffic in Persons Prevention Act of 1986 (ITPPA), would calculate the girl's "debt" at Rs. 20,000 [$666], plus interest. The owners then take one hundred percent of her earnings until that amount is paid off.

A woman's earnings depend on the type of brothel in which she is employed, her age and appearance, and the nature of the sex acts she is compelled to perform. Devi said that all the women and girls where she worked were dependent on tips for food to supplement the meager meals provided by the brothel, but that as a newcomer without regular customers, and an older woman at that, she got few tips.

Devi told Human Rights Watch/Asia that although she was never allowed to handle any money in the pillow houses where she worked, she heard from other women that the owners charged Rs.30 [$1] for five minutes.

In the bungalow, where she took the money from customers beforehand and turned it over to the management, the rate was Rs.110 [$3.66], again for a very short time. A villager in Nuwakot district who had travelled to Mumbai several times told Human Rights Watch/Asia that in his experience a typical pillow house charged Rs.50 [$1.66] for fifteen minutes, and that a woman earned between Rs.1500-2500 [$50-83] a day which she turned over to the owner.

In a day she might have more than twenty-five customers and she could earn small tips of Rs. 2-5 [five to fifteen cents] from customers. A bungalow-style brothel charged about Rs.100 [$3.33] for an hour and the girls kept the tips.

Although most business is conducted in the brothel, and is charged by the minute or hour, customers can pay extra to take women outside. For Rs. 500-1000 [$16-$33] a girl will be sent to a client's house or a hotel for the night.

If a customer buys a woman's services for a longer period her debt resumes upon her return. For example, one Mumbai customer paid Rs.12,000 [$400] and kept a woman in his home for two weeks. He returned her to the brothel, where she worked to repay the remaining debt. A girl who has managed to escape, but finds that she has no way to support herself may negotiate her return to a gharwali, resulting in a fifty-fifty division of her earnings.

Sometimes the woman attaches herself to a local thug to support her in her negotiations with the gharwali. However, this type of an agreement frequently results in indebtedness of a different sort, since the girl is often convinced to take a loan from the gharwali to see herself through. None of the Nepali girls or women we interviewed knew about the monetary arrangements between the brothel owner, the agents and their families.

Because the women did not know how much money had been exchanged or how much they earned, they did not know the amount of their debt. But all were frequently reminded that they had to work to pay off their debts, and many were threatened or beaten for not earning enough:

- "Santhi" said she worked in three low-grade brothels or "pillow houses" and one fancier brothel commonly called a "bungalow." In the pillow house she had fifteen to twenty customers a day and, except for regulars, customers paid Rs.15 [50 cents] for five minutes. She also worked for four months in a bungalow which charged Rs.100-Rs.300 [$3-$10] per hour. Some customers would pay to take the girls out all night, or sometimes for days at a time. If they were taken out to a hotel they were paid at least Rs.1,000 [$33.]. Although Santhi does not know how much she was originally sold for, she was told that each time she was sold it was for a higher price. None of the owners ever told her how much she had to repay, but the brothel managers kept track of how many customers each girl served per day and claimed to figure that against their debt.

Some of the women had a vague understanding that they would have to work for a specific length of time to pay off the debt, and that there was an agreed-upon amount of payment given at the end of the time. We were told both by returnees from brothels and other people from their villages that there were rules in Mumbai brothels about how long girls should work and how much they would be paid. But although this was a persistent rumor, none of the girls we spoke with earned anything like the amounts typically mentioned, or knew anyone who had.

- "Santhi" had heard there was a rule that the brothel can keep you three years, but after three years they have to give you Rs.20,000 [$666], gold and clothes. But they did not give heranything like that. Most of the money she brought out with her was her tips, and she managed to send a box of clothes to her father. After she was there seven years, her father came to see her, but the owner said she had to stay another two years before she could leave. After two more years, her father came to the brothel and brought her out. When she left the brothel she was given Rs.5,000 [$166] which she turned over to her father.
- "Sita" was told that she had to pay off her purchase price of Rs.20,000 [$666], and that was used to force her to work when she did not want to. She worked in the same brothel for ten years and was never told she had paid off her debt. She told Human Rights Watch/ Asia, "Nobody was allowed to leave after four years like people say they are." Sita had no idea what the brothel charged her customers because the money was given to the owner. She had nine or ten customers a day and worked from 10 a.m. to 11 p.m. Sometimes customers gave the girls tips, which they were allowed to keep. The owner provided one meal a day and they had to pay for the second meal with their tip money. They also had to pay for clothes and make-up with tip money they saved. The owner paid for treatment at a private clinic when they were sick, and added it to their debt. They received injections once a month, but Sita did not know what they were for, and they were given pills to induce abortions. The price of the monthly injections was also added to their debt.

According to "Maya," brothel inmates got about five days leave after an abortion before they had to start working again. One woman she knew had abortedtwice. The cost of abortions, plus interest, was added to the debt. One owner said that the abortions had cost her Rs.1,000 [$33] each time and then charged interest on top of it, increasing the woman's debt by Rs.4,000 [$133].

In addition to the money earned by parents from the sale of their daughters (a few hundred rupees if she is sold to a local recruiter, or several thousand if the family sells her directly to a broker), male relatives also make periodic trips to India to collect the girls' earnings.

In villages in places like Nuwakot and Sindhupalchowk, if a village has several women in Mumbai brothels, a prominent member of the village may be appointed to travel to India, collect the money they earn and bring it back to their parents. For the girls, this means that not only are they under pressure to pay off their debt to the brothel owner, but out of whatever earnings they do receive, in the form of tips primarily, they are expected to help support their families.

ILLEGAL CONFINEMENT

There are other aspects of the work in brothels which reinforce its non-voluntary nature. One of these is illegal confinement. Debt bondage is enforced by the near total confinement of the women and girls to the brothel premises. Women and girls are generally not allowed to leave the brothel or its immediate surroundings without escorts and are threatened with a range of consequences, including arrest by the Indian police or capture by other brothel owners, should they attempt to do so.

The women and girls we interviewed explained that they would be beaten severely if they tried to escape. With few exceptions, the Nepali women are unable to communicate with anyone outside of the brothel and some are even forbidden to take Nepali clients out of fear that the latter might be more likely to help the women escape.

Even conversation with customers is sometimes forbidden. A villager in Nuwakot who was familiar with Mumbai's brothels told Human Rights Watch/Asia, "Only girls who pay off their 'loan,' have gone on a holiday to their village and come back, are allowed to leave the brothel alone. Before that they are not allowed out alone."

In Sita's case, no one in the brothel was allowed to go out unescorted. Everything was brought by vendors into the brothel to sell — food, clothes, even videos. They were allowed no contact with their families. Sita, who could not read or write herself, said that none of the women in the brothel were permitted to write or to have pens and paper. Santhi also stated that the girls in her brothels were never allowed out for fear they would run away.

Everything was brought to the house, and shopkeepers charged very high prices. None of the interviewees were in regular communication with their families, none were from villages with telephones and several were illiterate. One woman was lucky enough to find a customer who was willing to send word to her family.

A Nepali man she met in the brothel wrote a letter to her family telling them what had happened to her, and her brother went to Mumbai to try and see her there, but he was not allowed to do so. Her family then brought charges against her trafficker, who was arrested and then released on bail after a month and a half. The case was proceeding, but she was not informed of its progress.

Fear of beatings, arrest or recapture by other brothel agents keeps many girls from trying to escape. Devi stated that the brothel had a window so that all the girls could be observed by the management. When she was seen trying to escape, she was beaten. Whenever there was a police raid the owner would hide all the girls; those who tried to come out would be beaten. Devi said that only newcomers tried to run away; the older ones would not try to escape.

"Maybe they know that those who run away would be sold to another brothel by men on the street, so they don't run."

The girls were also afraid of the police. In September or October 1993, a girl who had escaped was taken into custody and raped by the police. The next day the police brought her back to the brothel and told the owner to bring out all the new girls and leave only the "licensed" ones. The owner gave the police Rs.10,000 [$333,] and they went away.

WORKING CONDITIONS

Tips provide the only source of income for most newcomers to the brothels. Without tips, girls are entirely dependent on the brothel owner for food, sometimes only one meal a day, and the women have to supplement the meager food and clothing provided by the brothel by using their own tips. Most owners permit girls to keep tips, which amount to only a few rupees per customer, but in some cases even this avenue of earning is restricted.

For the first two or three years "Santhi" was in the brothels she was forbidden to ask for tips. In one house where she worked, the girls were supposed to give the owner any tips they received.They were made to swear in front of the brothel altar that they would not keep tips from customers. But Santhi said the brothel owner provided only one meal a day, in the morning, and girls would secretly hoard their tip money to pay for an evening meal.

Sometimes customers would bring them special food, like chicken, which was a treat because meat in the brothel was very rare. But they had to hide the food or the owner would become angry. In one brothel where Santhi worked, girls were only allowed to sleep in a bed if they had a customer, otherwise they slept on the floor.

"Devi" did not get many tips because newcomers got fewer regular customers. The brothel owner provided them with two meals a day, but the food was not very good. With tips they could buy tea and snacks.

"Sita's" owner gave the women in her brothel one meal a day. They had to pay for the second meal. They also had to pay for clothes and make-up. For all these things they would save up their tips, and buy from vendors who would come to the brothels and who charged very high prices.

None of the women interviewed by Human Rights Watch/ Asia was allowed to refuse customers. In some cases they were not even allowed to speak to them. Their days were spent waiting in line for customers or serving them, and they were beaten and humiliated for refusing.

In the bungalow where Devi worked, the girls stood or sat in a row in their make-up and the customers, who also stood in a queue, chose the girl they wanted. They were given only a very short time with each customer and sometimes, if customers tried to ask newcomers too many questions, they ran out of time before they had time to have sex. If the owner found out that a customer had been asking a new girl about herself, the girl would be beaten.

In the pillow houses in which Devi worked, the day started at 8:00 a.m. and they worked until late at night. In the bungalow, the day started at 4:00 p.m. and went until 2:00 a.m. The girls were expected to stand or sit in line the entire time, whether or not there were customers. They were given no time off, even when they were menstruating.

Devi said the happier you made the owners, the nicer they were to you, so sometimes if she was menstruating she took the customer's money first and then told him she wasmenstruating. If she was lucky, he would go away. Girls very rarely refused a customer, because those who refused were beaten. Sita also said the women in her brothel were not allowed to refuse customers. They were made to sit in a room and the customers would choose the girl they wanted.

If the girls refused, they were hit and verbally abused by the owner in front of the customer: "If you won't go, maybe your mother will." Besides being compelled to serve customers, brothel owners sometimes force workers to perform personal housework or childcare chores. Santhi said that the brothel madams lived in separate rooms with their husbands and children. Santhi and the others were sent to clean these rooms.

Every Saturday they had to clean the room, wash the family's clothes and bathe the children. Devi said that besides sleeping with customers, the women and girls in the brothels were expected to do housework for the owner, including washing the floors at the owner's house and doing her laundry, which they brought to the brothel to wash.

THE ROLE OF THE NEPALI AND INDIAN GOVERNMENTS

Despite the fact that both Nepal and India have numerous laws criminalizing trafficking and prescribing severe penalties for abusers, trafficking in women and girls flourishes between the two countries. Human Rights Watch/Asia's investigation reveals the involvement of police and other government officials at various points along the trafficking routes, but there has been little effort on the part of either government to investigate charges of official complicity or to punish those responsible.

Police demand bribes as payment for not arresting traffickers and brothel owners, or are themselves involved in trafficking. Government officials protect traffickers who are politically influential.

POLICE CORRUPTION AND COMPLICITY

The Bharatiya Patita Udhar Sabha, in its letter to the Home Minister in 1993, charged that police regularly extorted large sums of money in red-light areas in the name of protection — up to Rs. 26,000 [$866] per day in Delhi alone. The organization president, Khairati Lal Bhola, complained that out of the Rs.55 [$1.83] paid by a customer in one of the city's better brothels, Rs.10 [.33] went to the police. On a daily basis, he charged, the local police station received cuts according to rank: a constable could expect Rs.25 [$.83], a head constable received Rs.40 [$1.33], and an Assistant Sub-Inspector (ASI) received Rs.80 to Rs.100 [$2.66-$3.33].

The groups charged that the Station House Officer (SHO) received Rs.500 [$16.66] per month, and the district special branch police, which addresses special categories of crimes, collected monthly payments of about Rs.300 [$10] per *kotha* [brothel compound] of ten girls, and Rs.500 [$16.66] for larger kothas. In the case of recently trafficked girls and women, the organization charged that police were involved in the staged process called "registering" the victims. In this process, the madam would notify the police of the arrival of a new victim in her establishment and pay a bribe for their silence.

The madam routinely paid between Rs.5000 and Rs.25,000 [$166-$833] to the police station on scale with her purchase price. In the case of a minor, the police took their bribe from themadam, kept the girl for a day in lock-up, and produced her in court the next day along with a falsified First Information Report (FIR) attesting to her adult status, thereby protecting the brothel owner from any future charges related to the prostitution of a minor. The released minor girl, newly registered with the authorities as twenty-one years of age or older, would be handed back to the madam.

For this service, the madam paid the police Rs. 500 to Rs. 1000. [$16-$33] Sometimes the girl was given falsified papers and brought before the magistrate on a trumped-up charge of seduction in a public place, and handed back to the madam on payment of a fine of about Rs. 1000 [$33] for her release. Thus, for a fee, the madam is assured of police collusion in keeping the trafficking victim captive, while the performance of a few legal routines protects the police from complaints of negligence.

In the words of one Indian journalist: The entry of Nepalese girls into the flesh market is an ingeniously conceived mouse-trap. The exchange of money takes place under the eyes of the girl. A pimp in the G.B. Road area was fairly glib about it. "The money is paid to the concerned area's cops for registering an FIR (so that if the girl is a minor, her age is entered as 18 officially), and a fine of Rs. 1,000 is paid to the magistrate for her release — the charge is fabricated as seduction in a public place."

This total cost of the transaction, including a heavy packet for the police –is entered by the "madam" of the brothel in her ever-thickening notebook as "karz" (debt) on the girl, which she will, through selling her body, repay along with 10 percent interest. Thus, she has to work for five or six years in the brothel as no-wage worker, after which she can save and send back home something.

The testimony of Devi, Tara and other women interviewed by Human Rights Watch/Asia supported charges of police collusion with pimps and brothel owners to profit from the trafficking and arrest of minor girls. Judging from Devi's testimony, the Mumbai police also appear to participate in a similar "registration" or "licensing" charade to that described in Delhi's red-light areas.

Bharatiya Patita Udhar Sabha also charged that to set up a new brothel, large amounts of money ranging from Rs. 50,000 [$1,666] and Rs. 200,000 [$6,666] had to be paid to the police. The purchase of a new kotha of fifty or more inmates by a well-to-do owner required a police payoff of about Rs. 300,000 [$10,000].

While they know that police corruption occurs, the trafficking victims themselves are often kept in the dark about the details of these transactions. "Padma" said she thought that the Criminal Investigation Department (CID) at Marwari Chowk and Dilli Darbar (neighborhood police stations in Mumbai) were each paid Rs. 60 per month. She said that CID cars came by the brothel every five or six months, and that fines of Rs.100 [$3.33] had to be paid by the brothel keeper for each girl they picked up in order to get them released.

The "Tulasa case" of 1982, which involved the rescue of a young Nepali girl who was abducted into the brothels of Mumbai and subsequently infected with multiple sexually-transmitted diseases, first revealed to the general Indian public the extent of police complicity in trafficking from Nepal into India.

In 1982, a thirteen-year-old girl, Tulasa, was abducted by an acquaintance from her home village of Thankut, near Kathmandu, and smuggled into Mumbai via the border town of Birganj. She was beaten into submission by the acquaintance and his colleagues. She was sold to three different brothels in Mumbai, at prices ranging from Rs. 5,000 to Rs. 7,500.

In addition to the sex work she was forced to do in the brothel at a minimum of three customers per night, she was sent to various city hotels to entertain mostly Arab customers, for Rs.180 a night. The abuse of the girl continued until she collapsed with three venereal diseases and tuberculosis. Rescue efforts began when she was brought to Mumbai's J.J. Hospital for treatment in November 1982. At the hospital, Tulasa was given police protection against possible reprisals from the prostitution industry.

After a period of stay in the Dongri Remand Home, she returned to Nepal to take up residence in the Cheshire Home for the disabled in Jorpatti. Doctors evaluated Tulasa and found her to be severely damaged physically and psychologically. Over the years, she remained incoherent and rambling in her speech. She was confined to a wheelchair and complained that her stomach hurt all the time, and that she could not go to the toilet. Her family no longer visited her. In 1994 Tulasa broke her leg in a suicide attempt.

Tulasa's story supported what everyone in the business understood as the norm: police were involved in the highly organized and systematic business of trafficking. One of the leaders of the team that rescued Tulasa, Dr. I.S.Gilada of the Indian Health Organisation (IHO), noted the help of the then Police Commissioner and the local police station in the arrest of thirty-two persons — including three brothel owners — implicated in Tulasa's ordeal, and concluded that the police had known all along what was transpiring in the trafficking industry.

The IHO's records on the Tulasa case demonstrate the longevity of several patterns of trafficking which Human Rights Watch/Asia has documented in Nepal and India to date, notably: abduction carried out on home ground in Nepal, violence used to break down the trafficking victim, exchange of money at all levels of trafficking transactions, victim's high-level exposure to disease and lack of medical treatment, and complicity of police and other governmental authorities at various levels in Nepal as well as in India.

Activists attribute the successful prosecution and stiff penalties given in Tulasa's case to the wide publicity accompanying her rescue and rehabilitation.

Tulasa's abductors were given twenty years in prison. Following the public outcry, the governments of India and Nepal signed a 1985 cooperation agreement addressing the rescue and repatriation of Nepali girls trafficked into brothels in India.

THE RESPONSE OF THE COURTS

The Indian courts have occasionally recognized official complicity in the sex trade. For example, in February 1994, a division bench of the Supreme Court found two police officers — Additional Superintendent of Police Pratap Singh and Circle Officer B. K. Chaturvedi — in Uttar Pradesh guilty of contempt for disobeying the court's December 1993 order to rescue a twenty-year-old woman named Nasreen from a local red-light area after it had been shown that her husband had sold her into prostitution, and that she had been kept captive with police collusion.

Two other police officers, Senior Superintendent of Police R. N. Kataria and Sub-Inspector Prempal Singh, were ordered to show cause for lying to the court. The court also warned the police against intimidating and harassing Nasreen's family, which had filed the initial complaint.

Nasreen's mother had contended that the police refused to act when she first approached them, and in fact one officer demanded a bribe of Rs. 4,000 before throwing her out of the police station.

Court proceedings showed that the police colluded in moving Nasreen out of the red-light area and across state lines until the Supreme Court ordered that she be produced.

Chief Justice M.N. Venkatachalliah was reported to have opined that harassment "seems to be the police culture," and expressed determination to impose "constitutional culture on the police force."

However, the court did let off several police officers and constables on their unconditional apology, including Senior Superintendent of Police Mr. Jamal Ashraf, Deputy Superintendent of Police S. N. Singh, and Inspector S. N.

Yadav. In the November 1993 disposal of a twelve-year-old case, Justice G. N. Ray of the Indian Supreme Court noted that important local politicians were involved in trafficking in the Morena-Dholpur zone which falls in three states, Uttar Pradesh, Madhya Pradesh, and Rajasthan.

The case under review had been filed ten years earlier, when a journalist proved the ease with which women could be bought and sold by purchasing a woman called Kamala and subsequently writing about it.

At the time, the deputy inspector general of the Criminal Investigation Department had submitted a report in which he had asked that sympathetic police officers posted in the sex market areas ought to be given an assurance that they would not be transferred out for at least three years. The report maintained that this was necessary to prevent interference in the police officers'work from politicians and other influential persons who were involved in the sex trade.

POLICE RAIDS IN INDIA

Activists and trafficked women told Human Right Watch/ Asia that although police harassment of commercial sex workers in Mumbai was commonplace, the Mumbai police rarely undertook formal raids or "rescues" in the city's red-light districts.

Activist Preeti Pai Patkar said that when these raids did occur, they appeared to be made to fulfil police quotas or to carry out political vendettas. She thought international pressure also sometimes led to raids, but that on the whole women in prostitution were viewed as criminals by the police and by society at large and were not thought worthy of extra rescue efforts.

Police in Mumbai maintained that they did conduct regular raids on brothels, although high-level criminal cases took precedence. But most law enforcement against prostitution appears to be aimed at the arrest of individual sex workers for solicitation and other public offenses, rather than against traffickers, brothels owners or pimps.

A press report from March 1993 estimated that more than forty women were charged every week under Section 110 of the Mumbai Police Act in the jurisdiction of the Victoria Terminus Railway Station for misbehavior in a public place.

Figures for the total number of brothel raids and prosecutions of individuals for trafficking and brothel keeping have not been made public by Mumbai's Vigilance Cell [vice squad] since the mid-1980s, but statistics in a widely-referred-to study by sociologist Jean D'Cunha in 1986 indicated that between 1980 and 1985, almost six times as many women were arrested for soliciting and "indecent behaviour" as men or women were for trafficking, pimping or running brothels.

According to police records, during that five-year period, 44,663 women were arrested for "indecent behaviour" under Section 110(b) of the Mumbai Police Act, and an estimated 7,600 were arrested under Sections 7 and 8of the Suppression of Immoral Traffic in Women and Girls Act of 1956 (SITA) which prohibit soliciting and prostitution "in or near a public place." (Of those arrests, 6,845 were confirmed by the authorities; statistics for women arrested under Section 8(b) for 1980 were not available, but the average number of arrests per year for the following four years was 830.)

In contrast, of the 409 brothel keepers arrested between 1981 and 1985, only two were convicted. One was fined Rs. 150 or one day of rigorous imprisonment; the other was fined Rs. 10. In all, 469 brothel keepers and 1,116 pimps were arrested between 1980 and 1985 under SITA and the Mumbai

Police Act respectively; 304 "procurers" were also arrested under SITA between 1980 and 1984.

A female police officer in the Women-in-Distress Cell of the Mumbai headquarters of the CID, who had participated as an accompanying officer on three brothel raids between 1992 and 1994, described the "rescue" process to a Human Rights Watch/Asia researcher. She said that on an average of once or twice a month, a customer came to police headquarters to report that he had encountered a girl who wished to escape from a brothel.

After approaching the Women-in-Distress Cell with his story, he would be taken upstairs to Vigilance Cell officials to make a statement. The customer would then be asked to accompany the police on the "rescue." As a matter of procedure, police undertaking such a raid would formally ask the girls and women they approached if they wished to continue in the business, or if they wanted to go home to their families.

The officer noted that minors approached by police generally wished to go home, as did adult women from other parts of India, notably South India. But she observed that most Nepali women she encountered did not wish to return to Nepal.

The reasons given by Nepali women and activists to the Human Rights Watch/Asia researcher were similar to those given to the police officer during raids: the Nepali women feltviolated and "spoiled" and therefore social pariahs; they believed they would never be free to leave for reasons of crushing "debt" to their madams or because they feared violent reprisals; they had nothing to return to; they feared the contempt and rejection of family members; they had no resources, either to make a new life for themselves or to placate their families.

Because these women told the police that they did not want to return home, the officers apparently made no effort to free them from the brothel or investigate conditions there or charges of abuse. The police appeared oblivious to the fact that the brothel owners were in violation of the law and that the debt bondage the women described was itself illegal.

One of the women we interviewed, "Santhi," said police raids had been frequent in the brothels where she worked from 1980 to 1991, and when there was a raid the women would hide their customers. There was a special false ceiling where they could hide people. Santhi was arrested once when one night some Bangladeshi police came to the brothel in civilian dress and found a Bangladeshi girl working there who had been sold by her husband to the brothel.

All the women in the brothel were rounded up and held in police custody for about three hours. They were not given anything to eat or drink and because the police station was in the middle of town everyone was looking in at them. After some time the brothel owner came, paid the police some money and got them out. The woman from Bangladesh was returned to her village, and everyone else was returned to the brothel. The policemen demanded that the brothel owner pay money to send the Bangladeshi girl back home.

Activists who work with women in prostitution, as well as the brothel inmates interviewed by Human Rights Watch/Asia charged that local policemen regularly took advantage of their power to frequent the kothas as customers. In Calcutta's Sonegachi red-light area, a 1993 study by two epidemiologists with the All India Institute of Hygiene and Public Health found two policemen among every one hundred clients. Testimony from women interviewed by Human Rights Watch/Asia supports their findings.

THE ROLE OF THE NEPALI POLICE

The Nepali police are also complicit in the trafficking of Nepali girls and women to Indian brothels. Villagers and officials in Nuwakot District told Human Rights Watch/Asia that traffickers routinely pay protection money to local policeand Nepali politicians as "a sort of commission" to prevent arrests and prosecutions. "If a trafficker ends up in prison it means he or she hasn't paid off the police," one villager observed. A journalist who has researched trafficking patterns in Nepal told Human Rights Watch/Asia:

[E]very point of the border, the police come if they suspect trafficking. But they don't try to arrest, they just take bribes. You can see them go down through the bus collecting money. It's very visible." Activists and police have confirmed that there is a link between international trafficking and local prostitution in Nepal, and that both industries are on the rise, particularly in urban areas, border towns, and villages along the main east-west highway.

In the same towns where reports of trafficking to India are on the increase — Kathmandu, Birganj, Biratnagar, Nepalgunj — local prostitution also appears to be growing, with the complicity of local police and officials, according to local activists. At the lower levels police are common and frequent customers who take their pleasure free of charge — and often violently — as compensation for their "protection."

At the higher levels, activists say, an alarming number of ex-Panchayat government officials were involved in both trafficking and local prostitution, and border police still play a major role. Trafficking of girls, especially to India where the demand for young Nepalese increases every day, is probably one of the country's most lucrative "black" industries.

An officer in Birganj told Human Rights Watch/Asia that prostitution was increasing in the town's local guesthouses and wine shops, and also that women who used to be involved only in local prostitution were now also being trafficked to India. The same has been reported of girls from the Badibadini community in thewestern town of Nepalgunj — "traditional" prostitutes who are now recruited for Indian brothels.

Human rights organizations in Nepal also report consistent complaints of corruption and abuse by police attached to the Hanuman Dhoka district police headquarters in Kathmandu. Most complaints involve torture and mistreatment in detention, arbitrary and unacknowledged arrests, and extortion.

In the case described below, which was widely reported in the Nepali press, Thilu Ghale, a woman arrested by police from the Hanuman Dhoka police station in Kathmandu, accused police of torture and of attempted rape and extortion. She reported that in an attempt to secure a large bribe, the police at Hanuman Dhoka police station threatened to sell her to a brothel in India.

THE CASE OF THILU GHALE

According to a complaint lodged by Thilu Ghale, age twenty-six, a resident of Lazimpat and the owner of a carpet factory, she was arrested while shopping on September 22, 1994, by a group of five or six police officers and taken to Hanuman Dhoka police station in Kathmandu where she was beaten and tortured with electric shocks. In her written complaint, she charged that the police officers also attempted to extort money from her.

Press accounts reported that a police officer threatened to sell her to a brothel in India if she did not pay him Rs. 1,300,000 [$26,000]. Soon after her arrest, Ghale was allowed to telephone her mother, but despite two visits to the police station, her mother was not allowed to see her. Thilu Ghale's mother filed a *habeas corpus* petition with the Supreme Court on September 26. On September 28, the court ordered a written response from the police within twenty-four hours.

In a written reply to the court, delivered on September 30, the Kathmandu police denied having arrested Ghale. Ghale was then transferred to the office of the Bhaktapur deputy superintendent of police, about fifteen kilometers fromKathmandu. According to Ghale's complaint, she was further mistreated at the Bhaktapur station and was denied food for two days. She was, however, able to get a message to her mother.

On October 3, the Supreme Court ordered the deputy inspector of Police for Nepal to locate and produce Ghale within twenty-four hours. On October 5, Ghale was produced before the court by the police, who claimed she had been arrested on October 3 and charged before the district court with selling one gram of heroin. A detention order dated October 3 had been issued by the Kathmandu District Court.

The case was heard by the Supreme Court on October 6, and Ghale submitted a written account of her arrest and detention, which included the date of her arrest and her treatment in police custody. The court placed her in judicial custody and ordered an inquiry. While in custody, Thilu Ghale was reportedly visited by a senior Home Ministry official who tried to convince her to drop the *habeas corpus* case. In November, the Supreme Court found that Ghale had indeed been arrested in September.

It ordered her release, pending a hearing in Kathmandu District Court on charges of selling drugs. Superintendent of Police Rewat Bahadur Thapa was charged with contempt for lying to the Supreme Court, but to Human Rights Watch/ Asia's knowledge, Ghale's allegations of police mistreatment and attempted extortion were not investigated, and no disciplinary action was taken.

Despite consistent reports by human rights groups and journalists that trafficking occurs in Kathmandu, particularly from its carpet factories, and complaints from trafficking victims that they had been trafficked to India from Kathmandu, when Human Rights Watch/Asia visited the Hanuman Dhoka police station in March 1994 and spoke with Superintendent Thapa, the officer denied that trafficking of women was occurring in Kathmandu.

"Girl trafficking is not in Kathmandu district. They are all from Sindhupalchowk and Nuwakot — most are from Sindhupalchowk. None is happening in Kathmandu." Thapa also rejected charges that brokers for Indian brothels were using Kathmandu's carpet factories for recruitment. Brokers are not using carpet factories. Brokers are not trying to use Kathmandu because people know them. Brokers are not able to recruit from within carpet factories because they are connected to old village ladies. We get no news from carpet factories — there are no reports of this type, of criminal activity.

DENIAL OF RESPONSIBILITY

Nepali officers interviewed by Human Rights Watch/Asia acknowledged that although they had received directives from police headquarters "to take [trafficking] seriously," there has been no systematic attempt to train police officers to identify possible culprits. The decision to stop and question a suspected trafficker or, more commonly, a suspected trafficking victim, rests solely with the individual officer on duty, who makes the determination based on his subjective assessment of a suspect's appearance.

Based on interviews with many police officers, it was clear that their individual perceptions about who was a likely trafficker varied. One police officer described traffickers as typically "men from the Mongolian communities." Another said "most traffickers are women — ladies, with good relations in Mumbai, who bring girls and sell them."

Another said his post arrested mostly young men, and a fourth said he stopped mostly girls. An officer in Butwal explained, "If two people don't look alike we suspect something is wrong. We make an arrest if we suspect somebody..." And at the Briganj customs post, an officer told Human Rights Watch/Asia, "We can't arrest everybody. We look at people on rickshaws — if they have kids we leave them alone. If they look suspicious, we stop them."

This would have been little reassurance to "Sita," who was twenty and had a small child when she and the toddler were trafficked to India by a man who offered to marry her. As noted above, once Sita arrived in Mumbai, her son was taken from her and she never saw him again. The police in Butwal told Human Rights Watch/Asia they knew the town was a transit point for trafficking, but that it was difficult to apprehend traffickers because they often lied about their relationship to the girls, posing as brothers or husbands, or about the nature of their travel.

A police officer at the border disagreed: "If a couple who are arrested claimed to be married, but their stories differ or if the second names are different, we arrest them. If they claim to be married we ask them to bring a letter from their VDC [Village Development Community] to prove it. Then only do we allow them to go. On average we have about fifteen cases a month where people are told to return to their villages or asked to bring letters from their VDC."

He said that most people who are asked to bring a letter from home do return with one, but also expressed discomfort about requiring such letters, because of the expense and difficulty it posed for people who had travelled long distances. In general, girls and women attract the most attention at border posts and bus stands, and police target them for arrest. The police at the Sunauli border said that the great majority of people stopped at the border were suspected traffickingvictims, but seldom are the trafficker and trafficked arrested together.

All police personnel in the border towns were unanimous in asserting that the reason for arresting the girls was that they had no money and needed help getting home. Local police said they arrested girls to get information about their traffickers. In most interviews with Nepali police, the officers alleged that the problem was worse in other towns, or that primary responsibility for investigations and arrests was with other branches of the police force.

The Sunauli border police told Human Rights Watch/Asia that traffickers were rarely identified or arrested at the border. This was usually done in the village from which the girls were taken. They said girls got arrested more frequently because groups typically split up at the border, and the police can only identify the girls. If a girl could not say where she was going or why, she was arrested and sent back to her home district.

They also claimed that the criminal gangs who control trafficking operated in Butwal and Narayanghat, not at their border post. Officers at Birganj likewise alleged that the traffickers did not operate in their jurisdictions. An officer in Butwal, who had earlier acknowledged that Butwal was a transit point for trafficking, later downplayed the problem, saying it was more severe elsewhere. "Generally the traffickers don't want to stop here now. Now they stop on the other side or they go to other small places along the border." He also denied there was an organized gang operating in Butwal.

The Butwal police told Human Rights Watch/Asia that the majority of people they arrested were victims who were sent home, not traffickers. But since they cannot stop to question everyone, they said they only board a bus when they suspect there may be traffickers inside, and they rarely made arrests. The Butwal police claimed it was the border police who made most arrests. Occasionally, police in Butwal said, they receive a complaint from a family that a daughter has disappeared. These reports are sent on to the border police.

If someone filed a complaint that someone had disappeared from a village, we would send a letter to the border police to look for them. There is also an NGO in Mumbai and we would send a letter to them also. In the five months the inspector had worked in Butwal, he had never located anyone as a result of sending such a letter.

The U.N. Special Rapporteur on the Sale of Children found similar "burden shifting" on the issue of police responsibility for investigating the sale of children to illegal factories in Nepal and concluded, "This type of obfuscation...does not bode well for law enforcement and child protection..."

Another major problem is that there is no provision in the Nepali civil code to protect women against intimidation by those they accuse of being traffickers– who are normally allowed out on bail after a short time in detention. Police complain that women are pressured or bribed to drop cases they file against their traffickers. And the cases are difficult to win because it takes years for most women to escape the brothel system, and the trail is very cold.

An officer in Butwal claimed never to have been pressured to release anyone held in a trafficking case and said he did not know anyone who had. But he admitted that when a trafficking case went to court, there was a potential for intimidation and harassment of the witness. He told Human

Rights Watch/Asia that the length of time it takes to complete an investigation and the pressures on the victim encourage many of them to drop their cases. "Until the case actually goes to court, there is a lot of social pressure on the girl, and [public] interest drops after a while, too. Also the traffickers pay off the girls to drop the cases."

The logistical difficulties of arresting a suspected trafficker are compounded by Nepal's terrain, lack of infrastructure, poor communication technology and inefficient procedures. After a family reports its missing daughter to a local constable, the police must convey the report to the district center to obtain an arrest warrant. In some cases this requires traveling for many hours on footpaths in the mountains. If the suspect is found and an arrest is made, the suspect is brought back to the district headquarters for registration and detention pending investigation. Cases filed by the returned victims are equally difficult to investigate, because often years have passed since the girl left home.

Although local police bear primary responsibility for the apprehension of traffickers, their ability to prevent abuse is circumscribed by senior officers who view them as "dangerously untrained." According to Junior Subinspector Shrestha of the Kharanitar village police in Nuwakot district, although arrests can take place in the village, arrest orders and registration of detainees must occur at the district headquarters in Trisuli, thirteen hours away on foot.

The Kharanitar police must travel to Trisuli, report the case and get written authorization before returning to the village to bring anyone in for questioning. Those arrested are then sent back to the district center for registration. Although many suspected traffickers from the area served by the Kharanitar police post have been identified, the police there said they had not apprehended a trafficker in the past two years.

We arrest girls to get to the traffickers, but this post has not arrested any traffickers. There are warrants that have been outstanding for two years for the arrest of traffickers. We have thirty or thirty-five warrants out for traffickers, but we can't findthem. We haven't seen them. Anyway, once the girls are gone, it's useless to find the traffickers. The local police said that they detained women who had returned from India for questioning.

The girls have a right to go to India, but we have a right to question them. Trafficking is an offense against the state, and we have orders to question suspected victims. A letter comes from the district office ordering the questioning of a girl returning ... Sometimes parents register a case of a girl disappearing, and if she's found we need to question her.

Or somebody from the village reports it to the police, the police report it to the central district and the central district gives written authorization for questioning.

Police and other government officials at the national level defended these procedures by pointing out that the local police were "uneducated" and ill-trained and would be likely to abuse detainees if they were not required to report to the district center before and after arrest.

IMPUNITY FOR TRAFFICKERS AND BROTHEL OWNERS

Senior police officials interviewed by Human Rights Watch/ Asia acknowledged that there is political pressure, or perceived political pressure, to be lenient with accused traffickers, such as when a parliamentarian called a district officer to get information on a particular case.

They argued, however that it was not an institutional problem, but one individual's weakness of character and that it was up to the individual officers to resist such pressure.

But A.R. Panday, chief district officer for Nuwakot District, told Human Rights Watch/Asia that trafficking cases were notoriously difficult to prove, and that traffickers frequently used political influence and bribes to avoid prosecution.

Complicit parents avoid arrest by reporting their daughter missing to the police after enough time has passed to ensure that she and her trafficker have alreadycrossed the border into India. Local police also come under pressure from criminal gangs involved in trafficking.

According to Panday, the chief district officer is a civil servant, not a member of the police force. He is the highest level government servant in a district. The chief district officer is responsible for law and order but does not have prosecutorial powers. His office can support investigations, but the prosecution and police work is the responsibility of the deputy superintendent of police and the government prosecutor.

In a typical trafficking case, a women who has returned from Mumbai with the help of the Indian police or an Indian social service organization lodges a complaint against her trafficker with the police in her district. The chief district officer orders a police investigation. If the complaint is deemed credible, a case is filed in the district court by a government prosecutor.

An assistant superintendent of police in Birganj told Human Rights Watch/Asia that the Birganj police station did not keep records on the trafficking arrests they made; the records were sent on to the district of origin where the case is lodged with the district court. A CWIN newspaper survey between April and September 1992 found that 35 percent of all reported cases of sexual offenses implicated police or politicians. Regarding trafficking, CWIN reported:

Accusations of state corruption and complicity in the trade are fueled by ministers and politicians frequently ordering the release of offenders held by the police in Sindhupalchowk, Nuwakot and Makwanpur districts. Whereas reports of rape or abduction are frequent, those recording punishment of offenders are rare. Political parties reportedly play an important role in trafficking in Nuwakot district where traffickers were said to make campaign contributions in return for protection.

The chief district officer for Nuwakot explained that Nuwakot district was especially complicated because there were three MPs from three different parties represented — Nepali Congress, Communist Party and the Rastriya Prajatantra Party — each with its own constituency. When someone does a crime he tries to buy protection from politicians, MPs.

The MPs are silent on this [trafficking] issue. There is no political or social commitment, they are most interested in getting votes from their voters... Kansa Lama, he was a trafficker who was arrested, was protected by politicians, bailed himself out and escaped. The arrest of Ranjeet Lama in June 1993 and Simla Tamang in September 1993 brought into unprecedented public focus the role of Nepali officials in the trafficking industry and the influence wielded by wealthy brothel owners.

Simla Tamang, who was convicted of trafficking in January 1994, admitted in court to owning some 500 prostitutes in Mumbai. Ranjeet Lama, her nephew, admitted to trafficking girls to brothels in Mumbai owned by his wife Sita, who reportedly owned nearly 400 girls and women. Both Ranjeet and Simla have been linked to public officials, who were reported to have intervened on their behalf after they were arrested.

The chief district officer of Sindhupalchowk, Dhruba Wagley, complained to the press in September 1993 that a Rastriya Prajatantra Party (RPP) member of parliament and former cabinet minister, Pasupati Shamsher Rana, and other local leaders were pressuring him to release Ranjeet from custody. Wagley told a journalist with the *Kantipur Daily* that Ranjeet had contributed five million rupees to Pasupati Shamsher's last campaign.

According to local journalists, Simla was in her own right an important public figure, who reportedly threatened to run against Pasupati Shamsher Rana in the 1981 Rastriya Panchayat election. In 1986, journalists report that she donated one million rupees to then Prime Minister Marich Man Singh for earthquake relief. She has reportedly donated large amounts of money for the construction of schoolsand temples in Sindhupalchowk district. Simla Tamang's husband is reported to be a member of the Nuwakot District Development Committee.

Simla grew up in Mahankal, Sindhupalchowk, where her parents still live. Soon after her arrest, Simla Tamang accused her uncle, Gyan Bahadur Tamang, of selling her to a brothel twenty-five years before. According to the *Kathmandu Post*, on September 13, 1993, just days after the arrest of Simla Tamang, Kamala Lama, the wife of Dawa Phintso, a former Rastriya Panchayat member from Rasuwa District, was also arrested in Kathmandu on trafficking charges. Arrested along with her were four others, Dhan Bahadur, Jama Bahadur, Lila Tamang and Asha Tamang.

Research and surveys on the trafficking of women have revealed that there is a close link between police and politics where prostitution is concerned....Quite often the local administration or police of Sindhupalchok, Makawanpur and Nuwakot districts have released accused persons due to the direct command of ministries and politicians. In the same light, a photo album consisting of 125 young women was found during a police raid of Mr. D.B. Lama's home. Mr. D.B. Lama, the former Inspector General of Police (IGP), was arrested in connection with the trafficking of women.

Fortunately, newspapers often disclose facts about police involvement in protecting criminals and in sexual violence such as rape and abduction. Unfortunately, the criminals are rarely punished. The home of former IGP D.B. Lama was raided in 1987. He was arrested, and the Royal Army took over investigation of his case. No further information regarding the charges against him or the sentence served is available.

THE DANGERS OF DISSENT

The trafficking network is vast, reaching from India's largest cities to Nepal's most remote villages, yet the brothel owners and managers in Mumbai, the brokers, the agents and the victims are frequently from the same villages and communities. Local residents in Nepal's hill villages who oppose trafficking said they were afraid of the criminal gangs that operate in their areas.

The few individuals who were outspoken in their opposition complained that they were shunned and harassed by their neighbours. Villagers in Dupche, Nuwakot, told researchers with the human rights organization INSEC (Informal Sector Service Centre) in early 1993 that influential people from the area were running brothels in India and that "gallas" (centers from where girls are recruited) had been set up in the village itself. They charged that two daughters of a village leader were working in Mumbai at the time, as was the niece of a national-level politician from the area.

These charges were repeated frequently by Nuwakot residents and others in Nepal when Human Rights Watch/ Asia visited in 1994. One Nuwakot resident told Human Rights Watch/Asia that almost every household in his village had daughters in India, and some had three or four.

In 1993 he said he had tried to start an educational campaign against trafficking, but his neighbours got angry. He gave up when he found he could not interest local police or politicians in the project. He believes the trafficking network in Nuwakot operates with police complicity.

People who protest trafficking are in the minority. It is very difficult to fight because everyone is unified — all are involved in trafficking in one way or another. The families are profiting, so no one will talk. There is such a big gang nobody can do anything. They have so many agents. This is very high level. The gang uses adult women from the village itself who know the police.

If a girl goes through the gang they will guarantee safe passage all the way to the border. They use a lot of people. Only families who try to sell on their own get arrested. Even if the police do arrestsomeone, they just take their money and release them. But through the gang there is no problem at all. Only individuals get arrested. This man told Human Rights Watch/Asia that although he had been criticized by his neighbors for his outspokenness, and that a man who owed him money had refused to pay him, so far nothing more serious had happened.

In Sindhupalchowk, advocacy against trafficking has proven more dangerous. According to CWIN, in Mahankal, Villagers hate individuals, government agencies and nongovernmental organisations that campaign for the abolition of prostitution and girl trafficking. These villagers take the individuals and social organisations as their enemies who are trying to deprive them of a livelihood. They, in connivance with the agents, are reported to have made attempts on the lives of some social workers working for the abolition of trafficking and have often warned them not to create any obstacles to their activities.

CWIN noted that trafficking agents had told villagers not to cooperate with outsiders asking questions about trafficking, and that the organization's researchers had found "a couple of villagers... advising other villagers not to talk to social workers, law enforcement personnel or journalists."

This antagonism reached a peak after a major trafficking ring that recruited in the village was exposed in 1993 with the arrest of Simla Tamang, the infamous brothel owner mentioned above. After the arrests began in June 1993, traffickers with ties to rival political parties apparently engaged in a campaign to expose their competitors.

Shortly after her arrest Simla [who is said to have links to both the Rastriya Prajatantra Party and the Nepali Congress] accused her uncle, Jyam Bahadur, of having arranged her own trafficking years before. Jyam Bahadur was subsequently arrested, reportedly on the basis of information provided by Juthe Tamang, another Sindhupalchowk resident suspected of ties to the trafficking industry. Juthe Tamang, whose arrest was ordered by Sindhupalchowk's chiefdistrict officer in September, was reportedly affiliated with the Communist Party of Nepal-Unified Marxist Leninist (CPN-UML) as was the deputy superintendent of police for Sindhupalchowk, Krishna Kumar Tamang.

Juthe Tamang disappeared in January 1994. The human rights organization INSEC reported that two other residents of Sindhupalchowk suspected of involvement in the trafficking industry, Sonam Lama and Purna Tamang, may be responsible for his disappearance because he exposed their activities. The two were said to be affiliated with the Nepali Congress Party and had evaded arrest.

HEALTH CARE, BIRTH CONTROL AND AIDS

The first AIDS cases in Nepal were discovered in 1986 among Western tourists and Nepali women who had returned from Indian brothels. By February 1994, Nepal's Ministry of Health had recorded 199 confirmed cases of HIV infection in Nepal; the figure has continued to climb. The majority of those who have tested positive for HIV in Nepal do not know they carry the virus because they were tested anonymously by Nepal's Ministry of Health as part of a survey it conducted for statistical purposes.

The World Health Organization (WHO) estimates that there are over 5,000 people infected with HIV in Nepal and that by the end of the twentieth century, the infection rate in Nepal will reach 100,000. Low literacy rates in Nepal's villages contribute to misinformation and ignorance about HIV-related illness and death. Nepali men who go abroad for work have also contributed to the spread of the disease within their communities.

Many of these men, who come to India to work as domestic servants, laborers and watchmen, visit brothels in India and carry the disease back to their home villages in Nepal. Nepali health workers estimate that 300,000 migrant laborers cross the border annually for seasonal work in Indian urban centers, and many will bring back the "Mumbai disease" on reentry into Nepal.

A government health official in Nepal, interviewed in March 1994, told Human Rights Watch/Asia:

Women who are HIV positive are thrown out of the Indian brothels. The Indian police hand them over to the Nepali police.

I haven't heard of cases of girls being turned away at the Nepal border, but it's possible. It may be the police aren't well trained, aren't informed of the policy and don't want to deal with them. The government's policy is to accept them.

During a girl's time in [police] detention, if she is sick and a doctor strongly suspects HIV, the doctor very likely will test her. The ministry recommends consent. It is the official policy that the doctor should get her consent before testing for HIV, but often the doctor just says, "I want to do this test" and doesn't explain, and the girl doesn't know to refuse. We are trying to discourage this.

In Kathmandu there are six hospitals that do blood screening. The ministry has tested a total of 150,000 samples since they began testing. They have found 199 positive cases; there have been twenty-sex cases of full-blown AIDS and thirteen have died. There is no AZT or other drug available for treatment although India may soon begin producing AZT at a price that may make it affordable. There is no access to the drug at present, and as a matter of policy we are not giving the drug.

In India, WHO estimates that as many as 1.5 million people in India may be infected with the HIV virus, with the state of Maharashtra leading the nation in HIV infections. The Indian Council of Medical Research, which estimates that there are a total of about one million commercial sex workers in India, predicts that there will be around 2.5 million sexually transmitted HIV infections in India by the year 2000.

Clinical surveys done by the Indian Health Organisation (IHO) find that 80 percent of sex workers are infected with a sexually transmitted disease (STD), with 50 percent having two or more STDs concomitantly.

The most common STDs seen are syphilis, chancroid, gonorrhea, Donovanosis, and venereal warts. Instances of herpes genitalis are on the increase. A newspaper report quoted Maharashtra state officials as estimating that 50 percent of the sex workers in Mumbai are infected with HIV.

Dr. I.S. Gilada of the IHO has an even higher estimate of over 60 percent infected, a dramatic increase from the finding of 0.6 percent in the IHO's first Mumbai red-light study in 1986.

The organization's studies show that red-light districts in other metropolitan cities have an HIV infection rate ranging from 30 percent to 50 percent. The same press source quotes one young infected Nepali girl in prostitution, who was lured from her home with the promise of a job and subsequently sold to a brothel in Mumbai, as saying: "I am not living even now. So, how does it matter if I die."

Awareness of AIDS among potential customers has driven the sex industry to supply more and more young girls, who can be sold as virgins and therefore AIDS-free. By the same token, the turnover rate among those working as prostitutes is also likely to accelerate as more customers demand "clean" girls, particularly virgins.

Because many of the girls now contract AIDS sooner or later, there is a growing demand for "fresh meat" that the traditional villages cannot meet, and traffickers have begun looking for Nepali girls of all castes and localities.

Girls who test positive for AIDS are immediately dismissed and, visibly sick and without money, are either ostracized by their families or unwilling to go home. Some of them stay in India to die, while many of them come home to work in the streets and brothels of Kathmandu and other Nepalese cities.

The Nepalis are powerless to negotiate any terms of sex in order to protect themselves from HIV infection. They have virtually no say over whether or not to "service" a particular customer, how many customers to accept in a given day, condom use or the type of sex, much less payment.

Young girls, some only thirteen or fourteen years old, may be particularly at risk. Not only are they often too intimidated even to attempt to negotiate the terms of sex, but preliminary medical research suggests that the younger the girl, the more susceptible she may be to HIVinfection for physiological reasons.

Nepali women and girls who attempt to refuse customers often face retaliation. The owners and pimps threaten them with physical harm, beat them, or allow the customers to do so. People who worked with returnees in Nepal said that there was HIV testing in some Mumbai brothels, and that some brothels did appear to discard girls who tested positive. But girls are not always told of their status.

There have been only four recorded cases in Nuwakot district of returnees testing positive for HIV, but people in Nuwakot have very little knowledge about the transmission of the virus, and girls who are infected with sexually transmitted diseases remain hesitant to contact physicians. Activists there have also encountered cases of forced sterilization of brothel inmates, hysterectomies during abortion being the most typical.

What emerges from the girls' testimonies is a pattern of transmission from male customers to young girls that calls into question the common perception that prostitutes are the "source" of HIV/AIDS. To be sure, once infected, the Nepali girls in the brothels are likely to infect their customers. But whereas their clients can choose to use condoms or to abstain from sex, the women and girls have no such choice; they are captive partners.

ACCESS TO INFORMATION ABOUT HIV/AIDS

The Indian government has thus far failed to summon the necessary political will and financial resources to inform and educate Nepali women and girls in brothels. Brothel operators are allowed to dictate the terms of access for health educators, and to limit visits to clinics. The language barrier is also a major obstacle: most Nepali women and girls do not speak or read sufficient Hindi or Marathi to communicate in all but the simplest of terms with non-Nepali speakers; many are illiterate.

There are no official educational materials in the Nepali language, whether written pamphlets or public service announcements for television or radio, the latter two being the most common sources of information for our interviewees. In our interviews, Human Rights Watch/Asia learned that only a small percentage of the Nepali women and girls who hadworked in brothels in India had any knowledge about the transmission of HIV/AIDS.

- "Sita" said she had heard about AIDS, but only that it was a dangerous disease. She thought you only got infected by blood, but she wasn't sure what kind of blood was meant.
- "Devi" said condoms were not available in any of the brothels in which she worked and that the girls did not seem to know anything about AIDS. She thought if they really knew about the dangers of AIDS they would have tried to run away. Devi had only heard about AIDS on the radio since she returned to Nepal, but did not understand much about it. She thought it might be transmitted if you ate the food of someone with the disease. She said that in the brothels, old prostitutes used to give the younger girls their leftovers because they got more to eat, but Devi did not like to eat their food. She had not been to a doctor since she got back, but she is not afraid of diseases. She feels fine.
- "Maya" never asked clients to use condoms because she did not know they could prevent AIDS. She said she had heard about AIDS but did not know anything about it. Because she stayed in the brothel only a short time, she did not know the symptoms.
- "Santhi" said when she began working in the brothels condoms were not available, but after three or four years, girls began buying them themselves and would offer them to the customers. They knew nothing about AIDS, but "if customers used them we felt clean." The girls in the brothels where Santhi worked also tried to make a profit on condoms, buying them for 25 p. [less than a cent] a piece and selling them for two rupees. Most customers refused to use them.

- After "Neela" was arrested in a raid on the brothel where she worked, she was placed in a shelter for children and her blood was tested for HIV. She was told the doctors wanted a blood sample because she might have a contagious disease, but they never told her what disease they were testing for. Afterwards shewas told by the shelter staff that she had tested positive for HIV and that all the other girls had tested negative. Neela said she knew little about HIV before she returned to Nepal, but that in the brothel one girl was supposed to have been HIV positive and the manager told the girls not to eat her food.

Brothel owners and managers paint a rosier picture of AIDS awareness in Mumbai, and one of the ways health organizations in Mumbai attempt to convince local brothel owners to use condoms is to appeal to their desire to turn a profit. Women exposed to these programs know the dangers of AIDS and claim to use condoms, but in practice, customers frequently refuse them.

A gharwali in Mumbai, who was also a client of a local AIDS awareness program, told Human Rights Watch/Asia that she thought AIDS was one of the reasons for a troubling decrease in business. Customers are falling off in great numbers. Three to five a day is a large number these days. But somehow, for some reason, they also still keep coming. Those men who want to live stay away. Young unmarried men who don't care that much, don't worry that much about living, or responsibilities to wife and kids, they keep on coming.

THE APPLICABLE LAW

There is no shortage of applicable law addressing trafficking in women and other abuses typical of the brothel industry. Both international and domestic laws prohibit slavery and all similar practices, including the sale of persons, forced labor and debt bondage. There are also specific prohibitions against the trafficking of adults and children for prostitution and other forms of sexual exploitation.

Among those fundamental human rights guaranteed by international law but frequently denied trafficking victims are state protection against arbitrary detention, torture, including sexual assault and rape, and other cruel, inhuman or degrading treatment. International law obligates the state to protect individuals against such abuse, even when it is committed by a private actor. Such crimes are also prohibited under Indian and Nepali law. The problem lies in enforcement, which is rare and inconsistent, and in the active perpetuation of trafficking-related abuse by corrupt and complicit officials.

INTERNATIONAL LAW

India is a signatory to most international human rights instruments relevant to trafficking in women and girls, including the Convention for the Suppression of Traffic in Persons and of the Exploitation of the Prostitution of Others (The Trafficking Convention), the International Covenant on Civil and Political Rights (ICCPR), and antislavery conventions.

While Nepal has not ratified the Trafficking Convention, it is a party to the ICCPR and to the Supplementary Convention on the Abolition of Slavery, the Slave Trade and Institutions and Practices Similar to Slavery (1956). Both governments have ratified the Convention on the Elimination of All Forms of Discrimination Against Women (CEDAW) and the Convention on the Rights of the Child (CRC), which obligate states parties to ensure protection against discrimination and to take all appropriate measures to suppress all forms of trafficking in women and children.

Articles 34 and 35 of the Convention on the Rights of the Child direct states parties to "take all appropriate national, bilateral and multinational measures to prevent the abduction, sale or traffic of children for any purpose or in any form"and specifically charge signatories with the protection of children from sexual exploitation and abuse.

While CEDAW does not set forth specific measures with regard to the suppression of trafficking of women, earlier conventions do. The 1949 trafficking convention calls on states parties to punish traffickers and to protect all persons against such abuse. As a signatory to this convention, India has a clear obligation under international law to take action against traffickers and protect victims from the abuses documented in this report.

India is also a party to ICCPR and is thus obligated to ensure that persons are not subjected to arbitrary detention and torture or cruel, inhuman or degrading treatment or punishment.

Forced labor and slavery are prohibited by Article 8 of the International Covenant on Civil and Political Rights and Article 4 of the Universal Declaration of Human Rights. In addition, the International Labor Organization passed the Forced Labor Convention (No. 29) in 1930, to which India is a party.

This convention calls on its signatories to "suppress the use of forced or compulsory labour in all its forms in the shortest period possible." At its 40th session in 1957, the ILO further clarified its definition of forced labor to specifically incorporate debt-bondage and serfdom and it passed the Abolition of Forced Labour Convention (No. 105). India has not ratified ILO Convention No.105.

INDIA'S LAWS

Trafficking in human beings and the abuses associated with it are also explicitly prohibited under a wide range of India's domestic laws, including the Indian constitution, specific anti-trafficking acts, the Indian penal code, and in state and local ordinances. The Indian constitution specifically prohibits trafficking in persons.

Article 23, in the fundamental rights section of the constitution, states, "traffic in human beings...and other similar forms of forced labour are prohibited."

Article 39 guarantees equal treatment of men and women and obligates the state to ensure "that the health and strength of workers, men and women...and children are not abused...and that children and youth are protected against exploitation..." Article 42 provides protection against inhumane working conditions.

The two principal laws that address trafficking and prostitution are the Suppression of Immoral Traffic in Women and Girls Act of 1956 (SITA), and the Immoral Traffic in Persons Prevention Act of 1986 (ITPPA), colloquially called PITA, an amendment to SITA. Neither law prohibits prostitution *per se*, but bothtarget commercialized vice and forbid soliciting. SITA's chief drawback was its criminalization of the female practitioner of prostitution.

The language of the law defined the prostitute as female, thereby exempting males in prostitution from criminalization. Even the sentencing procedures discriminated against the woman: a woman arrested for soliciting under SITA could be imprisoned for up to a year, but a pimp for only three months. SITA allowed prosecution of persons other than the women only if the persons involved "knowingly" or "willingly" made women prostitute themselves.

Accordingly, pimps, brothel owners, madams, and procurers could feign ignorance of prostitution and escape punishment. Similarly, the client was not viewed as an offender and could not be penalized under SITA. In addition, SITA only addressed street prostitution; prostitution behind closed doors was left alone — a condition that actually promoted the establishment of brothels.

The Immoral Traffic in Persons Prevention Act of 1986 (ITPPA), amended the 1956 SITA in important ways. However, its basic goals and premises remain much the same as those of SITA. Although prostitution as such is not prohibited under ITPPA, ITPPA contains nine punishable conditions, including brothel keeping, abetting in brothel keeping, living off brothel earnings, procuring, detaining, activity in vicinity of public places, seducing or soliciting.

By implication, ITPPA recognizes that men and children can also be sexually exploited for commercial purposes. ITPPA includes new categories of offenses and punishments, making it easier to prosecute brothel-keepers and others involved in trafficking. Procurers of prostitutes or those found guilty of inducing someone to undertake prostitution are subject to a prison sentence of three to seven years and a fine of Rs.2000 [$66]; a second conviction carries a mandatory sentence of seven to fourteen years.

A first conviction for brothel-keeping under the ITPPA carries a mandatory prison term of one to three years of rigorous imprisonment and a fine of Rs.2000 [$66]. A second conviction is punishable by two to five years of rigorous imprisonment and a fine of Rs.2000. A person convicted of living on the earnings of a prostitute is subject to seven years of imprisonment and a fine of Rs.1000[$33] or ten years if the prostitute is a child.

Any person who engages in prostitution in a public place and any customer with whom the prostitution is carried out is subject to up to three months of imprisonment. If the offense involves a minor, the prison term can range from seven years to life. However, while the act has expanded the circle of persons subject to prosecution, the woman herself remained among those subject to arrest, and in the case of soliciting, subject to much longer terms of imprisonment than a man found guilty of the same offense.

ITPPA also expanded police power to prevent trafficking, but also recognized the potential abuse of power, such as verbal, physical and sexual harassment, by the police during raids. SITA had empowered a Special Police Officer to conduct a search of any premises without a warrant, but now ITPPA extended these powers to the accompanying trafficking police officers who entered the premises. However, ITPPA prohibited male police officers empowered under the act from making a search unless accompanied by two female police officers.

Questioning of women and girls had to be undertaken by female police officers. If this was not possible, the women and girls could be questioned only in the presence of a female member of a recognized welfare organization. The act also mandated rehabilitation in "protective homes," shelters or reformatories where education andliving facilities were to be provided. ITPPA did not give police the power to actually close brothels.

Unlike SITA, ITPPA was concerned about prostitution of minors and children, and introduced stiff penal measures against those who profited with punishment of not less than seven years and not more than ten years. ITPPA's additional clause addressing the offense of procuring carried rigorous imprisonment of seven to fourteen years in the case of a minor, and seven years to life in the case of a child. Similarly, prostitution of a minor or child in a public place was punishable with seven years to life, or up to ten years along with a fine.

However, these measures were effectively weakened by the discretionary powers given by ITPPA to the court to reduce the term of imprisonment to below the sevenyear minimum for offenses such as detaining a person for prostitution or seduction of a person in custody. Other existing legislation, including the Bonded Labour System (Abolition) Act and article 376 of the Indian penal code (IPC), explicitly forbids the purchase and sale of human beings, forced labor and all forms of bonded labor.

The IPC also prohibits the trafficking and sale of minors. In addition, since many brothel inmates are under eighteen and most report the systematic use of threats and physical assaults to force new girls to serve customers, existing rape, assault, and abduction laws can be used to address the systematic abuse of women and girls in brothels.

Article 375 of the IPC defines rape as the act of engaging in sexualintercourse with a woman when the act is against her will; without her consent; with her consent, when her consent has been obtained by putting her or any person in whom she is interested in fear of death or injury; with her consent when she is incapable of understanding the consequence of her consent; or when she is under sixteen years of age.

Under the IPC a minimum term of seven years of imprisonment may be imposed for rape. Rape laws are applicable to both brothel staff and customers. A report released in May 1994 by the Ministry of Human Resources Development's (HRD)

Central Advisory Committee on Prostitution acknowledged the organized and international nature of the trafficking industry and the use of coercion and force in procuring women and girls for prostitution.

The report called for paramilitary forces to check the entry of females from abroad and advocated implementation of Section 13(4) of the ITPPA which authorizes the appointment of a centralized anti-trafficking force with interstate jurisdiction. In June 1994, the Central Bureau of Investigation (CBI) responded to the HRD Ministry's invitation and agreed to assume responsibility for trafficking enforcement, pending additional funding.

The state of Maharashtra, of which Mumbai is the capital, also addressed trafficking of women in its *Policy for Women*, announced in June 1994. The document highlighted the particular vulnerability of women who had been sold into prostitution and targeted funding for a wide range of programs of policereorganization and training designed to address women's protection and safety.

The Maharashtra government, the first and to date only Indian state to have an official policy on women, should be required to implement its own suggested measures with particular urgency regarding Nepali women in prostitution, who not only are the frequent victims of harassment and abuse by law enforcement officials, but who also have little understanding of or access to information about their rights in India.

NEPAL'S LAWS

Nepal's constitution, adopted in 1990, its civil code and several specific laws forbid the trafficking and sale of women and children and other forms of slavery and provide for prison sentences of up to twenty years for interstate trafficking and sale of human beings. Article 20 of the Nepali constitution states:

1. Traffic in human beings, slavery, serfdom or forced labour in any form is prohibited. Any contravention of this provision shall be punishable by law.

The constitution is supplemented by a national legal code called the *Muluki Ain*, which contains provisions against interstate and domestic trafficking in human beings. Section 1 of the law governing "traffic in human beings" decrees prison sentences of twenty years for international trafficking cases where the victim has already been sold and sentences of ten years of imprisonment for attempted sale, plus fines equivalent to the amount of the transaction. In cases where the purchaser is found within Nepal's borders, he or she is subject to the same punishment as the seller.

Section 3 of the *Muluki Ain* also forbids slavery and all other "transactions in human beings." Section 2 prohibits the enticement and separation of children under sixteen from their legal guardians. Pimping and solicitation of prostitutes isforbidden under Section 5 of a law entitled "Intention to Commit Adultery." Intercourse with a child under fourteen is considered rape, regardless of consent.

Article 4 of the Traffic in Human Beings (Control) Act of 2043 (1986/1987) expressly forbids the sale of "human beings with any motive; the transport of "any person abroad with intent of sale," the act of "compel[ling] any woman to take to prostitution through allurement or enticement, deceit, threats, intimidation, pressures or otherwise; and "conspiracy for committing any of the acts mentioned."

The act applies the same penalties to these offenses regardless of whether they are committed inside or outside Nepal's territorial boundaries and makes no distinction between crimes committed by Nepalis or by foreigners. The act dictates prison terms of ten to twenty years for trafficking in human beings and, disturbingly, reverses the burden of proof, requiring the accused in a trafficking case to disprove the charges.

In 1990, the newly elected government of Nepal ratified the United Nations Convention on the Rights of the Child. In May 1992, Nepal passed the Children's Act 2048. The act defines a child as any person under sixteen years of age and Section 15 states that: "No person shall involve or use any child in an immoral profession."

It also contains a number of provisions designed to prevent other kinds of sexual exploitation of children including child pornography andprohibits discrimination between daughters and sons, the use of children for begging, the sale of girl children as religious offerings to temple deities, or for child labor.

FINDINGS OF U.N. SPECIAL RAPPORTEUR

The 1993 report of then U.N. Special Rapporteur on the Sale of Children, Vitit Muntarbhorn, was particularly important in outlining the role of official forces in trafficking and in drawing the link between industrial recruiting, bonded labor and forced prostitution in Nepal, concluding that Nepal's "[l]aw enforcement authorities are often weak, understaffed, undertrained and corrupt..." and that "[t]here is an expansive web of criminality which exploits children and which abuses the open border with India."

Muntarbhorn added, "[t]here is still insufficient transfrontier cooperation both to prevent child exploitation and to ensure safe return and rehabilitation of children subsequently." He called for improved law enforcement, investigation and punishment of corrupt officials, better international cooperation on trafficking, including national cooperation with Interpol, and the establishment of national policy bodies to deal with child exploitation.

The report concluded that: "[w]hile the legislative and policy framework to respond to children's rights are in place to some extent in Nepal, there is evidently poor implementation and weak enforcement at the national and local levels," problems aggravated by legal inconsistencies in a variety of Nepali laws and discrepancies between international standards and national law regarding theage of majority (16 in Nepal, 18 under the Convention on the Rights of the Child).

The report noted that legal shortcomings were compounded by a widespread failure to register births, making it difficult to establish the age of Nepali children and child workers and thus to enforce international standards designed to protect them. The report found that in general legal remedies were not easily accessible to the victims of abuse and that law enforcement lacked both training and the will to confront child exploitation:

(a) Several laws, such as the Constitution, depend for their implementation upon various ministries and the bureaucracy. This means that, in effect, the rights inherent in such laws are not justiciable; it would be difficult to resort to courts to enforce them. In any case, in view of the physical and mental distance between the majority of the population, who are rural based and often illiterate, on the one hand, and the formal judicial structure, on the other hand, there is a wide gap between availability of legal remedies and genuine accessibility of those remedies.

(b) Law enforcement authorities are often weak, understaffed, undertrained and corrupt. Interestingly, during the Special Rapporteur's dialogue with the police, the latter complained that the labour laws did not clearly confer upon the police the power to raid illegal factories and that this was within the mandate of the labour inspectors. This type of obfuscation and "burden-shifting" does not bode well for law enforcement and child protection.

These findings correspond with those of Human Rights Watch/Asia. Despite the abundance of legislation aimed at preventing trafficking and other forms of slavery, neither India nor Nepal has adequately enforced existing laws, investigated reports of official complicity in the trafficking industry or prosecuted officials found profiting from the trade. The apparent apathy on the part of bothgovernments, the highly organized nature of trafficking networks which include influential government officials, and the temptation of easy money makes police corruption virtually inevitable.

Increased awareness in recent years of violence against women and children has helped focus international attention on the problem of trafficking and forced prostitution.

Ratification of the Convention on the Rights of the Child by many countries, the appointment in 1994 of a U.N. special rapporteur on violence against women, and the continuing work of the special rapporteur on the sale of children, child prostitution and child pornography, with mandates to investigate and report on abusive conditions and make recommendations to the governments in question to end abuse, have helped put pressure on the U.N. and its member states to recognize the seriousness of the trafficking problem.

But while the reporting of these agents has been accurate and detailed, and some countries have taken steps to curb the involvement of their citizens in trafficking and sexual exploitation, particularly of girls, much more needs to be done to control the trade, address the issue of official complicity, and protect women and girls against victimization. International attention to trafficking in women first focused on Thailand and its position at the epicenter of a global trafficking industry.

The international media did much to raised awareness about the phenomenon of sex tourism in Southeast Asia. U.N. agencies were soon asked to take up the issue of the sex trade in other countries, including Nepal and India, and to recognize the enormity of the domestic sex market.

The rapid spread of AIDS in India, the world's second most populous country, has been a crucial factor in this shift of focus. International aid agencies, including UNICEF and UNDP, and agencies concerned with the spread of HIV and AIDS like the World Health Organization, have also acknowledged the issue of trafficking and prostitution in relation to their education and relief efforts. What has been lacking so far is a well-organized, multilateral effort to control the industry.

Despite public acknowledgement of the problem and an Interpol initiative focused specifically on the trafficking of minors, governments have failed to make the control of human smuggling and forced prostitution issues of urgency for regional or global crime control initiatives, and virtually no effort has been made at those levels to address complaints of official involvement in trafficking. Securing state accountability for violations of fundamental human rights is an essential element of human rights protection. India, Nepal and theinternational community have an obligation to ensure that states rigorously pursue prosecution of those of its own forces found guilty of complicity with the industry.

TO NEPAL

Human Rights Watch/Asia is deeply concerned that as long as there remains a demand for Nepali girls and women in India's brothels, and a lack of alternative sources of income in Nepal's villages, trafficking in women will flourish as a profitable industry. The government of Nepal has an obligation to do everything in its power to check the trafficking and sale of Nepali women and girls from its territory and to protect them from the human rights violations associated with the industry.

(1) Nepal should accede to the international instrument most relevant to the trafficking in women and girls: the Convention for the Suppression of Traffic in Persons and the Exploitation of the Prostitution of Others.

(2) The government of Nepal should ensure that all reports of trafficking or attempted trafficking be promptly and thoroughly investigated and that those found guilty are prosecuted. The government of Nepal has a special obligation to investigate reports of official corruption and complicity in the trafficking and sale of persons and should hold all persons alleged to have involvement with the industry to the same legal standards. This includes police officers, government officials and influential private citizens.

(3) The quality of law enforcement personnel needs to be improved. Human rights training within the police force should include trafficking issues as a priority. The chain of command and responsibilities of the various levels of the police force need to be clearly articulated,

and police at all levels should receive frequent, clearly worded directives indicating their responsibility to investigate and arrest traffickers and warning that police found guilty of taking bribes or profiting from the trafficking industry will be prosecuted. Prosecutions should follow.

(4) Local village constabulary in particular need to receive better training, including human rights training, and direction in recognizing and investigating trafficking cases. At present village police are considered dangerously untrained by their superiors and are therefore unable to police their communities effectively. Systems of communication between local police posts and district-level police need to be improved and protections put in place which would allow local constables to resist the pressures of criminal gangs operating in their areas. At present these local stations are frequently remote and unprotected, and local police rely heavily on the good will of area bosses.

(5) In accordance with Article 20 of the Convention on the Suppression of Traffic in Persons, the Nepali government should monitor and investigate recruitment networks operating in known trafficking centers such as Nuwakot and Sindhupalchowk, carpet factories in Kathmandu, and border towns "to prevent persons seeking employment, in particular women and children, from being exposed to the danger of prostitution."

(6) Nepal should establish of a central registry of missing persons and should have information regarding the status of investigations easily accessible to concerned family members.

(7) Negotiations between Nepal and India regarding the status of their shared border should include establishing systems for monitoring the trafficking in women and girls and investigating and prosecuting the traffickers to the fullest extent of the law.

The government of Nepal should ensure that no trafficking victims repatriated from India or any other country is subjected to arrest, detention, or compulsory medical testing on return to Nepal. The system of shuttling Nepali women from police station to police station and holding returnees in detention until parents or guardians retrieve them is unacceptable and can be viewed as arbitrary detention. The practice of compelling women to undergo HIV testing in detention is equally unacceptable and leads to stigmatization.

TO INDIA

The demand for Nepali girls and women in India's brothels drives the trafficking from Nepal. This demand is fueled by a fear of AIDS and the tastes of the consumer and is made possible by the active support of Indian police. It is essential therefore that India take immediate steps to curb this demand.

(1) The government of India should move to reform its prostitution and trafficking laws to ensure they are non-discriminatory and in line with international human rights standards, particularly those designed to protect the victims of trafficking. While Human Rights Watch takes no position on prostitution *per se*, we consider the disproportionate application of those articles of ITPPA and the Mumbai Police Act which allow police to arrest persons for public prostitution but not brothel owners, pimps or traffickers to be discriminatory. At the same time, individuals forced into prostitution should be exempt from any punishment or involuntary remand to reform institutions.

(2) India and Nepal's five-hundred-mile open border makes it essential that both countries give priority to strict monitoring efforts to guard against thetrafficking in women and girls, including the inspection of vehicles. Special training should be given to law enforcement officials at the border in the problem of trafficking and their obligation to protect trafficking victims and investigate those who engage in such abuse.

(3) The government of India should actively investigate and prosecute all those involved in trafficking and brothel operations, with particular attention to its own police and officials who receive payoffs or protection money from brothel owners and/or agents, patronize illegal brothels, have financial holdings in, collect rent from, or in any other way are complicit in the operations of such brothels. Investigations of official involvement must be both thorough and impartial. A hotline might be established to receive allegations of official involvement, with safeguards established for the protection of witnesses. Information could then be turned over to a commission of inquiry for investigation, with the record of the proceedings public to the extent that witness security permits. Prosecutions of officials, including members of the police, should take place in civilian courts in proceedings that are open to the public.

(4) Officials found guilty of involvement in trafficking and/or brothel operations, or of failing to enforce the law with respect to those operations, should be prosecuted to the fullest extent of the law. Suspensions, transfers or public apologies for complicit law enforcement officials are not sufficient.

(5) All laws which can lead to the prosecution of all others involved in trafficking and brothel operations, including recruiters, agents, brothel owners and pimps, should be strictly enforced. Brothel owners, for example, are responsible for forcible procurement of women, outlawed under the IPTTA, each time that they compel one of their workers to have sex with a client. Clients who engage in sex with children below the age of sixteen could and should be arrested for rape under the Indian penal code.

(6) Any case involving the detention of a Nepali woman or girl following a raid on a brothel should be given particular attention with a view toward the speedy release of anyone found to be a trafficking victim. If

the status of a woman or girl as a trafficking victim is not clear and she is arrested, the Indian government should ensure that her civil rights are fully protected, including that she understands the nature of the charges against her, has access to an interpreter and legal counsel and is tried without undue delay before a fair and impartial tribunal, with the right of appeal thereafter. Special efforts should be made to protect women from having to decide between lengthy detentions or being bailed out by pimps or brothel owners claiming to be family members.

(7) To protect Nepali women and girls against abuse by Indian police, the Indian government should ensure the presence of women police officers in allplaces of detention. The government should also investigate any report of extortion and sexual abuse in detention and prosecute those responsible to the fullest extent of the law. The rights of detainees to be protected against abuse and the procedures for submitting complaints against officials should be available in the Nepali language in Indian jails and be explained fully to detainees on arrival. The Indian government should ensure that all detention facilities conform fully to the U.N. Standard Minimum Rules for the Treatment of Prisoners.

(8) The Indian government should ensure that arrangements with the Nepali government for the safe return of trafficking victims ensure the protections guaranteed by the Convention on the Suppression of Traffic in Persons. In the case of indigent women, it should bear the cost of their repatriation to the border and arrange for Nepal to bear any additional costs, a process that is now *ad hoc* at best. The agreement with the Nepali government should contain guarantees for the legal protection and privacy of women and girls returning from India. Under no circumstances should the Indian government agree to selective and discriminatory repatriation on the basis of the ethnic or racial background of the women and girls concerned. Because of the danger posed by organized crime, and the social

stigmatization associated with prostitution, both governments should protect the women's right to privacy by prohibiting access to confidential or biographical information about the women. The Indian and Nepali press should also agree on an ethical code that would restrict the use of names or identifiable photographs of these women from appearing in the print or broadcast media unless the women in question have specifically consented.

(9) The Indian government should ensure that all HIV testing of prostitutes is of a non-compulsory nature and that when it is undertaken with the informed consent of the women and girls, those tested should be informed of the results if they so request.

TO THE INTERNATIONAL COMMUNITY

The Secretary-General of the United Nations and the United Nations High Commissioner for Human Rights should ensure that all United Nations agencies pay particular attention to the issue of trafficking in women and develop programs and strategies designed to curb that abuse and encourage accountability.

U.N. agencies that have AIDS programs in India and Nepal, including WHO, UNDP and UNICEF should use these programs to focus attention on the human rights implications of the AIDS pandemic, including the role of official forces in thetrafficking of women and the dangers of discrimination against victims of the disease.

Because the Nepali women and girls in the brothels are trapped in virtual slavery, unable to negotiate any aspect of their situation, or count on police protection, information on AIDS is admittedly of limited practical use. Nonetheless, it is one of their only remaining lines of defense against contracting and transmitting the AIDS virus.

AIDS education for the Nepali women will help them assert some control over their lives by informing their decisions about marriage and children if they return to their home villages. And information for the general public, including potential male customers, may hopefully deter some from high-risk behaviour.

The World Health Organization's Global Program on AIDS lists public information and education as critical elements of the fight against AIDS. Trafficking of women is an increasingly global industry. The Beijing Women's Conference in September 1995 provides an ideal forum in which to promote the issue of trafficking in women as a primary human rights concern worldwide. The members of SAARC should also be encouraged to make trafficking in women and children a regional priority at their periodic meetings.

Influential countries such as Japan, which have good relations with both India and Nepal and which have ratified the relevant international instruments related to trafficking, should urge the latter two countries to ratify or accede to those instruments and to work out an agreement on repatriation and protection of trafficking victims.

Other Asian countries and donor countries in other regions should encourage India and Nepal to adopt the recommendations outlined above and should use every opportunity to raise the problem of trafficking both publicly, at international meetings, congressional or parliamentary hearings, and in press conferences; and privately, in meetings with relevant officials.

They should work to develop programs and strategies for bilateral and multilateral aid programs to India and Nepal that would make funds available for certain kinds of training, education, information dissemination and legal reform programs related to trafficking, but would also make some assistance programs conditional on evidence of effective prosecution of officials, brothel owners, agents and pimps.

Interpol, the Nepali police, the Indian police, and the South Asian Association for Regional Cooperation should cooperate to identify international trafficking networks that exploit women and children. India and Nepal should have a special police force mandated to deal with trafficking. Communication and joint training sessions between border personnel should be improved and encouraged, as should extradition agreements and information exchanges.

11

Aspects of Cultural Policy in Nepal

The main and distinct feature of Nepali culture is that it is colourful, diversified, plural and highly traditional with enough room for modernisation and functionalisation. That is so because some traditions and customs persist over time owing to their relevance while others need to go. New ideas and practices tested by time gradually weed out the unnecessary rules, practices and customs. That is, however, traditional it might be, there is always room for timely changes and modification in a culture.

Years ago, UNESCO started a campaign of compiling a monograph on the cultural policy of member nations. No exact data are available as to how many nations actually compiled such a monograph, but this scribe had an opportunity to browse through some monographs in the libraries of the University of California decades ago. The monographs were of almost uniform size and shape and covered nearly similar topics and issues relevant to their respective countries.

The idea of having such a monograph was to make the information globally accessible to all the member nations. The main objective was, however, to help nations have their cultural policy in hand so that preservation, study, research and other projects could be designed. A little later, perhaps in the early 1990s, there was a monograph on the cultural policy of Nepal written by none other than Dr. Saphalya Amatya, former Director General of the Department of Archaeology, and a well known scholar.

It is difficult to imagine whatever happened to the monograph and its expected circulation, but it is heard that the government has assigned some scholars and agencies to work on the project all over again. In any case, this is a welcome step if proper and qualified personalities are involved to compile the cultural policy of Nepal in a more comprehensive and acceptable way.

NATIONAL NEED

The compilation of the nation's cultural policy is especially important not only because we are a nation of many cultures, traditions, faiths and belief systems but also because this is the time to look into ourselves and make as well as redesign the potential impact of culture on the lives of the people concerned in the present context. Many of our age-old traditions and beliefs have had a negative impact on our social development.

Due to the lack of proper education and resources, awareness and advocacy programmes have not reached places where such impacts are found. On the other hand, many of our resources such as traditional wisdom have not been highlighted, promoted and fully utilised or listed for preservation. The cultural policy to be drafted and finalised for publication needs serious attention in this regard.

It is worthwhile to note here that the primary work of listing the priorities and main issues to be addressed in the making of a cultural policy of Nepal was commissioned at the Central Department of Nepali History, Culture and Archaeology years ago.

The Ministry of Culture and Tourism had initiated and entrusted this to the said Department of TU, and a team of professors led by the then Head had duly and precisely compiled the outline of the work within the given time frame. The file must be sitting in some corner of the Ministry or the Department of Archaeology (DOA) of the Government of Nepal. But, as is the normal practice in Nepal, the whereabouts of this primary work was almost forgotten even by the contributors who had meticulously worked on the project and had signed out.

Interestingly enough, now a new team has been created and entrusted once again for finalising the work. In any case, it is highly gratifying to see that Nepal will be finally showing to the world its cultural policy in the new and changing context. If, and only if, the newly chosen team bothers to dig out the files and dust them off carefully, it will find many useful tips as outlines, if not the final form, and proceed on with its new assignment.

Nepal (then Royal) Academy some years ago launched a project entitled 'intangible cultural heritage listing'. In about three years' time, the listing was complete for the Eastern and Far Western Development Regions. Currently there is a plan to continue the work in the Western region. The study indicated that there is so much to list, study, publish and preserve. The listing of tangible heritage can be a separate project in its own right.

The indigenous communities, the minority groups and regions have specific cultural traditions that need support and study. There is an urgent need to complete the listing of the heritage in all the five regions of the country. The report submitted to the Academy includes preservation and study plans along with the approximate budget.

The objective of this mention here is that the cultural policy of the country must focus on the need to list, study/research, publish and preserve all the cultures of the country. Nepal Academy could be the focal point to plan and carry out a more comprehensive study of Nepali culture.

However, the recent constitution of this institution does not indicate this concern.

Finally, as the country braces up to move gradually towards federalism, each federation constituting the Union will be a replica of the national culture - a harmonious existence of scores of divergent yet accommodating people, scores of languages, traditions and beliefs, and wisdoms, to name a few features. Therefore the new cultural policy to be designed, drafted and finalised must address the need to not only incorporate the value of pluralism but also to frame a policy to uplift the cultures of the minority, enable them to foster their cultures, and make them able to modify, use and sustain them.

RESPECT FOR OTHER CULTURES

Our cultural policy must reflect our concern to uphold the basic strands that have always preserved national unity, fraternity and respect for other cultures against disintegration, domination and fragmentation. Let us hope New Nepal will be a much cherished home for all cultures and their carriers, the colourful and ever friendly people regardless of their roots, branches and skins.

Nepal thus is not a special case for us anymore even if it is a Hindu kingdom. It is a part of the general problem of the Hindus under siege, encircled by the anti-Hindu forces. Hindus are under a camouflaged siege and hence most Hindus do not even realise it. To lift this siege, Hindus need a new mindset based on an implementable Agenda.

It is not enough anymore for the Hindus to be just pious, or religious or observe rituals to defend their faith. Hindus have to awaken to the reality of this siege and become organised with a mindset to repulse the threats. The siege is manifested in terrorism, illegal immigration, religious conversion, and the geo-political encirclement of the present day India by hostile forces.

Everyone of these threats is directed at only one target.the Hindus and the Hindu foundation of India. The developments in Nepal also have to be seen and understood as a part of this siege that the Hindus face today. So when we seek to formulate India's Nepal policy, it cannot be just a question of whether we support the Nepal King or not, or we favour democracy or not.

The core question to the answer is whether the policy will safeguard India's national security and the fundamental interest of protecting her ancient culture. India that is Hindustan, is and shall of course forever remain an ancient nation of the Hindus and of those who accept and are proud that their ancestors were Hindus.

India is not a new nation founded by the British imperialists or foreign marauders who came before them. Instead, the territory of Akhand Hindustan is the cradle of the Hindu civilization of a people indigenous to it, with a small fusion of foreigners who came sporadically to this land. Just as Ganga remains Ganga even if other rivers merge into it, India remains Hindu in character, even if other cultures have influenced it. India today may be of composite culture, but the core and distinguishing feature is 'Hindu'.

If the Muslims and the Christians of India accept and cherish this fact and also that their ancestors were Hindus, then Indian identity is established, and we all would become one family and equal legatees of Hindu civilization. The moment a Muslim or Christian owns this heritage, we cannot doubt his or her patriotism. At the same time those Hindus who believe in the Aryan-Dravidian race theory are not real Hindus but stooges of foreigners. The Hindustani identity is thus established.

But through terrorism, illegal immigration, religious conversion, and encirclement of India by hostile forces, this identity is sought to be undermined with a long run aim to Balkanize India much as Soviet Union and Yugoslavia had been and unravelled. Nepal thus is not a special case for us anymore even if it is a Hindu kingdom. It is a part of the general problem of the Hindus under siege, encircled by the anti-Hindu forces.

Bhutan is under threat from the ULFA, an anti-India terrorist organisation, Bangladesh has come under the influence of Al Qaeda, Srilanka is under attack by the LTTE dominated by Christians and Jaffna Church, and of course, Pakistan which has become the hothouse of all Islamic terrorists. Hence, India is geo-politically surrounded by forces which target the Hindus and nobody else.

It is with this perspective that we should formulate India's policy on Nepal. Such a policy should enhance our national security, protect the Hindus by ensuring that our neighbourhood is freed from sanctuaries breeding anti-Hindustani terrorists, and also further the cause of democracy.in that order of priority. In Nepal there are three main forces on the ground.the King, the seven party alliance of political parties, and the Maoist terrorists.

The King is anti-democratic unlike his predecessor, King Birendra. If it was just a question of democracy, the solution would have been simple. Unlike in the past, there is no agreement in Nepal amongst the three main forces on what would constitute democracy. For the seven party alliance [SPA] democracy is just the revival of the dissolved Parliament.

For the Maoists, it is a Constituent Assembly for a new Constitution and for adopting the concept of 'people's democracy', a euphemism for dictatorship by the Maoists. The King has proclaimed fresh elections in April 2007 but left unclear the terms of it. So restoring democracy cannot be a solution till there is agreement on it's form and structure.

Today, however, the Nepal question for India is multi-dimensional. In one dimension it is how to crush terrorism before it spills over dangerously into India. In another dimension, it is how to cleanse Nepal of anti-Indian foreign intelligence forces who are abetting a coup d'etat. But the foreign-dominated UPA government with a spineless Prime Minister whipped into action by the communist parties of India acting at the behest of their foreign benefactors, are forcing India to support the Maoists for a spurious concept of democracy. This is disastrous for India.

12

Problems and Prospects of India: Nepal Bilateral Trade Relations

Even after India had achieved independence from Britain in 1947, Nepalese-Indian relations continued to be based on the second Treaty of Sagauli, which had been signed with the government of British India in 1925. Beginning in 1950, however, relations were based on two treaties.

Under the Treaty of Peace and Friendship, ratified in July 1950, each government agreed to acknowledge and respect the other's sovereignty, territorial integrity, and independence; to continue diplomatic relations; and, on matters pertaining to industrial and economic development, to grant rights equal to those of its own citizens to the nationals of the other residing in its territory.

Agreements on all subjects in this treaty superseded those on similar matters dealt with in the previous treaties between Nepal and Britain. In the Treaty of Trade and Commerce, ratified in October 1950, India recognized Nepal's right to import and export commodities through Indian Territory and ports. Customs could not be levied on commodities in transit through India.

India's influence over Nepal increased throughout the 1950s. The Citizenship Act of 1952 allowed Indians to immigrate to Nepal and acquire Nepalese citizenship with ease—a source of some resentment in Nepal. And, Nepalese were allowed to migrate freely to India—a source of resentment there. (This policy was not changed until 1962 when several restrictive clauses were added to the Nepalese constitution.)

Also in 1952, an Indian military mission was established in Nepal. In 1954 a memorandum provided for the joint coordination of foreign policy, and Indian security posts were established in Nepal's northern frontier. At the same time, Nepal's dissatisfaction with India's growing influence began to emerge, and overtures to China were initiated as a counterweight to India.

King Mahendra continued to pursue a nonaligned policy begun during the reign of Prithvi Narayan Shah in the mid-eighteenth century. In the late 1950s and 1960s, Nepal voted differently from India in the UN unless India's basic interests were involved. The two countries consistently remained at odds over the rights of landlocked states to transit facilities and access to the sea.

Following the 1962 Sino-Indian border war, the relationship between Kathmandu and New Delhi thawed significantly. India suspended its support to India-based Nepalese opposition forces. Nepal extracted several concessions, including transit rights with other countries through India and access to Indian markets. In exchange, through a secret accord concluded in 1965, similar to an arrangement that had been suspended in 1963, India won a monopoly on arms sales to Nepal.

In 1969 relations again became stressful as Nepal challenged the existing mutual security arrangement and asked that the Indian security checkposts and liaison group be withdrawn. Resentment also was expressed against the Treaty of Peace and Friendship of 1950. India grudgingly withdrew its military checkposts and liaison group, although the treaty was not abrogated.

Further changes in Nepalese-Indian relations occurred in the 1970s. India's credibility as a regional power was increased—and Nepal's vulnerability was reinforced—by the 1971 Indo-Soviet Treaty of Peace, Friendship, and Cooperation; the 1971 IndoPakistani War, which led to the emergence of an independent Bangladesh; the absorption of Sikkim into India in 1974; increased unofficial support of the Nepali Congress Party leadership in India; rebellions fomented by pro-Beijing Naxalite elements in 1973-74 in West Bengal State bordering Nepal; and India's nuclear explosion in 1974.

Nepal adopted a cautious policy of appeasement of India, and in his 1975 coronation address King Birendra called for the recognition of Nepal as a zone of peace where military competition would be off-limits. India showed some flexibility in placating Nepal by distancing, if not disassociating, itself from the Nepalese opposition forces based in India, agreeing to a favourable trade and transit arrangement in 1978, and entering into another agreement on joint industrial ventures between Indian and Nepalese firms.

The latter agreement, by opening the possibilities of India's investment, indirectly furthered India's domination of Nepal's economy. India also continued to maintain a high level of economic assistance to Nepal. In the mid-1970s, Nepal pressed for substantial amendments to the 1971 trade and transit treaty, which was due to expire in 1976. India ultimately backed down from its initial position to terminate the 1971 treaty even before a new treaty could be negotiated.

The 1978 agreements incorporated Nepal's demand for separate treaties for trade and transit. The relationship between the two nations improved over the next decade, but not steadily. India continued to support the Nepalese opposition and refused to endorse Nepal as a zone of peace. In 1987 India urged expulsion of Nepalese settlers from neighboring Indian states, and Nepal retaliated by introducing a work permit system for Indians working in Nepal.

That same year, the two countries signed an agreement setting up a joint commission to increase economic cooperation in trade and transit, industry, and water resources. Relations between the two countries sank to a low point in 1988 when Kathmandu signed an agreement with Beijing to purchase weapons soon after a report that China had won a contract for constructing a road in the western sector to connect China with Nepal.

India perceived these developments as deliberately jeopardizing its security. India also was annoyed with the high volume of unauthorized trade across the Nepalese border, the issuance of work permits to the estimated 150,000 Indians residing in Nepal, and the imposition of a 55 percent tariff on Indian goods entering Nepal. In retaliation for these developments, India put Nepal under a virtual trade siege.

In March 1989, upon the expiration of the 1978 treaties on trade and transit rights, India insisted on negotiating a single unified treaty in addition to an agreement on unauthorized trade, which Nepal saw as a flagrant attempt to strangle its economy.

On March 23, 1989, India declared that both treaties had expired and closed all but two border entry points. The economic consequences of the trade and transit deadlock were enormous.

Shortages of Indian imports such as fuel, salt, cooking oil, food, and other essential commodities soon occurred. The lucrative tourist industry went into recession. Nepal also claimed that the blockade caused ecological havoc since people were compelled to use already dwindling forest resources for energy in lieu of gasoline and kerosene, which came mostly via India.

To withstand the renewed Indian pressure, Nepal undertook a major diplomatic initiative to present its case on trade and transit matters to the world community. The relationship with India was further strained in 1989 when Nepal decoupled its rupee from the Indian rupee which previously had circulated freely in Nepal. India retaliated by denying port facilities in Calcutta to Nepal, thereby preventing delivery of oil supplies from Singapore and other sources.

A swift turn in relations followed the success of the Movement for the Restoration of Democracy in early 1990. In June 1990, a joint Kathmandu-New Delhi communiqué was issued pending the finalization of a comprehensive arrangement covering all aspects of bilateral relations, restoring trade relations, reopening transit routes for Nepal's imports, and formalizing respect of each other's security concerns.

Essentially, the communiqué announced the restoration of the status quo ante and the reopening of all border points, and Nepal agreed to various concessions regarding India's commercial privileges. Kathmandu also announced that lower cost was the decisive factor in its purchasing arms and personnel carriers from China and that Nepal was advising China to withhold delivery of the last shipment.

The communiqué declared that Kathmandu and New Delhi would cooperate in industrial development, in harnessing the waters of their common rivers for mutual benefit, and in protecting and managing the environment. India and Nepal has signed a new trade treaty in Kathmandu on October 27, 2009, reviewing a 13-year-old pact to create a more stable framework for greater bilateral trade and investment.

Indian Minister of Commerce and Industry Anand Sharma and Nepal's Minister of Commerce and Supplies Rajendra Mahato signed the 2009 India-Nepal Treaty of Trade as well as an Agreement of Cooperation to Control Unauthorized Trade, giving a shelf life of seven years to the trade treaty instead of the earlier five and including a provision to have it automatically extended every seven years.

"A new trade treaty was needed keeping in mind the changes in Indo-Nepal bilateral relations, regional and international trade and the demands of the present times," Mahato said.

The new treaty revises the 1996 pact that Sharma called "rewarding" with rich benefits. It had resulted in bilateral trade soaring from Rs.28.1 billion in 1995-96 to Rs.204.8 billion in

2008-09. Nepal's exports to India increased from Rs.3.7 billion in 1995-96 to Rs.40.9 billion in 2008-09 while Indian exports to Nepal increased from Rs.24.4 billion in 1995-96 to Rs.163.9 billion in 2008-09.

India remains Nepal's biggest trade partner accounting for over two-thirds of Nepal's foreign trade. The new trade treaty will provide further access to Nepali products to India with the scrapping of discrimination in respect of tax, including central excise, rebate and other benefits.

This, Sharma said, will bring the bilateral trade conducted in Indian rupees at par with trade in convertible currency and will end the existing cumbersome mechanism of Duty Refund Procedure.

It will also allow Indian exports to avail benefit of export promotion schemes prevailing in India, making them more competitive for further sale or value addition in Nepal. India will now open its port at Vishakhapatnam. Earlier, only the Kolkata Port was open to Nepali traders. The time limit for temporary import of machinery and equipment for repair and maintenance has been raised from three to 10 years and new items of export interest to Nepal added to the list of primary products giving these items duty free access to India without any quantitative restrictions.

These include floriculture products, atta, bran, husk, bristles, herbs, stone aggregates, boulders, sand and gravel. Four additional Land Customs Stations will be established to facilitate bilateral trade: at Maheshpur/Thutibari (Nawalparasi); Sikta-Bhiswabazar; Laukha-Thadi; and Guleria/Murtia, bringing the total number of such stations to 26.

Also, for the first time, bilateral trade will be allowed by air through international airports connected by direct flights between Nepal and India (Kathmandu/Delhi, Mumbai, Kolkata and Chennai). The Indian side has agreed to review and simplify the existing administrative arrangements for operationalisation of fixed quota for acrylic yarn, copper products and zinc oxide.

India has agreed to assist Nepal to increase its capacity to trade through improvement in technical standards, quarantine and testing facilities and related human resource capacities. The Agreement of Cooperation to Control Unauthorized Trade will allow export of goods imported by Nepal from India to the third countries without the necessity of carrying out any manufacturing activity in Nepal.

This will enhance exports from Nepal to third countries where it has a better market access as compared to India. It will also allow export of the goods imported by India from Nepal to third countries, thus helping Nepali exporters to take advantage of the third country market access developed by the Indian export houses.

During the early 1970s, India absorbed almost all of Nepal's exports and accounted for nearly 90% of Nepal's imports but the bilateral trade dropped below 30% by mid-1990s. The 1996 trade treaty, combined with India's rapid economic growth and industrial transformation in the 1990s as also the fixed exchange rate between Indian and Nepalese currency (INR 1= NRS 1.6) since 1993, has helped reverse the trend.

The 1996 trade treaty can be considered as a turning point in the trade relations between the two countries. It bestowed a unique relationship, providing Nepalese goods non-reciprocal preferential access to the Indian market. The treaty helped diversify and expand Nepal's industrial base, and attract Indian investments, although the overall impact on the economy can only be modest, as the manufacturing sector accounts for less than 10% of Nepal's GDP, and primary products exported to India account for a small fraction of its agricultural GDP.

Nepal's export basket to India also diversified. Some changes were introduced while renewing the Treaty in 2002 to encourage genuine industrialization in Nepal and to provide greater clarity and transparency. These included detailed rules of origin (value addition criterion) to qualify for preferential access, quantitative restrictions on 4 items and safeguard clauses.

Since 1996, Nepal's exports to India have grown more than eleven times and bilateral trade more than seven times; the bilateral trade that was 29.8% of total external trade of Nepal in year 1995-96 reached 64.3% in 2007-08. The bilateral trade grew from IRs. 1,755 crores in 1995-96 to IRs. 12,803.5 crores in 2008-09. Exports from Nepal to India increased from IRs. 230 crores in 1995-96 to IRs. 2,560 crores in 2008-09 and India's exports to Nepal increased from IRs. 1,525 crores in 1995-96 to IRs. 10,243 crores in 2008-09.

Although Nepal's trade deficit with India reached a peak of 63.8% of total trade deficit of Nepal in 2007-08, Nepal's export-import ratio with India continues to remain higher than its export-import ratio with the rest of the world. Further, a significant part of the trade deficit is due to petroleum imports from India, which account for about 25-30% of Nepal's imports from India.

Bilateral trade takes place generally in Indian rupees, but Nepal's central bank (Nepal Rashtra Bank) maintains a list of items that can be imported from India in dollars. Currently, there are about 135 items in the list. Exports from India in hard currency are exempt from excise duty in India, which makes them more competitive, wherever import duty in Nepal is less than excise duty in India.

In respect of exports from India against Indian currency, either the exports are made under a bond without payment of excise duty or the duty is collected by India and refunded to the Government of Nepal through the Duty Refund Procedure (DRP) to the extent of import duty chargeable on them by Government of Nepal. The new Trade Treaty signed in October 2009 will bring the bilateral trade conducted in Indian Rupees at par with trade in convertible currency and will end the existing mechanism of DRP.

The deficit of Indian currency is partially covered by transfers like remittances, pension payments, investments, grants etc. from India to Nepal and the remaining shortfall is met by Nepal by purchasing Indian currency through sale of convertible currency in the Indian market.

Nepal's main imports from India are petroleum products (25.2%), motor vehicles and spare parts (9.8%), machinery and spare (4.4%), medicines (4%), coldrolled sheet in coil (3.7%), cement and M. S. billet. Nepal's export basket to India mainly comprises textiles (7.7%), Zinc sheet (6.8%), Threads (6.1%), Polyster yarn (6.1%), Juice (4.7%), readymade garments (4.1%), Jute goods (3.1%), large cardamom (2.9%) and range of other semi-processed and processed food products.

With a view to facilitate Nepalese trade and promotion of high value agricultural product exports to Indian markets, the two countries have agreed to constitute a Joint Task Force to enhance investment for domestic production and exports of high value agricultural products from Nepal to India.

TRADE IN SERVICES

The main components of India's service exports to Nepal are education, transportation, travel, recreation, communication, insurance, professional & technical services.

INVESTMENTS

Indian firms are the largest investors in Nepal, accounting for 44% of total approved FDI commitments. Many of these ventures were established after the introduction of liberal economic reforms and fiscal incentives in Nepal in the early 1990s. At the end of 2008-09, the total FDI approved by Government of Nepal stood at IRs. 3151.7 crores, of which Indian FDI commitments are IRs. 1372 crores. As of 15 July, 2009, there were a total of 1726 registered FDI projects in Nepal. India leads the list with 440 projects. 37 Indian ventures with FDI commitment of about IRs. 280 crores were registered in Nepal during 2007-08 and 34 Indian ventures with FDI commitment of IRs. 156.2 crores were registered in 2008-09.

The Indian ventures are engaged in manufacturing, services (banking, insurance, dry port, education and telecom), power sector and tourism industries. The Indian ventures in Nepal have contributed significantly to the economic growth of Nepal and increase in Nepal's exports to India. In recent years, Hydropwer sector has emerged as an attractive sector for Indian investments.

BILATERAL FRAMEWORK

The bilateral framework for trade is provided by the India-Nepal Treaty of Trade and Agreement of Co-operation to Control Unauthorised Trade 2009. The Trade Treaty, valid for seven years was signed on October 27, 2009 after successful conclusion of bilateral consultations, which began in August 2006, to modify the provisions of the trade treaty to make it a more effective instrument of bilateral trade.

The main features of the previous Trade Treaty retained in the 2009 Treaty are:

- Duty free access to each other's primary products as per agreed list, which has been expanded in 2009 Treaty.
- Nepalese manufactured products are allowed non-reciprocal access to the Indian market, free of basic customs duty, on the basis of Certificate of Origin issued by a GoN designated authority – FNCCI, if the goods are manufactured in Nepal with Nepalese and/or Indian inputs; or, with at least 30% local value addition, if third country inputs are used; and, involves substantial manufacturing process leading to change in HS classification at four-digit level;
- Annual quotas for duty free access in respect of four items – vegetable fats (100,000 tonnes) acrylic yarn (10,000 tonnes), copper products (10,000 tonnes) and zinc oxide (2,500 tonnes);
- MFN list of three items – cigarettes, alcohol (excluding beer) and cosmetics with non-Nepalese and non-Indian brands;
- Nepalese goods attract Countervailing Duty (CVD) equal to excise duty on similar products in India;
- Goods manufactured by small scale units in Nepal enjoy the same benefits as SSIs in India with regard to tax exemption;

- The exports and imports of goods not subject to prohibitions or duties are also allowed to move through the traditional routes on common border.

The main changes introduced in the 2009 Trade Treaty are:

- The validity of the Treaty has been increased from five to seven years, along with the provision of automatic extension for further periods of seven years at a time.
- No discrimination will be made in respect of tax, including central excise, rebate and other benefits to exports merely on the basis of payment modality and currency of payment of trade.
- The time limit for temporary import of machinery and equipment for repair and maintenance has been raised from 3 to 10 years.
- Several new items of export interest to Nepal have been added to the list of primary products giving these items duty free access to India without any quantitative restrictions. These include floriculture products, atta, bran, husk, bristles, herbs, stone aggregates, boulders, sand and gravel.
- Criterion for calculating value addition for gaining preferential access to India has been changed from ex-factory basis to FOB basis.
- India will consider waiver, on request from GON, of any additional duty that may be levied over and above CVD.
- Both sides will exempt exports of goods, which are already covered under forward contract, from imposition of restrictions on exports.
- Both sides will grant recognition to the sanitary and phyto-sanitary certificates issued by the competent authority of the exporting country based on assessment of their capabilities.
- Articles manufactured in Nepal, which do not fulfil the criteria for preferential access will be provided MFN

access to the Indian market. The certificate of origin in case of such exports has been prescribed.

- The provisions regarding safeguard measures in case of serious injury to the domestic industry have been streamlined.
- A joint mechanism, comprising local authorities will be established to resolve problems arising in clearance of perishable goods.
- An Inter-Governmental Sub-Committee (IGSC) at the joint secretary-level has been established. Existing Inter-Governmental Committee (IGC) at the Secretary level will meet once in six months and the IGSC will meet at the interval of the two IGC meetings.
- Four additional Land Customs Stations (LCSs) will be established to facilitate bilateral trade: Maheshpur/Thutibari (Nawalparasi); Sikta-Bhiswabazar; Laukha-Thadi; and Guleria/Murtia, bringing the total number of Stations to 26.
- Bilateral trade will be allowed by air through international airports connected by direct flights between Nepal and India (Kathmandu/Delhi, Mumbai, Kolkata and Chennai).
- India will review and simplify the existing administrative arrangements for operationalisation of fixed quota for acrylic yarn, copper products and zinc oxide.
- Several additional products will be considered as wholly produced or manufactured in Nepal for the purpose of gaining preferential access to the Indian market. It includes articles collected in Nepal fit only for recovery of raw materials and waste and scrap resulting from manufacturing operations in Nepal. It also includes products taken from seabed/ ocean floor/ sub-soil for which Nepal has exclusive rights under UNCLOS.
- India will assist Nepal to increase its capacity to trade through improvement in technical standards, quarantine and testing facilities and related human resource capacities.

AGREEMENT OF COOPERATION TO CONTROL UNAUTHORISED TRADE

A revised Agreement of Cooperation to Control Unauthorised Trade between India and Nepal was signed on 27 October 2009. The new Agreement removes restriction imposed in the previous Agreements on export of goods imported by one party from the other to the third countries, without involving any manufacturing activity.

TRANSIT ARRANGEMENTS BETWEEN INDIA AND NEPAL

India and Nepal have a Treaty of Transit, which confers transit rights through each other's territory through mutually agreed routes and modalities. The treaty of transit was last renewed for seven years in March 2006. The key features are:

- India offers 15 transit routes from Kolkata/Haldia to Nepal for its third country trade.
- Goods can move by road or rail. The creation of ICD in Birgunj and extension of railway line from Raxaul to Birgunj has facilitated direct movement of goods in transit by rail to Nepal.
- A simple customs procedure has been put in place for Nepal's third country traffic.
- Since 1993, India also allows movement of goods from one part of Nepal to another through a simple process of customs undertaking.
- India has extended Nepal direct transit routes to Bangladesh for bilateral and third country traffic. One road route and one rail route have been notified. The road route is through Kakarbitta-Panitanki-Phulbari-Banglabandha corridor. The rail route is through Radhikapur-Birol.

In response to request from Nepal, India has agreed to allow an alternate rail route through Rohanpur-Sighabad as the Radhikapur-Birol route has been rendered unusable after the gauge conversion of the rail track on the Indian side. India has also agreed to allow Vishakhapatnam port as an additional port for Nepal's trade with other countries.

OTHER BILATERAL AGREEMENTS IN THE ECONOMIC FIELD

India and Nepal signed a Double Taxation Avoidance Agreement (DTAA) in 1987. The two countries are currently engaged in negotiating a revised DTAA. The two governments are also negotiating a Bilateral Investment Protection and Promotion Agreement. India and Nepal signed a Rail Services Agreement (RSA) in May 2004, which was modified in December 2008.

The two governments are currently engaged in a comprehensive review of the RSA. A Motor Vehicles Agreement (MVA) for passenger vehicles was initialled in February 2004. The two countries initiated a revised Air Services Agreement on September 9, 2009.

US$ 100 MLN. LINE OF CREDIT FROM EXIM BANK OF INDIA TO GOVERNMENT OF NEPAL

India agreed to provide a USD 100 million Line of Credit (LoC) to Nepal in June 2006 for execution of infrastructure development projects as prioritized by Nepal. Exim Bank of India and GON signed an agreement in September 2007, following which, LoC was operationalised in January 2008.

The projects identified for implementation under the LoC include ten road development projects, rehabilitation of 15 MW Devighat Hydro Power Project (HEP), development of 27 MW Rahughat HEP, Nepal portion of the Muzaffarpur-Dhalkebar cross-border transmission line and rural electrification projects.

TRADE RELATED INFRASTRUCTURE

The Government of India is providing extensive assistance to Nepal to develop its skill base and trade related infrastructure. During the visit of the Prime Minister of Nepal to India in August 2009, India has agreed to provide following additional assistance:

- Construction of a polytechnic at Hetauda at an approximate cost of IRs.22 crores.
- Construction of Integrated Check Posts (ICPs) at Birgunj-Raxaul and Biratnagar-Jogbani at an estimated cost of IRs.200 crores. These modern facilities would contribute to an effective and integrated border management system and considerably facilitate people-to-people contact and trade.
- To enhance connectivity of feeder and lateral roads in the Terai (hulaki roads), twenty roads of a total length of about 660 kms would be undertaken with Indian assistance in the first phase at an estimated cost of IRs.805 crores.
- To improve rail connectivity between the two countries, two cross-border rail links would be constructed with Indian assistance at the following two points along the India-Nepal border at an estimated cost of IRs.680 crores:
  - — Jogbani-Biratnagar (18 Kms)
  - — Gauge conversion of Jayanagar to Bijalpura (51 kms) and extension of the same to Bardibas (17 kms).
- For accelerated development of financial markets in Nepal the Government of India would provide technical assistance for establishment of a Central Depository System (CDS) in Nepal at an estimated cost of IRs.9.2 crores towards consultancy, development of application software and training.
- In order to further assist with human resource development in Nepal, the Government of India agreed to double the number of scholarships, and also increase the number of slots for training and exchange programmes for Government of Nepal officials to further strengthen capacity building and expand interaction between the civil servants of the two countries.

Bibliography

Allen M. R.: "Buddhism without Monks: The Vajrayana Religion of the Newars of the Kathmandu Valley", *South Asia*, 1973.

Appadurai A.: "Is Homo Hierarchicus?", *American Ethnologist*, 1986.

Aris M.: *Bhutan*, Vikash Publication, Delhi, 1980.

Bajracharya P. H.: "Newar Marriage Customs and Festivals", *South-Western Journal of Anthropology*, 15: 418-28, 1959.

Barré V., Berger P., Feveile L., and Toffin G.: *Panauti: Une ville au Népal*, Collection Architectures; Paris: Berger-Levrault, 1981.

Basham A. L.: *The Wonder that was India: A Survey of the History and Culture of the Indian Sub-Continent before the Coming of the Muslims*, Calcutta: Rupa & Co., 1967.

Bayly C.: *Indian Society and the Making of the British Empire* (*The New Cambridge History of India*, Cambridge University Press, 1988.

Beal S.: *Si-Yu-Ki: Buddhist records of the Western World*, Paragon, New York, 1970.

Chakravarti, P. C.: *India's China Policy*, Indiana University Press, Bloomington, 1962.

Chatterji, Bhola. *A Study of Recent Nepalese Politics*. Calcutta: World Press, 1967. 190 pp.

Chatterji, Dr. Nandalal. "The First English Expedition to Nepal," *Proceedings of the Indian History Congress*, 2nd session. Allahabad, 1938.

Chatterji, Sunita Kumar: *Kirata-Jana-Krti the Indo-Mongoloids: Their Contribution to the History and Culture of India*. Calcutta: Royal Asiatic Society of Bengal, 1951.

Chaudhuri, K. C.: *Anglo-Nepalese Relations, From the Earliest Times of the British Rule in India till the Gurkha War*, Modern Book Agency, Calcutta, 1960.

Das, Sarat Chandra: *Journey to Lhasa and Central Tibet*, Murray, London, 1902.

Dial, Roger: *Flexibility in Chinese Foreign Relations: Nepal a Case Study*, University of California, Berkeley, 1967.

Digby, William: *1857 — A Friend in Need: 1887 — Friendship Forgotten*, Indian Political Agency, London, 1890.

Eden, Ashley: *Political Missions to Bootan*, Bengal Secretariat Press, Calcutta, 1865.

Filippi, Filippo de: *An Account of Tibet: The Travels of Ippolito Desideri of Pistoia, S.J., 1712-1727*, G. Routledge and Sons, London, 1932.

Fisher, Margaret W. and Joan V. Bondurant: *Indian Views of SinoIndian Relations*, Indian Press Digests Project Monograph No. 1. University of California Press, Berkeley, 1956.

Giri, Tulsi: *Some Speeches of Dr. Tulsi Giri*. Kathmandu: Department of Publicity, 1964.

Gupta, Anirudha: *Politics in Nepal; A Study of Post-Rana Political Developments and Party Politics*, Allied Publishers, Bombay, 1964.

Hasrat R. J.: *History of Nepal, as Told by its Own and Contemporary Chroniclers*, V. V. Research Institute Book Agency, Punjab, 1970.

Hazlehurst L.: "Caste and Merchant Communities", in M. Singer and B. Cohn (eds.), *Structure and Change in Indian Society*, Aldine, Chicago, 1968.

Hocart A. M.: *Caste: A Comparative Study*, Methuen, London, 1950.

Hodgson B. H.: *Miscellaneous Essays relating to Indian Subjects*, Trubner & Co., London, 1880.

Holmberg D.: *Order in Paradox: Myth, Ritual, and Exchange among Nepal's Tamang*, Cornell University Press, London, 1989.

Hutton J. H.: *Caste in India: Its Nature, Function, and Origins*, University Press, Cambridge, 1946.

Inden R. B.: *Marriage and Rank in Bengali Culture*, University of California Press, Berkeley, 1976.

Ishwaran K.: *Tradition and Economy in Village India*, Routledge & Kegan Paul, New York, 1966.

Joshi B. L., and Rose L. E.: *Democratic Innovations in Nepal: A Case Study of Political Acculturation*, University of California Press, Berkeley, 1966.

Kane P. V.: *History of Dharmauastra*, Bhandarkar Research Institute, Poona, 1941.

Ketkar S. V.: *The History of Caste in India*, Taylor & Carpenter, NY, 1909.

Kirkpatrick Col.: *An Account of the Kingdom of Nepal*, Asian Publication Series, Delhi, 1975.

Lamb H. B.: "The Indian Merchant", in M. Singer (ed.), *Traditional India*, American Folklore Society, Philadelphia, 1959.

Landon P.: *Nepal*, Ratna Pustak Bhandar, Kathmandu, 1976.

Levy R. I., with Rajopadhyaya K. R.: *Mesocosm: Hinduism and the Organization of a Traditional Newar City in Nepal*, University of California Press, Los Angeles, 1990.

Lynch O. M.: *The Politics of Untouchability: Social Mobility and Change in a City of India,* Columbia University Press, New York, 1969.

Macdonell A. A.: *A Practical Sanskrit Dictionary,* Oxford University Press, London, 1929.

Mahar J. M.: *The Untouchables in Contemporary India,* University of Arizona Press, Tucson, 1972.

Majupuria I. and T. C.: *Marriage Customs in Nepal,* Indra Majupuria, Kathmandu, 1978.

Mandelbaum D. G.: *Society in India,* University of California Press, Los Angeles, 1970.

Moffatt M.: *An Untouchable Community in India: Structure and Consensus,* University Press, Princeton, 1979.

Nepali G. S.: *The Newars: An Ethno-Sociological Study of a Himalayan Community,* United Asia Publications, Bombay, 1965.

Oldfield H. A.: *Sketches from Nepal,* Cosmo Publications, Delhi, 1974.

Opler M., and Singh R. D.: "The Division of Labour in an Indian Village", in C. S. Coon (ed.), *A Reader in General Anthropology,* Henry Holt, New York, 1950.

Owens B. M.: *The Politics of Divinity in the Kathmandu Valley: The Festival of Bungadya/Rato Matsyendranath,* University Microfilms International, Columbia, 1989.

Parry J.: *Caste and Kinship in Kangra,* Routledge & Kegan Paul, London, 1979.

Pieper J.: "Three Cities of Nepal", in P. Oliver (ed.), *Shelter, Sign and Symbol,* Barrie & Jenkins, London, 1975.

Pradhan B.: *The Newar Women of Bulu,* (Status of Women in Nepal, Field Studies) Tribhuvan University, CEDA, Kathmandu, 1981.

Raheja G. G.: *The Poison in the Gift: Ritual, Prestation, and the Dominant Caste in a North Indian Village,* University of Chicago Press, London, 1988.

Regmi D. R.: *Medieval Nepal,* Firma K. L. Mukhopadhyay, Calcutta, 1965.

Rose H. A.: *A Glossary of the Tribes and Castes of the Punjab and North-West Frontier Province,* Samuel T. Weston, Lahore, 1914.

Rowe W. L.: "The New Chauhans: A Caste Mobility Movement in North India", in J. Silverberg (ed.), *Social Mobiliy in the Caste System in India,* Mouton, Paris, 1968.

Rudolph L. I. and S. H.: *The Modernity of Tradition: Political Development in India,* University of Chicago Press, London, 1967.

Russell R. V.: *The Tribes and Castes of the Central Provinces of India,* Macmillan, London, 1916.

Sahlins M.: "On the Sociology of Primitive Exchange", in M. Banton (ed.), *The Relevance of Models for Social Anthropology,* ASA Monographs, London, 1965.

Sakya Hemraj: *Samyak Mahadan Guthi,* Jagatdhar Tuladhar, Kathmandu, 1979.

Sayami D.: *The Lotus and the Flame: An Account of Nepalese Culture,* Ratna Pustak Bhandar, Kathmandu, 1980.

Searle-Chatterjee M.: *Reversible Sex Roles: The Special Case of Benares Sweepers,* Pergamon, Oxford, 1981.

Shaha R.: *Essays in the Practice of Government in Nepal,* Manohar Publication, Delhi, 1982.

Shepard J. W.: *Symbolic Space in Newar Culture,* Ph.D. thesis, University Microfilms International, Michigan, 1985.

Shulman D.: *The King and the Clown in South Indian Myth and Poetry,* University Press, Princeton, 1985.

Sjoberg G.: *The Preindustrial City,* Free Press, Glencoe, 1960.

Slusser, M. S.: *Nepal Mandala: A Cultural Study of the Kathmandu Valley*, University Press, Princeton, 1982.

Snellgrove D. L.: *Indo-Tibetan Buddhism: Indian Buddhists and their Tibetan Successors,* Serindia, London, 1987.

Srinivas M. N.: *Religion and Society among the Coorgs of South India,* Clarendon Press, Oxford, 1952.

Strong J. S.: "Rich Man, Poor Man, Bhikkhu, King: Aúoka's Great Quinquennial Festival and the Nature of Dâna", in R. F. Sizemore and D. K. Swearer (eds.), *Ethics, Wealth, and Salvation: A Study in Buddhist Social Ethics,* University of South Carolina Press, Columbia, 1990.

Thapa Y. S., and Tiwari P. N.: *In-Migration Pattern in Kathmandu Urban Areas,* Tribhovan University, Kathmandu, 1977.

Turner R. L.: *A Comparative and Etymological Dictionary of the Nepali Language,* Allied Publishers, Delhi, 1980.

Uprety P. R.: *Nepal-Tibetzz Relations,* Puja Nara, Kathmandu, 1980.

Wheatley P.: *City as Symbol,* University College, London, 1967.

Wright D.: *History of Nepal,* Nepal Antiquated Book Publishers, Kathmandu, 1972.

Index

A

Air Services Agreement, 292.

Ancient Times, 3.

B

Bagmati Zone, 190, 217.

Balamba Hang, 5.

Bilateral Framework, 103, 288.

Bilateral Investment Protection and Promotion Agre, 292.

Bilateral Relations, 20, 21, 25, 88, 89, 90, 91, 95, 98, 104, 148, 165, 283.

British Indian Army, 175, 178.

Buddhist, 8, 38, 189.

C

Civil Strife, 2, 19, 58.

Civil War, 27, 142, 152.

Communist Party of Nepal, 21, 22, 27, 58, 72, 94, 98, 129, 134, 135, 149, 151, 165, 166, 249.

D

Democratic Reform, 16.

Double Taxation Avoidance Agreement, 292.

E

Economic Achievement, 120.

Economic Factors, 192.

Electrification Projects, 292.

F

Federal Democratic Republic, 2, 58, 80, 105, 106, 107, 110, 111, 128, 148.

Foreign Minister, 25, 66, 68, 96, 99, 134.

Foreign Policy, 11, 19, 20, 59, 61, 65, 66, 68, 101, 131, 154, 162, 280.

G

Gautam Buddha, 6, 8.
Gorkha Rule, 14.
Gurkha Military Rank System, 178.

H

Hriti Hang, 5.
Human Rights, 19, 23, 71, 75, 77, 79, 81, 137, 138, 142, 170, 173, 184, 186, 187, 192, 195, 196, 197, 200, 201, 202, 203, 204, 206, 209, 211, 212, 217, 220, 222, 224, 226, 228, 229, 231, 233, 236, 237, 238, 239, 240, 241, 242, 243, 244, 245, 246, 249, 250, 251, 252, 253, 256, 257, 258, 259, 266, 268, 269, 270, 272.
Humati Hang, 5.
Hydro Power Project, 116, 292.

I

Indian Union, 15, 22, 62, 64.
Indo-Nepal Treaty, 1, 20, 21, 151.
Indo-Nepalese Relationship, 151.
Invincible Defence Technology, 60.

J

Joint Press Statement, 109.

K

Koirala Dynasty, 117, 118.

L

Lichavi Dynasty, 8.
Limbu Kingdoms, 13.
Limbuwan-Gorkha War, 13.
Local Healers, 38, 44.

M

Malla Dynasty, 9.
Medieval Times, 1.
Motor Vehicles Agreement, 292.
Multilateral Relations, 22.

N

National Defence Council, 68.
National Sadbhavana Party, 95.
Nepal Transit and Warehousing Company Limited, 84.
Nepal-India Transit Treaty, 84.
Nepalese Civil War, 27, 152.
Nepalese Parliament, 99, 141, 143.
Nepali Congress, 16, 17, 18, 58, 71, 72, 73, 74, 92, 94, 95, 99, 108, 134, 142, 160, 163,

166, 167, 168, 171, 172, 191, 192, 246, 249, 250, 281.
Nepali Police, 194, 209, 236, 241, 250, 272.

P

Pari Hang, 5.
People-Oriented Budget, 106.
Prithvi Narayan Shah, 10, 11, 14, 17, 56, 57, 162, 280.

R

Rail Services Agreement, 292.
Rashtriya Prajatantra Party, 95.
Rastriya Panchayat, 15, 16, 18, 191, 246, 247.
Royal Coup, 15, 17.

S

Shah Dynasty, 10, 14.
Sher Bahadur Deuba, 58, 95, 99, 141.
Skandhar Hang, 5.
Social Identity, 36, 37, 53.
Sociopolitical Landscape, 77, 79.

T

Trade, 1, 9, 10, 20, 22, 23, 24, 37, 52, 56, 74, 83, 85, 86, 94, 96, 97, 100, 113, 147, 148, 150, 162, 163, 164, 165, 168, 184, 187, 188, 189, 190, 192, 193, 194, 197, 205, 219, 232, 233, 245, 256, 264, 265, 279, 281, 282, 283, 284, 285, 286, 287, 288, 289, 290, 291, 292, 293.
Transcendental Meditation, 60.
Transit Arrangement, 163, 281.

U

UN Security Council, 68.
Universal Zone, 155.

W

Western Nepal, 12, 55, 108.

Y

Yellung Hang, 5.

Z

Zinc Sheet, 287.

